RICHARD ROHR

Essential Teachings on Love

Selected with an Introduction by

JOELLE CHASE
and
JUDY TRAEGER

ORBIS BOOKS
Maryknoll, New York 10545

Second Printing, April 2018

Founded in 1970, Orbis Books endeavors to publish works that enlighten the mind, nourish the spirit, and challenge the conscience. The publishing arm of the Maryknoll Fathers and Brothers, Orbis seeks to explore the global dimensions of the Christian faith and mission, to invite dialogue with diverse cultures and religious traditions, and to serve the cause of reconciliation and peace. The books published reflect the views of their authors and do not represent the official position of the Maryknoll Society. To learn more about Maryknoll and Orbis Books, please visit our website at www.maryknollsociety.org.

Center for
Action and
Contemplation

Published by Orbis Books, Box 302, Maryknoll, NY 10545-0302.

Sources and Acknowledgments listed on pages **xv–xxii** represent an extension of this copyright page.

Manufactured in the United States of America

Library of Congress Cataloging-in-Publication Data

Names: Rohr, Richard, author. | Chase, Joelle, editor.
Title: Richard Rohr : essential teachings on love / selected with an
  introduction by Joelle Chase and Judy Traeger.
Description: Maryknoll : Orbis Books, 2018. | Series: Modern spiritual
  masters series
Identifiers: LCCN 2017041850 (print) | LCCN 2017048563 (ebook) |
  ISBN 9781608337354 (e-book) | ISBN 9781626982697 (pbk.)
Subjects: LCSH: Love—Religious aspects—Catholic Church.
Classification: LCC BV4639 (ebook) | LCC BV4639 .R64 2018 (print) |
  DDC 241/.4—dc23
LC record available at https://lccn.loc.gov/2017041850

Love is who you are. When you don't live according to love, you are outside of being. You're not being real. When you love, you are acting according to your deepest being, your deepest truth. You are operating according to your dignity.

—*Richard Rohr*

Contents

Timeline of Significant Events in Richard Rohr's Life

1943   Born in Topeka, Kansas

1957   Left home to begin thirteen years of Franciscan formation

1961   Graduated from high school, St. Francis Seminary, Mount Healthy, Ohio

1961–1962 Novice, St. Anthony Friary, Cincinnati, Ohio

1962–1966 Duns Scotus College, Southfield, Michigan; received Bachelor's degree in Philosophy. (The Second Vatican Council took place from 1962 to 1965.)

1966–1970 St. Leonard College, Centerville, Ohio; received Master's degree in Theology from the University of Dayton

1969   Ordained as a deacon

1970   Ordained to the priesthood

1972   Founded the New Jerusalem Community in Cincinnati, Ohio

1973   First talks on cassette tape, *The Great Themes of Scripture,* were released by St. Anthony Messenger Press (now Franciscan Media)

1973–2013 Preached, led retreats around the world

1987   Founded the Center for Action and Contemplation in Albuquerque, New Mexico

2002   Began Men As Learners and Elders (M.A.L.Es; now Illuman)

2013   Reduced travel to teach primarily from New Mexico

2013   Launched the Living School for Action and Contemplation

2013   Spoke alongside the Dalai Lama in Lexington, Kentucky

2015   Appeared on Super Soul Sunday with Oprah Winfrey

Sources and Acknowledgments

Most of Richard's writings selected for this book were drawn from his own *Daily Meditations* on love, edited by Judy Traeger and Joelle Chase and published online by the Center for Action and Contemplation in 2016. These and other teachings have been adapted for this context with Richard's blessing. The editors are grateful for the support of several individuals: Lauren Brandt, Robert Ellsberg, Vanessa Guerin, Morgan Overton, Lee Staman, and Therese Terndrup. We also thank the publishers listed below for permission to reprint from the following copyrighted material (abbreviations of titles are used throughout the book):

AC   *Adult Christianity and How to Get There* (Albuquerque, NM: Center for Action and Contemplation, 2004), CD, MP3 download.

ALG   *The Art of Letting Go: Living the Wisdom of Saint Francis* (Louisville, CO: Sounds True, 2010), CD.

AR   *Adam's Return: The Five Promises of Male Initiation* (New York: Crossroad Publishing, 2004).

ATWS   *The Authority of Those Who Have Suffered* (Albuquerque, NM: Center for Action and Contemplation, 2005), MP3 download.

B   Richard Rohr's personal Blog, no longer available.

BSHM   *Beloved Sons Series: How Men Change* (Albuquerque, NM: Center for Action and Contemplation, 2009), CD, DVD, MP3 download.

BSMG   *Beloved Sons Series: Men and Grief* (Albuquerque, NM: Center for Action and Contemplation, 2005), CD, MP3 download.

BUW   *Breathing Under Water: Spirituality and the Twelve Steps* (Cincinnati, OH: Franciscan Media, 2011).

C2016   *CONSPIRE 2016: Everything Belongs* (Albuquerque, NM: Center for Action and Contemplation, 2016), MP4 video download.

CC   *The Cosmic Christ* (Albuquerque, NM: Center for Action and Contemplation, 2009), CD, MP3 download.

CCC   *Creating Christian Community* (Albuquerque, NM: Center for Action and Contemplation, 1994), MP3 download.

CP   *Contemplative Prayer* in *CAC Foundation Set* (Albuquerque, NM: Center for Action and Contemplation, 2007), CD, MP3 download.

DD   with Mike Morrell, *The Divine Dance: The Trinity and Your Transformation* (New Kensington, PA: Whitaker House, 2016).

DDEMT   *The Divine Dance: Exploring the Mystery of Trinity* (Albuquerque, NM: Center for Action and Contemplation, 2004), CD, MP3 download.

DSS   *Dancing Standing Still: Healing the World from a Place of Prayer* (Mahwah, NJ: Paulist Press, 2014).

EB   *Everything Belongs: The Gift of Contemplative Prayer* (New York: Crossroad Publishing, 2003).

ECP with Andreas Ebert, *The Enneagram: A Christian Perspective* (New York: Crossroad Publishing, 2001).

EDS *The Enneagram: The Discernment of Spirits* (Albuquerque, NM: Center for Action and Contemplation, 2004), CD, DVD, MP3 download.

EENN *Exploring and Experiencing the Naked Now* (Albuquerque, NM: Center for Action and Contemplation, 2010), CD, DVD, MP3 download.

EG *The Enneagram and Grace: 9 Journeys to Divine Presence* (Albuquerque, NM: Center for Action and Contemplation, 2012), CD, MP3 download.

EL *Eager to Love: The Alternative Way of Francis of Assisi* (Cincinnati, OH: Franciscan Media, 2014).

ES *Emotional Sobriety: Rewiring Our Programs for "Happiness"* (Albuquerque, NM: Center for Action and Contemplation, 2011), CD, DVD, MP3 download.

ETSJ *The Enneagram as a Tool for Your Spiritual Journey* (Albuquerque, NM: Center for Action and Contemplation, 2009), CD, MP3 download.

ET *Eucharist as Touchstone* (Albuquerque, NM: Center for Action and Contemplation, 2000), CD, MP3 download.

FF "Francis Factor," an unpublished talk, December 6, 2015, Trinity Church Wall Street, New York.

GCCA *Gospel Call for Compassionate Action (Bias from the Bottom)* in *CAC Foundation Set* (Albuquerque, NM: Center for Action and Contemplation, 2007), CD, MP3 download.

FM   *Franciscan Mysticism: I AM That Which I Am Seeking* (Albuquerque, NM: Center for Action and Contemplation, 2012), CD, MP3 download.

FMNG   *Following the Mystics through the Narrow Gate* (Albuquerque, NM: Center for Action and Contemplation, 2010), CD, DVD, MP3 download.

FMU   "Franciscan Mysticism," an unpublished talk, April 12, 2012.

FU   *Falling Upward: A Spirituality for the Two Halves of Life* (San Francisco: Jossey-Bass, 2011).

GCB   *The Great Chain of Being: Simplifying Our Lives* (Albuquerque, NM: Center for Action and Contemplation, 2007), MP3 download.

GTP   *Great Themes of Paul: Life as Participation* (Cincinnati, OH: Franciscan Media, 2002), CD.

H   Homily (Albuquerque, NM: Center for Action and Contemplation), https://cac.org/category/homilies/.

HAD   with John Feister, *Hope Against Darkness: The Transforming Vision of Saint Francis in an Age of Anxiety* (Cincinnati, OH: Franciscan Media, 2001).

HDWB   *How Do We Breathe Under Water?: The Gospel and 12–Step Spirituality* (Albuquerque, NM: Center for Action and Contemplation, 2005), CD, DVD, MP3 download.

HDWG   *How Do We Get Everything to Belong?* (Albuquerque, NM: Center for Action and Contemplation, 2004), CD, MP3 download.

HOV   *Healing Our Violence through the Journey of Centering Prayer* (Cincinnati, OH: Franciscan Media, 2002), CD.

HTJ   *Hierarchy of Truths: Jesus' Use of Scripture* (Albuquerque, NM: Center for Action and Contemplation, 2014), CD, MP3 download.

HTP   *Holding the Tension: The Power of Paradox* (Albuquerque, NM: Center for Action and Contemplation: 2007), CD, MP3 download.

HTU   *Holding the Tension*, an unpublished talk, 2007, in Houston, Texas.

ID   *Immortal Diamond: The Search for Our True Self* (San Francisco: Jossey-Bass, 2013).

IDA   *Intimacy: The Divine Ambush* (Albuquerque, NM: Center for Action and Contemplation, 2013), CD, MP3 download.

IDM   "Introduction to the 2016 Daily Meditations," December 27, 2015, https://cac.org/2016-daily-meditations-overview/.

IFF   *In the Footsteps of Francis: Awakening to Creation* (Albuquerque, NM: Center for Action and Contemplation, 2010), CD, MP3 download.

IFP   *In the Footsteps of St. Paul* (Cincinnati, OH: Franciscan Media, 2015), CD.

L   Lineage, Living School for Action and Contemplation, https://cac.org/living-school/program-details/lineage-and-themes/.

LEN   *Living the Eternal Now* (Albuquerque, NM: Center for Action and Contemplation, 2005), CD, MP3 download.

LS   Curriculum, Living School for Action and Contemplation.

M   *the Mendicant* (Albuquerque, NM: Center for Action and Contemplation):"Things Learned While Recuperating," 6, no. 1 (2016); "Mercy, within Mercy, within Mercy," 6, no. 2 (2016).

MN   *Mary and Nonviolence* (Albuquerque, NM: Center for Action and Contemplation, 2002), CD, no longer available.

NC   *A New Cosmology: Nature as the First Bible* (Albuquerque, NM: Center for Action and Contemplation, 2009), CD, MP3 download.

NGTS   *New Great Themes of Scripture* (Cincinnati, OH: Franciscan Media, 2012), CD.

NJC   "On the Occasion of Its 14th Birthday," sermon and letter written to New Jerusalem Community, November 8, 1985.

NN   *The Naked Now: Learning to See as the Mystics See* (New York: Crossroad Publishing, 2009).

NOG   *Near Occasions of Grace* (Maryknoll, NY: Orbis Books, 1993).

NWS   *A New Way of Seeing . . . A New Way of Being: Jesus and Paul* (Albuquerque, NM: Center for Action and Contemplation, 2007), CD, MP3 download.

O   *Oneing* (Albuquerque, NM: Center for Action and Contemplation): "The Perennial Tradition," *Oneing* 1, no. 1 (2013); "The Trap of Perfectionism: Two Needed Vulnerabilities," "Perfection," *Oneing* 4, no. 1 (2016).

OT   *On Transformation: Collected Talks* (Cincinnati, OH: Franciscan Media, 1997), CD.

RG   *Radical Grace* (Albuquerque, NM: Center for Action and Contemplation): 4, no. 4 (1991); Anniversary Edition (December 1999).

RRWP   "Richard Rohr on White Privilege," interview with Romal Tune, January 19, 2016, https://sojo.net/articles/richard-rohr-white-privilege.

S   *Simplicity: The Freedom of Letting Go* (New York: Crossroad Publishing, 2004).

SB   *Soul Brothers: Men in the Bible Speak to Men Today* (Maryknoll, NY: Orbis Books, 2004).

SC   *Silent Compassion: Finding God in Contemplation* (Cincinnati, OH: Franciscan Media, 2014).

SE   "Creation as the Body of God," in *Spiritual Ecology: The Cry of the Earth,* ed. Llewellyn Vaughan-Lee (Point Reyes, CA: Golden Sufi Center, 2013).

SG   *The Shape of God: Deepening the Mystery of the Trinity* (Albuquerque, NM: Center for Action and Contemplation, 2005), CD, DVD, MP3 download.

SL   *Scripture as Liberation* (Albuquerque, NM: Center for Action and Contemplation, 2002), MP3 download.

SPMM   *St. Paul: The Misunderstood Mystic* (Albuquerque, NM: Center for Action and Contemplation, 2014), CD, MP3 download.

STHL   *A Spirituality for the Two Halves of Life* (Cincinnati, OH: Franciscan Media, 2004), CD.

TH   *Things Hidden: Scripture as Spirituality* (Cincinnati, OH: Franciscan Media, 2007).

THTT   *Taking Heart in Tough Times* (Albuquerque, NM: Center for Action and Contemplation, 2009), CD, no longer available.

TSFS   *True Self/False Self* (Cincinnati, OH: Franciscan Media, 2003), CD.

TTM   "Today Is a Time for Mercy," December 10, 2015, St. Paul Church, Princeton, New Jersey, https://cac.org/richard-rohr-on-mercy-mp3.

TW   *Transforming the World through Contemplative Prayer* (Albuquerque, NM: Center for Action and Contemplation, 2013), CD, MP3 download.

TMT   *The Two Major Tasks of the Spiritual Life* (Albuquerque, NM: Center for Action and Contemplation, 2004), CD, MP3 download.

UIG   "Universal, Inherent Dignity," an unpublished talk, February 2015, at the Albuquerque, NM: Center for Action and Contemplation.

YA   *Yes, And . . . Daily Meditations* (Cincinnati, OH: Franciscan Media, 2013).

A note on Bible versions: Unless otherwise stated, Richard uses his own translation, paraphrase, or a combination of several versions, particularly the *Jerusalem Bible, New American Bible, New English Translation, Revised Standard Version, J.B. Phillips New Testament,* and *The Message.*

Introduction

BACK TO THE BASICS

"It's so simple that it's hard to teach." Respected Franciscan author and speaker Father Richard Rohr often says this about his work. His mission, as he sees it, is simply to awaken us to what we already know is true: the foundation of everything is love because "God is love" (1 John 4:8). God's love in us is seeking to love and be loved and to bring healing and wholeness to a suffering world. Father Richard says love is our basic identity *in God*; "I am that which I am seeking."

Why have we made things so complicated? "Most of us were taught that God would love us if and when we change," Richard says. "In fact, God loves you so that you can change. What empowers change, what makes you desirous of change, is the inner experience of love. This alone becomes the engine of positive change."

For nearly fifty years, Richard's own experience of God's infinite and reliable love has inspired him to be a channel of divine love for others. He tries to remove the barriers—created by immature religion, bad teaching, culture, ego, and our own woundedness—that keep us from knowing God's love for ourselves. Richard takes us back to the basics that have been forgotten for so long and for so many reasons. Jesus summed up the entire law and prophets with these words: "Love God and love others" (Matthew 22:36–40; Luke 10:25–28; Mark 12:28–31).

Jesus demonstrated how to love in very practical ways by himself living "a downwardly mobile, nonviolent, and eminently sharable life in this world," as Richard says. Our lives are most fruitful by simply imitating Jesus in this regard. The Franciscan worldview concluded that the Divine Incarnation was already

1

"redemption" and Christmas was already Easter. Thus Earth is good and being human is good. In Jesus, God fully revealed to humanity the "face of God" so we could personally fall in love with what most of history had presumed was a distant and judgmental God. Our own acts of compassion and justice are to be the natural outflowing of such inflowing love—rather than ways to earn what we already have. Richard observes that Jesus did not say, "Worship me," but he often said "Follow me." And, as John's Gospel puts it, "I shall return to take you with me, so that where I am you also may be" (14:3).

Methodologically, Richard's work reunites Scripture, Tradition, and Experience as the three wheels of a tricycle that moves us forward in spiritual development.[1] He believes these three must regulate, balance, and validate one another, especially when each is critiqued in a reasonable way. This is his model for reconstruction, as opposed to mere deconstruction, rationalism, or fundamentalism.

> I pray that my words will not get in the way of what God is doing in your lives and in the world. I pray that these words will not just be words, but "spirit and truth" (John 4:24) that plant you firmly in the breach between the world as it usually is (Power) and the world as it should and could be (Love). Yet both love and power are the necessary building blocks of God's Reign on this earth; both are to be respected and given their full due, although love utterly redefines the nature of power. Power without love is mere brutality (even in the church), and love without power is only the sentimentality of private lives disconnected from the Whole. The Gospel in its fullness holds power and love together, and is always hope for the world—with this new kind of power. I draw strength from the words of Isaiah, who, like all of the prophets, was a radical

---

1. Richard borrows this analogy from Carolyn Metzler, spiritual director at the Center for Action and Contemplation.

traditionalist, which ironically made him into a liberal subversive:

The ancient ruins will be rebuilt,
You will build on age-old foundations,
You will be called "Breach-Mender,"
Restorer of ruined houses. —Isaiah 58:12

—NOG xv–xvi

THE PROPHETIC TRADITION

Not all would agree that Richard teaches orthodox Roman Catholic or Christian doctrine. Yet Richard follows in a long line of daring prophets "at the edge of the inside," those who love their Tradition enough to offer constructive criticism, speaking truth to power. Like St. Francis of Assisi, Richard focuses on an "alternative orthodoxy," emphasizing truths that have been neglected or misinterpreted, just as the prophets did for Israel. Richard recognizes what Pope Francis calls a hierarchy of truths: not all truths are equal; some deserve more attention than others, "and the greatest of these is love" (1 Corinthians 13:13). There are relative truths and there is absolute Truth. We need them both and in proper perspective.

Ever a Franciscan, Richard's "hermeneutic" (method of interpreting Scripture) is simply to interpret the Scriptures *the way that Jesus did*. Jesus clearly did not treat each of his own Jewish Scriptures equally. He ignored or openly disobeyed those that were violent, imperialistic, tribal, exclusionary, or merely cultural purity codes. He highlighted, against his own tradition, many ignored texts that were inclusive, merciful, and forgiving. Jesus consistently operated out of a worldview of abundance, because for him grace was not scarce but infinite. God is by definition the mender of all breaches, the filler for all the gaps of the universe. The Christian word for that is grace, which Richard says is his favorite word.

Like St. Francis, Richard is rebuilding the forgotten, falling parts of the church, setting the ancient teachings on a solid

foundation of love. Paula D'Arcy writes: "With the cutting skills
of a surgeon and the heart of a Franciscan, Richard exposes the
misperceptions and counterfeits that have shaped our faith. He
then promises and delivers a 'staggering change of perspective'
along with a taste of the intimacy of all love, both human and
divine. Every word is a rare gift from a true elder and a worthy
guide."

Richard's teachings come both from the Christian Tradition
and the ancient truths found along all sacred paths (the Perennial Tradition or Philosophy) that point to our common human
longing for union with divine love and with each other. Perhaps
because of this, Richard's teaching appeals to a vast audience—
from cradle and former Catholics, Anglicans, Evangelicals,
and mainstream Protestants, to "spiritual but not religious,"
to Buddhists, to agnostics—all around the world, with strong
followings in Germany, the United Kingdom, South Africa, and
Australia. Episcopalian pastor and author Nadia Bolz-Weber
writes: "Rohr has had such a profound influence on so many
Christians seeking to balance reason and mystery, action and
contemplation, not to mention faith and real life."

Throughout the years, Richard has joined numerous spiritual leaders, bringing his unique and down-to-earth perspective
on universal wisdom alongside a variety of teachers, including
Thomas Keating, Laurence Freeman, Joan Chittister, Ilia Delio,
Gerald May, Walter Wink, Daniel Berrigan, Barbara Brown
Taylor, Desmond Tutu, His Holiness the Dalai Lama, Brian
McLaren, James Wallis, Oprah Winfrey, fellow core faculty at
the Center for Action and Contemplation James Finley and Cynthia Bourgeault, and many others.

There is something about Richard's words and the way in
which he delivers them that resonates at a deep level, across
boundaries of age, ethnicity, socioeconomic status, and culture.
People often say, "I knew this [whatever Richard was explaining
in his unique way] all along, but he put it into words I can understand. It all makes sense now!" They intuited that, as the Beatles
sing, "all you need is love," and now they have the framework

by which to trust this is not just wishful thinking but the very
"force field" of the universe, the Holy Spirit. In Richard's teachings, many of us have found a God who is both universal and
personal.

LOVE GROUNDED IN TRINITY

Let's be clear from the beginning: This is not a book about love
as an emotion, as romance, as "being nice," or as having sentimental feelings. It is more about living in the Trinitarian *flow*
of love. Richard sees love as the metaphysical foundation of
everything because Trinity is the model for all reality. God is
all-vulnerable relationship—ever outpouring and ever infilling
love. God can only be experienced through friendship, not ideas.

To put it simply, if God is a "substance" instead of a relationship, then we too are merely "an individual substance of a
rational nature," which was the operative Western definition of
the human person for much of our history. But if God is *an
event of relationship*, and we are created in such an image, then
we also are an event of relationship—inherently in relationship
with God and thus with everything else, too. In other words, we
are love!

God is Being Itself more than *a* Being (Acts 17:28). In mystical and mature Christianity, God is seen as a verb more than
a noun, an action and a movement of love more than a solitary
monarch or a critical judge. God is forever actively involved
in evolving and creating new forms of life and love. The Early
Church Fathers found a term from Greek theater to describe
such a God: *perichoresis* or circle dance. All of creation inherently participates in this divine dance, a centrifugal force moving
outward from the inner circle of "Father, Son, and Holy Spirit."
Humans are blessed to consciously know and enjoy this dance.

We "are created in the image and likeness of God" (Genesis
1:26–27). Thus, human dignity is not attained, but rather inherent from the beginning. This was supposed to give us a foundational compatibility for and with God, instead of the fragility

of relying upon personal moral perfection, cultural position, or psychological wholeness. The Eastern Church's belief in divinization or *theosis* stayed true to the principle of our original blessing as created in the image of God. Unfortunately, this insight was lost in the Western Church, which overemphasized developing our likeness to God. Each of us, from the moment of conception, receives the free gift of the image of God; it is entirely unmerited. The word "image" describes our *objective* DNA that marks us as creatures of God. It is the Holy Spirit living within us. We only gradually come to discover our "likeness," which is our unique way of incarnating love. We all have the same gift, but how we say yes to it is quite different.

In Richard's view, the effects on Western Christianity of underemphasizing the divine indwelling have been tragic and lasting. The recognition of inherent goodness (love as our core) cannot be left to the whims and prejudices of the individual, as centuries of racism and classism have now proven. The theological and philosophical key is the rediscovery of a Trinitarian God—that is, love—as the template for all reality. Trinity is central to Richard's understanding and definition of love.

GROWING IN LOVE

Throughout this book, we will introduce many of the alternative teachings for which Richard has become known, all with a particular view for how they point to his overarching theme of love: Love is the foundation of everything; we love God by loving others, loving our self, and, finally, loving everything. We have drawn from Richard's work to illuminate a lifelong journey of growing in love. Experiences from Richard's life illustrate how the path has unfolded for him and how we each might come to know love more intimately. In Richard's words,

> This "pilgrim's progress" was, for me, sequential, natural, and organic as the circles widened. I was lucky enough to puddle-jump between countries, cultures, and concepts because of my public speaking; yet the solid

ground of the Perennial Tradition never really shifted. It was only the lens, the criteria, the inner space, and the scope that continued to expand. I was always being moved toward greater differentiation and larger viewpoints, and simultaneously toward a greater inclusivity in my ideas, a deeper understanding of people, and a more honest sense of justice. God always became bigger and led me to bigger places. If God could "include" and allow, then why not I? I did not see many examples of God "smiting" enemies; in fact, it was usually God's friends who got "smited," as Teresa of Avila noted! If God asked me to love unconditionally and universally, then it was clear that God operated in the same way.

—FU 107

Many of the biographical stories in this book emerged during several conversations we had with Richard in late 2016 and early 2017; a few came from talks he gave at an Illuman conference in 2016. His own words tell his story best! The teachings come primarily from his existing published work, adapted and reviewed by him. These meditations are, as Richard's friend and colleague Cynthia Bourgeault writes, "the ripe fruit of a life courageously and honestly lived."

We realize that love is a mystery too great for language. As Richard often says, his words are only a finger pointing to the moon, never the moon itself. He writes in *Falling Upward*, "All spiritual language is by necessity metaphor and symbol. The Light comes from elsewhere, yet it is necessarily reflected through those of us still walking on the journey ourselves. As Desmond Tutu told me on a recent trip to Cape Town, 'We are only the light bulbs, Richard, and our job is just to remain screwed in!'" (FU ix).

Love cannot be dissected into discrete components or stages; it is a dynamic dance. It is only for the sake of formatting this book that we have divided love into four parts or chapters. In reality, we grow in various aspects of love throughout our lives. It is rarely a chronological journey, but "three steps forward and two steps back," as Richard observes of Scripture, history, and human development. But as we talked with Richard and revisited familiar teachings, we saw a simple progression to help frame our exploration of his life in love.

We begin united in love with God, who is our *foundation*, the very "ground of our being," as theologian Paul Tillich suggested. We hopefully receive the love of parents and others to help us develop healthy psyches and egos. Through suffering and failure, we encounter a love not dependent upon our behavior but based upon grace. We practice loving and being loved with other humans and creatures, with our self, and with God. Richard writes in *Everything Belongs*, "Once I can see the Mystery here, and trust the Mystery even in this piece of clay that I am, in this moment of time that I am—then I can also see it in you. I am able to see the divine image in myself, in you, and eventually in *all things*" (EB 57). When you love God, you love everything. It's that simple . . . and it's that difficult!

Richard's own life began with, as he puts it, "an imaginarium very much formed by Catholic images of Incarnation, of a safe, loving, benevolent universe." In **Chapter 1 (1943–1957)**, we connect Richard's childhood in Kansas with his belief that **Love is the foundation of everything.** Richard has come to know **"God is love"** (1 John 4:8, 16) through his personal experience of divine and human love. That belief particularly shines through in his teachings on the Trinity, Creation, and Incarnation.

There are active and contemplative sides to love. Love must flow in and out for it to truly be love. Some people begin to experience love by loving someone else, perhaps a parent, child, partner, creature, or stranger. Others may start with an inner experience of being a beloved. Both action and contemplation need and feed each other. We must give and receive love; otherwise, we block the flow of God's love to us and, through us, to others. The second part of the book follows Richard as he joins the Franciscan Order where he hoped to learn to love like Jesus and Francis, by serving. First, he had to learn that he couldn't earn love or be perfect. Rather than being perfect, God calls us to love as God loves—without exception—which we can only do through God's own love. **Chapter 2 (1957–1985)** also shares Richard's experiences as pastor of New Jerusalem, the lay community he founded in Cincinnati, Ohio, in 1972. Here he continued to learn to see God in others, but "through many mistakes and trials," he insists. In this section, Richard's teachings focus on how **we love God by loving others.** "**Love one another as I have loved you**" (John 13:34).

As hard as we may try to love others, at some point we realize that unless we allow God to love us, we can never love unconditionally and unceasingly. Unless we receive God's love, we cannot continue giving love away. **Chapter 3 (1985–2000)** explores Richard's efforts to bring contemplation back to Christian awareness. After observing passionate activists, he realized that without the contemplative mind, those working to bring about social justice often become part of the problem themselves. Richard founded the Center for Action and Contemplation as a way to form healthy activists who could stay engaged for the long haul, grounding their compassionate action in God's love and nondual consciousness. In this chapter, we also share Richard's own struggles with self-doubt. Richard's experience during this period is tied to his teachings on how **we love God by loving our self; or really by allowing God to love us.** "**We love because God first loved us**" (1 John 4:19).

Finally, **Chapter 4 (2000–Present)** is about how we love God by loving what God loves. In other words, **we love God by loving everything.** In the end, "**God will be all in all**" (1 Corinthians 15:28). This section includes teachings on nondual thinking, the mystics, the evolution of consciousness, and living truthfully and in harmony with the infilling and outflowing that is the pattern of love in the universe. We see how Richard's desire to create a kind of seminary that emphasizes contemplation has come to fruition in the Living School for Action and Contemplation. And Richard shares how his dog, Venus, taught him love in one concrete place and helped him realize that love is stronger than death; love always wins.

Throughout his life, Richard has emphasized the importance
of incarnation, moving from the concrete to the universal, and
taking doctrine and dogma to the level of experience. Thus, it
only makes sense to let Richard's life experiences be the framework for his teachings on love. He explains:

> Humans are creators of meaning, and finding deep
> meaning in our experiences is not just another name for
> spirituality but is also the very shape of human happi-
> ness.   —FU 114

> Happiness is always a gift from first seeking union or
> love. *If love is your actual and constant goal, you can
> never really fail,* and happiness comes much easier and
> more naturally.   —SC 59

> This is because the heartfelt desire to do the will of God
> [i.e., to love], *is itself the truest will of God.*

No matter what religion or denomination we are raised in,
our spirituality still comes from our own life experience. And
we must begin to be honest about that instead of pretending
that any of us are formed exclusively by the Scriptures or our
Tradition! *There is no such thing as an entirely unbiased position; the best we can do is own and be honest about our filters.*
God allows us to trust our own experience, for we will anyway.
Scripture and Tradition hopefully keep our personal experiences
both critical and compassionate.

> The Great Traditions give name, shape, and ultimate
> direction to what our heart inherently knows from other
> sources. This is not new or unorthodox but exactly what
> Paul said to the Romans: "Ever since God created the
> world, God's everlasting power and divinity—how-
> ever invisible—have been there for the mind to see in
> the things of creation" (1:20). Similarly, as the Hebrew
> Scriptures say, "It is not beyond your strength or beyond
> your reach. It is not in the heavens, so that you need

to ask, 'Who will go up to heaven and bring it down to us?' Nor is it beyond the seas, so that you need to ask, 'Who will cross the seas and bring it back to us?' No, the Word is very near to you, it is in your mouth and in your heart" (Deuteronomy 30:11–14). We must honor the infinite mystery of our own life's journey to recognize God in it. Or is it the other way around? It seems that God is not going to let us get close unless we bring all of ourselves—in love—including our brokenness. That's why the Good News really is good news. Nothing is wasted.   —NOG 94–95

In summary, Richard loves to recite: "I write to you not because you do not know the truth, but because you know it already" (1 John 2:21). All true spiritual cognition is re-cognition.

1

1943–1957:
Love Is the Foundation of Everything

"God is love."—1 John 4:8, 16

I am more and more seeing that Love, God, and Consciousness are the same thing. They are the substratum of reality. As Teilhard de Chardin says, "The structural shape of the universe is love." —Richard Rohr

You see, faith in God is not just faith to believe in spiritual ideas. It's to have confidence in Love itself. It's to have confidence in reality itself. At its core, reality is okay. God is in it. God is revealed in all things.
—Richard Rohr (H April 10, 2016)

The Most Essential Teaching

The most powerful, most needed, and most essential teaching is always about Love. Love is our foundation and our destiny. It is where we come from and where we're headed. As St. Paul famously says, "So faith, hope, and love remain, but the greatest of these is love" (1 Corinthians 13:13).

My hope, whenever I speak or write, is to help clear away the impediments to receiving, allowing, trusting, and participating in a foundational Love. God's love is planted inside each of us as the Holy Spirit who, according to Jesus, "will teach you everything and remind you of all that I told you" (John 14:26). Love is who you are.

All I can do is remind you of what you already know deep within your True Self and invite you to live connected to this Source. John the Evangelist writes, "God is love, and whoever remains in love, remains in God and God in him or her" (1 John 4:16). The Judeo–Christian creation story says that we were created in the very "image and likeness" of God—who is love (Genesis 1:26; see also Genesis 9:6). Out of the Trinity's generative, loving relationship, creation takes form, mirroring its Creator.

We have heard this phrase so often that we don't get the existential shock of what "created in the image and likeness of God" is saying about us. If we could believe it, we would save ourselves thousands of dollars in therapy! If this is true—and I believe it is—our family of origin is divine. It is saying that we were created by a loving God to *be love* in the world. Our core is original blessing, not original sin. Our starting point is positive and, as it is written in the first chapter of the Bible, it is "very good" (Genesis 1:31). We do have a good place to go home. If the beginning is right, the rest is made considerably easier, because we know and can trust the clear direction of our life's tangent.

We must all overcome the illusion of separateness. It is the primary task of religion to communicate not worthiness but union, to reconnect people to their original identity "hidden with Christ in God" (Colossians 3:3). The Bible calls the state of separateness "sin." God's job description is to draw us back into primal and intimate relationship. "My dear people, we are already children of God; what we will be in the future has not yet been fully revealed, and all I do know is that we shall be like God" (1 John 3:2).   —TH 27–29

BUILDING THE CONTAINER

Richard was born in March of 1943, in the middle of World War II, a time of tremendous turmoil and tragedy in the wider world. He was somewhat sheltered from the global climate by his circumstances and location: the middle of Middle America in Topeka, Kansas, in a lower–middle-class German, Roman Catholic family. Richard's parents had grown up as wheat farmers during the Great Depression and the Dust Bowl of the 1930s. His father, also named Richard, found work painting trains for the Atchison, Topeka and Santa Fe Railway (AT&SF) and never missed a day in thirty-six years. He turned on the lights in the shops each morning.

Richard acquired the values of frugality, working hard, and being on time from his parents. It was only years later that he realized those were cultural values and not necessarily Gospel values. Richard recalls coming home as a young priest and saying, "Mother, did you know 'Cleanliness is next to godliness' is not in the Bible?"

"Yes, it is!" Eleanore asserted. He assured her it wasn't. She finally gave in, knowing her son the priest couldn't be wrong. But she added, "Well, it's still true!"

Richard credits his loving parents with giving him the container for a happy childhood. He says he had an ordinary, imperfect family like most others. He was the second of four children, two girls and two boys. Although he was the second born, he was the first son; and he thinks this is what made him his mother's favorite. His siblings are good-natured about it.

Richard's parents provided a combination of unconditional and conditional love. He recalls that his father, a Seven on the Enneagram,[1] was "extremely positive about everything, including me. He'd do little dances and was not afraid to get down on the floor and wrestle with us. He was a softie. I didn't have any father wounds, unlike many men." His mother, on the other

---

1. For an explanation of the Enneagram, see the section beginning with "Nine Faces of Love" on page 107 and the Appendix of this book.

hand, was an Enneagram Eight. Richard always knew she loved him, but she "was very demanding and strict. When you received her love, you felt like you'd earned it."

Richard reflects, "Now I know that my parents and the Catholic school culture of the 1950s created the whole container that made me feel safe enough and beloved enough so that when I went to seminary and studied the Gospels, I already had a template for a loving universe. It was not hard for me to believe I was God's beloved son, because I had been Mother and Daddy's beloved son. And the nuns always affirmed little Dickie!"

Unconditional and Conditional Love

The only happy people I have met are those who have found some way to serve. I do mean that. Such folks are not preoccupied with self-image, success, and power. They almost always began conservative and traditional with rules, discipline, and structure that created a kind of compression chamber. As we grow, the chamber becomes tight and oppressive and usually based on exclusion. So we begin to practice what we call "the sacred no" against self-serving laws, traditions, and cultural practices that pose as the will of God. We are no longer willing to prop up the status quo and believe this is all there is to life.

It seems many of the people raised in our culture in the last few decades grew up backward by beginning "liberal." This leaves the unconverted ego in the position of decider. I don't think we're doing our children any favors by raising them without boundaries or rules and largely letting them decide for themselves what is right. Basically, we're asking them to start from zero. In an overreaction to the generation before them, parents and the church have been trying hard to love unconditionally. I know this from doing it myself with the young people in the New Jerusalem Community in my early years as a priest. I was endlessly preaching about God's unconditional love. To be honest, although we drew thousands of young people, most did not take this very far in terms of a deep and lasting transformation or service to the world.

Eric Fromm, in his classic book *The Art of Loving*, states that the healthiest people he has known are those who received from their parents and early authority figures a combination of unconditional love and conditional love. This does seem to be true of so many effective and influential people, like St. Francis, John Muir, Eleanor Roosevelt, and St. Teresa of Calcutta. I know my siblings and I received conditional love from our mother and unconditional love from our father. We all admit now that Mom's demanding love served us very well later in life, although we sure fought her when we were young. And we were glad Daddy was there to balance her out.

I am convinced that Fromm is wise and correct, and his wisdom surely matches my own lifetime of observation. It seems we need a goad, a wall to butt up against, to create a proper ego structure and a strong identity. Such a foil is the way we internalize our own deeper values, educate our feeling function, and dethrone our own narcissism. We all need to internalize the sacred "no" to our natural egocentricity. It seems we need a certain level of frustration, a certain amount of not having our needs met. Then we realize there are other people who also have needs and desires and feelings. As my mother told me, "Dickie, your rights end at the end of your nose; that's where somebody else's nose begins."   —STHL discs 1–2 and FU 32–34

The Core Is Good

If I do have an ordered theology, I guess a secure childhood would be its beginning and foundation: reality can be trusted. The core is good. Despite all evidence to the contrary, *what is* is okay. As our Franciscan Doctor, St. Bonaventure (1221–1274), put it, "Being and Goodness are the same thing. They differ only in reason of words." That affirmation is not logically or even psychologically obvious. It is a gift of grace. Some call it faith, some call it hope, and some call it love. But it is surely the beginning of the spiritual journey. The Catholic Tradition calls these the theological virtues, which mean that both their source and their goal are the same—God. These virtues are not worked for, chosen, or achieved. They are given to those who ask and wait with anticipation. Until that foundational faith, hope, and love are received, most religion is a disguise, pretense, or a waste of time—more part of the problem than part of the solution.

Until God has elicited that primordial act of confidence in ourselves, in others, in the natural world, it is actually a dodge and a deception to talk about having confidence in "God-out-there." The words have no concrete meaning, and religion will only lead us to various forms of legalism, pharisaism, and fear which cover up our lack of confidence in anything or anybody. Virtue is of one piece. You cannot be cynical about yourself and confident in God, because you really have not gone to the school that teaches confidence: the world of adversity. You cannot love anyone unless you learn how to love everyone. Loving, as opposed to liking, is a gift of God's pure being; it is not called forth by some and withheld from others. It simply is and has nothing to do with the other meeting our needs. Hope is not occasioned by things working out as we expected. If our hope rises or falls according to circumstances, we do not have hope. As Paul says so well in Romans, "We can be happy right now. Our trials produce endurance, and endurance produces a stubborn hope, a hope that will not disappoint us. It is the love of God poured forth in our heart" (5:3–5).   —NOG 95–96

CHOSEN

Richard remembers visiting his Catholic parish as a little boy and seeing "all the statues, paintings, color, music, incense, and candles. It was just a mystical place, and I was in awe. It felt like a different world. To me it felt like the real world."

That "real world" feeling echoes Richard's earliest memory of a God-experience: "I was probably five years old. I was in the living room. All the family was in the kitchen talking, and the kitchen was bright. But the living room was dark with just the Christmas tree lit. I had the sense that the world was good, I was good, and I was part of the good world; and I just wanted to stay there. I remember feeling very special, very chosen, very beloved, and it was my secret. The family in the kitchen didn't know what I was knowing." With a chuckle Richard adds, "Do you see the ego involved in that?"

Richard notes how anyone's first spiritual experience can be very ego-inflating. But, like the Apostle Paul, he knows that, "Chosenness is for the sake of letting everybody else know they are chosen too!" Richard has spent his adult life doing just that, reminding people of their inherent belovedness.

Richard describes his Christmas tree experience as being taken to another world, the real world, the world as it's meant to be, where the foundation is love and God is in everything. It's a benevolent universe where God is on our side and God is more for us than we are for ourselves, where "my deepest me is God," as Catherine of Genoa says. Richard explains that the reason he is so intent on reforming things is not only because he's an Enneagram One, but because he's seen how the world can be and how much it is not that way!

Richard often tells of another early spiritual encounter in first or second grade, this time in church. He remembers going up to look at the Nativity scene on Epiphany when the three kings and their camels finally arrived to see Jesus, Mary, and Joseph. "I remember feeling how lucky I am to live in this world where it all makes sense and it's all good. It is all focused in the birth of this little baby." Richard lights up. "It's funny how both of these early God-experiences happened around Christmas: the Christmas tree and the Christmas crib. You can see why the Incarnation became the heart of my understanding of the Gospel and how good it was that I was led to the Franciscans, not yet knowing that they were the great teachers of incarnationalism!"

The Face of the Other

It was probably St. Francis of Assisi (c. 1181–1226) who first brought attention to the humanity of Jesus. Prior to the life of

St. Francis, paintings of Jesus largely emphasized his divinity, as they still do in most Eastern icons. Francis is said to have created the first live Nativity scene. Before the thirteenth century, Christmas was no big deal. The emphasis was on the high holy days of Easter, as it seems it should be. But for Francis, the Incarnation was already redemption. For God to become a human being among the poor, born in a stable among the animals, meant that it's good to be a human being, that flesh is good, and that the world is good—in its most simple and humble forms.

In Jesus, God was given a face and a heart. God became someone we could love. While God can be described as a moral force, as consciousness, and as high vibrational energy, the truth is, we don't (or can't?) fall in love with abstractions. So God became a person "that we could hear, see with our eyes, look at, and touch with our hands" (1 John 1:1). The brilliant Jewish philosopher, Emmanuel Levinas, says the only thing that really converts people is "the face of the other." He develops this at great length and with great persuasion. When the face of the other (especially the suffering face) is received and empathized with, it leads to transformation of our whole being. It creates a moral demand on our heart that is far more compelling than the Ten Commandments. Just giving people commandments on tablets of stone doesn't change the heart. It may steel the will, but it doesn't soften the heart like personal encounter can. So many Christian mystics talk about seeing the divine face or falling in love with the face of Jesus. There is no doubt that was the experience of Francis and Clare of Assisi. I think that's why Clare often uses the word "mirroring." We are mirrored not by concepts, but by faces delighting in us, giving us the face we can't give to ourselves. It is the gaze that does us in!

Jesus taught us what God is like through his words, his actions, his very being, making it clear that "God is love" (1 John 4:8, 16). If God is Trinity and Jesus is the face of God, then it is a benevolent universe. God is not someone to be afraid of, but is the Ground of Being and is on our side. —FM discs 2–3

INCARNATIONAL MYSTICISM

A few years ago, when asked how he would describe all of his teaching in two words, Richard replied: "incarnational mysticism." He's still happy with that response, which like all of his best stuff, came right from the gut. Richard doesn't write his talks. As a One on the Enneagram, he's a "gut" or "body" person. He says his ideas don't go through his head: he talks straight from his physical core.

Richard is the first to admit that his way of speaking doesn't work well if he's not "connected to the flow" or "aligned with God." But his listeners know he usually lives up to his name ("Rohr" is German for "conduit"). He has been a conduit of the Spirit for many of us, a humble, embodied example of incarnational mysticism. Richard's teaching joins together what never should have been thought separate: the secular and the sacred, the flesh and the spirit, earth and heaven, the world and God. "God is not 'out there'!" Richard continually reminds us, citing a holy recluse who once told him, "I do not get to preach to the people, but you do. Just tell them one thing: 'God is not out there!'" The hermit pointed to the sky and then quickly walked away.

God Is Not "Out There"

Incarnation is the overcoming of the gap between God and everything else. It is the synthesis of matter and spirit. Without incarnation, God remains separate from us and from creation. Because of incarnation, we can say, "God is with us!" In fact, God is in us, and in everything else that God created. We all have the divine DNA; everything bears the divine fingerprint, if the mystery of embodiment is true.

God, who is love, incarnates as the universe beginning with the Big Bang approximately 13.8 billion years ago. Then 2,000 years ago, God incarnates as Jesus of Nazareth, when humanity was ready for relationship and to personally comprehend that this mystery could be met, engaged with, and even loved. So matter and spirit have always been one, ever since God decided to manifest Godself in the first act of creation (Ephesians 1:3–10; Colossians 1:15–20).

It is crucial that we understand the importance of incarnation. The belief that God is "out there" is the basic dualism that is tearing us all apart. Our view of God as separate and distant has harmed our understandings of our sexuality; of our relationship to food, possessions, and money; and of our relationship to animals, nature, and our own incarnate selves. This loss is foundational to why we live such distraught and divided lives. Jesus came precisely to put it all together for us and in us. He was saying, in effect, "To be human is good! The material and the physical can be trusted and enjoyed. This world is the hiding place of God and the revelation of God!"

The final stage of incarnation is *resurrection*! This is no exceptional miracle only done once in the body of Jesus. It is the final and fulfilled state of all embodiment. Now even the new physics tells us that matter itself is a manifestation of spirit, and *spirit or shared consciousness is the real thing*. Matter also seems to be eternal. We do say in the Creed that we believe in "the resurrection of the body," whereas many Christians—still followers of Plato more than Jesus—only believe in the eternal nature of the soul.   —EB 117–19

Lover of All

Lord, lover of life, lover of these lives,
Lord, lover of our souls, lover of our bodies, lover of all that
   exists . . .
In fact, it is your love that keeps it all alive . . .
May we live in this love.
May we never doubt this love.
May we know that we are love,
That we were created for love,
That we are a reflection of you,
That you love yourself in us and therefore we are perfectly
   lovable.

May we never doubt this deep and abiding and perfect
   goodness
That we are because you are.   —HOV disc 4

CONDITIONAL LOVE

*Richard started teaching early. At the age of seven, he would
gather his siblings and neighborhood friends and have them sit
on a bench in the backyard. "I would hold my penny catechism
upside down since I could not read yet, and I would pretend to
teach 'about Jesus.' I must have been a weird little kid!" Richard
muses.*

*Regardless, he was a happy kid. Childhood photos show him
grinning. Richard's mother told him he was always screaming
with excitement. She'd admonish him, "If you want to scream,
go outside." So he would. At some point, Richard's spontaneous
joy turned into seriousness. He admits, "Somewhere during my
early years I became committed to being the good boy, the nice
boy. In grade school, I tried to please the sisters because I wanted
their love just like I had my mother's love."*

*Attending Catholic school—where the reward/punishment,
perfection/achievement system maintained order—reinforced
his mother's modeling of conditional love. "The God I was presented with was no unconditional lover," he says. "But that was
the whole Catholic world in the 1950s; all of us seemed to live
in it. Reality was shaped by a God who demands justice, who is
punitive." However, Richard does not have any Catholic school
"horror stories." Of his Irish priest and nun teachers, Richard
says, "I can see now that they were generous-hearted people,
even though the theology and morality they taught us was rather
pathetic. 'Be a good boy, and God will love you.' It makes for
conformity and very little disruption since we are all agreeing
together to abide by the same laws.*

*"When I was a little altar boy, I rode my bike at six in the
morning in the dark to serve at Mass. I see now that I was doing
just what Luther had observed during the Reformation. While*

not realizing it, I was 'saving my soul' by doing all these correct rituals and obeying commandments. Obedience was the highest virtue, not love. Even though I felt that most of the people who taught me were loving people, they didn't teach me how *to love, except by being rather nice people themselves. What they did teach me was obedience to law."*

When asked, "So, how did you learn how to love?" Richard responds in his characteristically honest and humble way, "Well, I don't know that I have. But first of all, by meeting loving people. It's that simple. And then contemplation became such a gift because, yes, I met these loving people, but I didn't know how to be like them because there was no one teaching us how to clean the lens of awareness and perception. Being loving was just about willpower. 'Obey the law and you will go to heaven.' So by willpower we tried to force ourselves to be loving. But when you are forcing yourself to do the loving thing, it doesn't feel like love to other people. It isn't a natural flow."

Creative Continuation

Mature Christianity is an invitation to share in the personal life of God, a dynamic flow of eternally generated love forever continued in space and time through God's creatures. *Thus, God's self-knowledge includes knowledge of us, and God's self-love includes love of us.* They are the same knowing, the same loving, and the same freedom.

Yes, in some sense we become an "other" that can be seen as a separate object from God, but from God's side we are always known and loved subject to subject, just as the persons of the Trinity know and love one another. God and the human person must (and can) know one another center to center, subject to subject; we will not and cannot know one another if we objectify one another.

This is perhaps the clearest way to describe God's unconditional acceptance of us, forgiveness of our mistakes, and mercy toward us in all circumstances: We are never an object to God.

God cannot *not* love God's image in us. This is the eternal covenant.

So, a fully Christian theology and philosophy of the human person must say that our personhood originates in the divine Logos, the eternal Christ, as imitations and reflections of God's relationship to Godself. We are constituted by the same relationship that exists between the Father, Son, and Holy Spirit!

Divine Personhood and human personhood are reciprocal, mutual concepts. God's nature as relationship creates ours; and our nature is constituted by this same bond, which is infinite openness and capacity to love. We must know that we are in fact objectively lovable to honestly be able to love ourselves. We cannot pretend. Our false self is never fully ready to trust in unconditional love. Maybe forgiveness and forbearance, but not unconditional love—at best a kind of highly conditional love, which is most practical Christianity when people do not go inside of the Living Mystery.

You cannot "get" to such a place; you can only rest and rejoice in such a place.   —DD 78–79

ALONE WITH THE PRESENCE

Richard speaks of one Catholic ritual that helped lay the foundation for contemplation in his life. "They used to have Forty Hours' Devotion where the Blessed Sacrament [the communion host] is displayed for forty hours and all members of the church are asked to spend an hour in adoration, so the church is never empty during that period. I remember riding my bike to church at four o'clock in the morning. (The nun probably signed me up for that time because she knew that little Dickie Rohr would show up—and on time, too!) It was a holy experience. There were no words, there was no music, just the bread exposed and candles lit. The church was totally silent. And at that time of the morning, it was just me and Jesus. There was nothing else to do but to be alone with the Presence."

Loving the Presence in the Present

We cannot *attain* the presence of God because we're already *in* the presence of God. What's absent is awareness. Little do we realize that God's love is maintaining us in existence with every breath we take. As we take another, it means that God is choosing us now and now and now. We have nothing to attain or even learn. We do, however, need to unlearn some things.

To become aware of God's loving presence in our lives, we have to accept that human culture is in a mass hypnotic trance. We're sleepwalkers. All great religious teachers have recognized that we human beings do not naturally see; we have to be taught how to see. Jesus says further, "If your eye is healthy, your whole body is full of light" (Luke 11:34). Religion is meant to teach us how to see and be present to reality. That's why the Buddha and Jesus say with one voice, "Be awake." Jesus talks about "staying watchful" (Matthew 25:13; Luke 12:37; Mark 13:33–37), and "Buddha" means "I am awake" in Sanskrit.

Prayer is not primarily saying words or thinking thoughts. It is, rather, a stance. It's a way of living in the Presence, living in awareness of the Presence, and even enjoying the Presence. The contemplative is not just aware of God's Loving Presence, but trusts, allows, and delights in it.

All spiritual disciplines have one purpose: to get rid of illusions so we can be present. These disciplines exist so that we can see what is, see who we are, and see what is happening. What *is* is love. It is God, who is love, giving away God every moment as the reality of our life. Who we are is love, because we are created in God's image. What is happening is God living in us, with us, and through us as love. —EB 29–31

FINDING GOD IN NATURE

A natural Franciscan, Richard has always been fascinated with creation. "When I was little I loved to look at trees, plant things and watch them grow, and know the names of different flowers and shrubs. I had a special patch of velvety green grass in a secret place on my cousins' farm in western Kansas where I would hide out and look at the stars at night. I called it my 'beautiful spot.' I have a feeling it is still there."

Infinite Presence, Infinite Love

If Christianity would have paid attention to the teachings and example of Jesus and St. Francis, our planet—"Mother Sister Earth," as Francis called her—would perhaps be much healthier today. But it took until the 21st century for a pope to write an entire encyclical, *Laudato Si': On Care for Our Common Home,* making this quite clear and demanding.

We have not honored God's Presence in the elemental, physical world. We made God as small as our own constricted hearts. We picked and chose, saying, "Oh, God is really only in my group, in baptized people, in moral people, etc." Is there that little of an Infinite God to go around? Do we have to be stingy with God? As Isaiah put it "the arm of God is not too short to save!" (59:1). Why pretend only *we* deserve God, and that God is not for other groups, religions, animals, plants, the elements, Brother Sun, and Sister Moon?

God is saving creation and bringing all creatures back where they began—into union with their Creator. God loves everything that God has made! All created things God proclaimed "good" (see Genesis 1:9–31 and Wisdom 11:24–12:1). But we, with our small minds, can't deal with that. We have to whittle God and love into small parts that our minds can handle and portion out. Human love is conditional and operates out of a scarcity model. There's not enough to go around, just like Andrew said about the boy's five loaves and two small fish (John 6:9). Humans can't conceptualize or even *think* infinite or eternal concepts. We cannot imagine Infinite Love, Infinite Goodness, or Infinite Mercy.

We don't come to the God Mystery through concepts or theories but by connecting with *what is*—with God's immediate, embodied presence which is all around us. Notice that almost all of Jesus' common stories and examples are nature based and relationship based—never once academic theory.

We have not recognized the one Body of Christ in creation. Perhaps we just didn't have the readiness or training. There is first of all the seeing, and then there is the recognizing; the second stage is called contemplation. We cannot afford to be blind any longer. We must learn to see and recognize how broad and deep the Presence is if we are to truly care for our common home.   —H August 16, 2016 and THTT disc 2

Created to Love

St. Augustine (354–430) said, "the church consists in the state of communion of the whole world."[2] Wherever we are connected, in right relationship—you might say "in love"—there is the Christ, there is the authentic "body of God" revealed. This body is more a living organism than any formal organization.

Non-human creation is invariably obedient to its destiny. Animals and plants seem to excitedly take their small place in the "circle of life," in the balance of nature, in the dance of complete interdependence. It is only we humans who have resisted our place in "the one great act of giving birth" (see Romans 8:22), even though we have the most powerful role! Humans, in fact, have frequently chosen death for themselves and for so many other creatures besides. We are, by far, the most destructive of all species.

Jesus clearly taught that if we seek first God's kingdom and the universal law of love ("love God and love one another," Matthew 22:37–40), all the rest would take care of itself (see Matthew 6:33). We would no longer blatantly defy the laws of nature but seek to live in harmony and sustainability with Earth and all her creatures. This radical lifestyle demands a sense of inherent dignity that is granted by God and not an off-and-on dignity determined by egocentric humans.

---

2. Augustine, "Ecclesiam in totius orbis communion consistere," from *De unitate ecclesiae* (*On the unity of the Church*), XX, 56.

As *Homo sapiens* ("Wise Humans"), we should have taken our place as what Teilhard de Chardin called "the pinnacle of evolution" or "the rocks come to consciousness." Then we could *join with the rest of creation* in obedience to our unique and full destiny. In poet Gerard Manley Hopkins' words:

Each mortal thing does one thing and the same:
. . . *myself* it speaks and spells,
Crying *What I do is me: for that I came.*[3]

When we get the "who" right and realize that *who I am is love*, then we will do what we came to do: *Love God and love all that this God has created.* I firmly believe that grace is inherent to creation and not an occasional additive, and that God and goodness—not Armageddon—have both the first and final word, which we call divine creation and final resurrection.

—SE 235–41

The Soul of All Things

Apprehend God in all things, for God is in all things.
Every single creature is full of God and is a book about
   God.
Every creature is a word of God.
If I spent enough time with the tiniest creature—even a
   caterpillar—
I would never have to prepare a sermon.
So full of God is every creature.   —Meister Eckhart[4]

Creation is the first and primary face of God. (See Romans 1:20.) The world itself is the universal religion that precedes all

---

3. Gerard Manley Hopkins, "As Kingfishers Catch Fire," in *Gerard Manley Hopkins: The Major Works* (London: Oxford University Press, 2009), 129.

4. Matthew Fox, *Meditations with Meister Eckhart* (Vermont: Bear & Company, 1983), 14. Used with permission.

organized religions. Do you really think that God would not have made Godself available to the Stone Age people and all historical peoples who were created in "the image and likeness of God," just like all of us? We monotheists should have been the first to recognize this because we believe in "one God who created *all* things!"

Or was God just waiting for the Catholics and Evangelicals to come along? Unfortunately, when we Catholics came, we loved to build fancy churches, without any encouragement from Jesus, I might add; and we went quickly inside them, disconnecting our minds and hearts from the natural world, probably because the natural world seemed wild and dangerous to us. Our very word *profane* comes from *pro*, meaning "in front of," and *fanum*, meaning "temple." We thought we lived "outside the temple." Without a nature-based spirituality, it was a profane universe, bereft of Spirit, so we had to keep building shrines and churches to capture and hold our now domesticated and tamed God. Soon we did not know where to look for the divine. We became like fish in a huge ocean looking for water, and often arguing about who owned the water!

Note that I'm not saying God *is* all things (pantheism), but that each living thing reveals some aspect of God's presence; God is both greater than the whole of our universe, and as Creator interpenetrates all created things (pan*en*theism). No exceptions. The Judeo–Christian conviction about this was so total, that the ancient myths even had Lucifer created by God (Isaiah 14:12–15) and Satan in the divine council (Job 1:6–12).

St. Francis is the earliest recorded Christian to grant animals and objects subjectivity, mutuality, even naming them as sister and brother. He could talk and listen to them. Few Christians are trained to see all created things in this way. Yet it is the heart of all contemplative seeing. We were told animals didn't have souls. I fully disagree.

Love is at the core of all beings. When you know this, as Thomas Berry says, the world becomes "a communion of subjects more than a collection of objects," to state it quite perfectly and profoundly.

When you love something, you grant it soul, you see its soul, and you let its soul touch yours. You have to love something deeply to know its soul. Before the resonance of love, you are largely blind to a thing's meaning, value, and its power to literally save you. In fact, until you can appreciate and even delight in the ecstatic wag of a dog's tail and other such ubiquitous signals, I doubt if you have discovered your own soul.   —NC disc 2

Nature Reflects God's Goodness

Nature itself is the primary Bible. The world is the locus of the sacred and provides all the metaphors that the soul needs for its growth.

If you scale chronological history down to the span of one year, with the Big Bang on January 1, then our species, *Homo sapiens*, doesn't appear until 11:59 PM on December 31. That means our written Bible and the Church appeared in the last nanosecond of December 31. I can't believe that God had nothing to say until the last moment. Rather, as both Paul and Thomas Aquinas say, God has been revealing God's love, goodness, and beauty since the very beginning through the natural world of creation. (See Romans 1:20.) "God looked at everything God had made, and found it very good" (Genesis 1:31).

Acknowledging the intrinsic value and beauty of creation, elements, plants, and animals is a major paradigm shift for most Western and cultural Christians. In fact, we have often dismissed it as animism or paganism. We limited God's love and salvation to our own human species, and even then we did not have enough love to go around for *all* of humanity! God ended up looking quite miserly and inept, to be honest.

Listen instead to the Book of Wisdom (13:1, 5):

> How dull are all people who, from the things-that-are, have not been able to discover God-Who-Is, or by studying the good works have failed to recognize the

Artist. . . . Through the grandeur and beauty of the creatures we may, by analogy, contemplate their Author.

All you have to do today is walk outside and gaze at one leaf,
long and lovingly, until you know, really know, that this leaf is
a participation in the eternal being of God. It's enough to create
ecstasy. The seeming value or dignity of an object doesn't matter;
it is the dignity of your relationship to that thing that matters.
For a true contemplative, a gratuitously falling leaf will awaken
awe and wonder just as much as a golden tabernacle in a cathe-
dral. —NC disc 1

MIRRORING

*In his teaching, Richard emphasizes the importance of early
mirroring. Neuroscience now shows that the gaze between a
newborn and his or her loving caregiver creates mirror neurons
that help a person become compassionate and have empathy for
others. Richard says, "All holiness is mirrored holiness." He adds
that although "none of us can experience absolutely unconditional divine love from another human being, we can experience
aspects of it. That helps us keep the doors open to God's love.
Our parents' love doesn't have to match divine love exactly, but
it has to be similar so that we can imagine what God's love
feels like."*

*When asked if he remembers other people who showed him
love in his early life, Richard recalls his second-grade teacher,
Sister Incarnata (note the name!). "She still keeps in touch! We
send Christmas greetings to one another. She's a very creative
musician and a beautiful woman. They must have put habits
on eighteen-year-old girls in those days. I remember I was one
of her favorites in the classroom, and I reveled in that. I'd stay
afterward to clean her blackboard because she was so good
to me.*

*"Then there was Bonnie, the girl I fell in love with in the
eighth grade. We danced together in every dance, and then I
went off to the seminary."*

Was it hard to leave her for the seminary?

"*I wouldn't say it was hard.*" Richard laughs at himself. "*I was so 'spiritual,' you know. My whole wonderful, sanctimonious future was ahead!*"

Richard knew he was to be a priest ever since the Christmas tree experience at age five.

"*It took me years to process this, but I think I also went away to the all-male world of a seminary to get away from an excess of feminine energy and attention. We lived a block from the Methodist Home in Topeka, Kansas, and my mother was a beautician. My dad built a little beauty shop adjoining our house. So all these little sweet ladies from the Methodist Home would come and have their hair done by my mother. I grew up being loved to death by Methodist women with blue hair. Then at school, we were taught by nuns in their full and enveloping habits. So I grew up surrounded by women: older sister, younger sister, doting mother, older cousin Julie who lived with us, and the Sisters of Charity of Leavenworth who taught us. I could do no wrong in their eyes, and I was going to keep all that specialness by being a good boy. Cute little Dickie was the center of everything. Little did I realize that I was basking in such immense affirmation. But that did give me a kind of brash self-confidence.*"

Big Love

We can't seem to know the good news that we are God's beloveds on our own. It has to be mirrored to us. We're essentially social beings. Another has to tell us we are beloved and good. Within contemplative prayer, we present ourselves for the ultimate gaze, the ultimate mirroring. Before this gaze of Love, we gradually disrobe and allow ourselves to be seen, to be known in every nook and cranny, nothing hidden, nothing denied, nothing disguised. It's like lovemaking. The wonderful thing is, after a while, we feel so safe that we know we don't have to pretend or disguise any more. We don't have to put on any kind of costume.

Letting your naked self be known by God is always to recognize your need for mercy and your own utter inadequacy and littleness. You realize that even the best things you've done have often been for mixed and selfish motives, not *really* for love. The saints often weep in the middle of prayer because they recognize how tiny they are in the presence of such Infinity. Your need for mercy draws you close to God. It's a wonderful and humiliating experience. Within contemplation, you stand under an immense waterfall of mercy, compassion, and forgiveness.

Knowing your need for mercy opens you to receiving mercy. Knowing your intimate need for mercy is in great part what it means to know, need, or fall in love with God, because *God is mercy itself and must be experienced as such*! If you live like the Pharisee in Jesus' parable (Luke 18:9–14), where you do everything perfectly and you are never in need of mercy, then you will never know God! So don't be too good, even in your own eyes. Make sure you always and happily stand on the receiving end of God, just like the Three Persons of the Trinity do with one another, where self-emptying always precedes any new infilling.

—TSFS discs 1–2

The Foundation Is Always Love

Only God in you can know God, through silence. You cannot know God in an intimate, experiential way with your mind alone. You are going to need full access knowing, which many of us call the contemplative mind, or even the "mind of Christ" (1 Corinthians 2:16).

Great religion seeks utter awareness and full consciousness, so that we can, in fact, receive all. Everything belongs and everything can be received. We don't have to deny, dismiss, defy, or ignore. *What is, is the great teacher.*

The purpose of prayer and religious seeking is to see the truth about reality, to see *what is*. And at the bottom of *what is* is always goodness. *The foundation is always Love.*

Enlightenment is to see and touch the big mystery, the big pattern, the Big Real. Jesus called it the kingdom of God; Buddha called it enlightenment. Philosophers might call it Truth. Many of us see it as Foundational Love. Here is a mantra you might repeat throughout your day to remind yourself of this:

> God's life is living itself in me. I am aware of life living itself in me.
> God's love is living itself in me. I am aware of love living itself in me.

You cannot *not* live in the presence of God. This is not soft or sentimental spirituality, but ironically demands confidence that must be chosen many times and surrender that is always hard won.   —EB 54–57 and DDEMT discs 1–3

What You Seek Is What You Are

Any authentic spirituality will emphasize a real equivalence and mutuality between the one who sees and what can be seen. There is a symbiosis between the heart/mind of the seer and what they will pay attention to. All *being* can rightly be spoken of with "one voice," as John Duns Scotus put it. What I am you also are, and so is the world. *Creation is one giant symphony of mutual sympathy.* Or, as Augustine loved to say, "In the end there will only be Christ loving himself."

To understand this, *I must know that I am, at least in part, the very thing I am seeking.* In fact, that is what makes me seek it! But most do not know this good news yet. God cannot be found "out there" until God is first found "in here," within ourselves, as Augustine profoundly expressed in his *Confessions* in many ways. Then we can almost naturally see God in others and in all of creation too. *What you seek is what you are.* The search for God and the search for our True Self are finally the same search. St. Francis' all-night prayer, "Who are you, O God, and who am I?" is probably a perfect prayer, because it is the most honest prayer we can offer.

A heart transformed by this realization of oneness knows that only love "in here," in me, can spot and enjoy love "out there."

Fear, constriction, and resentment are seen by spiritual teachers to be an inherent blindness that must be overcome. Those emotions cannot get you anywhere, certainly not anywhere good. Thus, all mystics are positive people—or they are not mystics! Their spiritual warfare is precisely the work of recognizing and then handing over all of their inner negativity and fear to God. The great paradox here is that such a victory is total gift from God and yet somehow you must want it very much (see Philippians 2:12–13).

The central practice in Franciscan mysticism, therefore, is that we must *remain in love* (John 15:9). Only when we are *eager to love* can we see love and goodness in the world around us. We must ourselves remain in peace, and then we will find peace over there. Remain in beauty, and we will honor beauty everywhere. This concept of remaining or abiding (John 15:4–5) moves all religion out of any esoteric realms of doctrinal outer space where it has been lost for too long. There is no secret moral command for knowing or pleasing God, or what some call "salvation," beyond becoming a loving person in mind, heart, body, and soul. Then you will see what you need to see. God did not say "Be right"; God said "Be in love."   —EL 7–10

The Hidden Secret

St. Bonaventure taught, "We are each loved by God in a particular and incomparable way, as in the case of a bride and bridegroom."[5] Francis and Clare of Assisi knew that the love God has for each soul is unique and made to order, which is why any "saved" person feels beloved, chosen, and even "God's favorite." Many biblical characters also knew and experienced this specialness. Divine intimacy is always and precisely particular and made to order—and thus "intimate."

---

5. Bonaventure, "The Breviloquium," in *The Works of St. Bonaventure* (St. Bonaventure, NY: St. Bonaventure University Press, 2005), 253.

The inner knowledge of God's love is described as joy itself (see John 15:11). This inner knowing is the Indwelling Presence. Which comes first? Does feeling safe and held by God allow you to deal with others in the same way? Or does human tenderness allow you to imagine that God must be the same, but infinitely so? I do not suppose it really matters where you start; the important thing is that you get in on the big secret from one side or the other.

Yes, "secret," or even "hidden secret," is what writers like the Psalmist (25:14, JB), Paul, Rumi, Hafiz, Bonaventure, Lady Julian, and many mystics called it. And for some sad reason, it seems to be a well-kept secret. Jesus praises God for "hiding these things from the learned and the clever and revealing them only to the little ones" (Matthew 11:25). Well, what is it that the learned and the clever often cannot see?

The big and hidden secret is this: an infinite God seeks and desires intimacy with the human soul. Once you experience such intimacy, only the intimate language of lovers describes what is going on for you: mystery, tenderness, singularity, specialness, changing the rules "for me," nakedness, risk, ecstasy, incessant longing, and of course also, necessary suffering. This is the mystical vocabulary of the saints.   —EL xviii and ID 163–65

Love Is Who You Are

Your True Self is who you are, and always have been in God; and at its core, your True Self is love itself. Love is both who you are and who you are still becoming, like a sunflower seed that becomes its own sunflower. Most of human history has referred to the True Self as your "soul" or "your participation in the eternal life of God." The great surprise and irony is that "you," or who you think you are, have nothing to do with your True Self's original creation or its ongoing existence. This is disempowering and utterly empowering at the same time. There's nothing you can do to make God love you more; and there's nothing you can do to make God love you less. All you can do is nurture your

True Self, which is saying quite a lot. It is love becoming love in this unique form called "me."

According to Paul (Romans 8:28), becoming my True Self seems to be a fully cooperative effort, and this is affirmed in my own limited experience. God never forces himself/herself on us or coerces us toward life or love by any threats whatsoever. God seduces us, yes; coerces us, no (Jeremiah 20:7; Matthew 11:28–30). Whoever this God is, he or she is utterly free and utterly respects our own human freedom. Love cannot happen in any other way. Love flourishes inside freedom and then increases that freedom even more. "For freedom Christ has set us free!" shouts Paul in his critique of all legalistic religion (Galatians 5:1).

We are allowed to ride life's and love's wonderful mystery for a few years—until life and love reveal themselves as the same thing, which is the final and full message of the Risen Christ. Life morphs into a love that is beyond space and time. Christ literally "breathes" *shalom* and forgiveness into the universal air (John 20:22–23). We get to add our own finishing touches of love, our own life breath to the Great Breath, and then return the completed package to its maker in a brand new but also same form. It is indeed the same "I," but now it is in willing union with the great "I AM" (Exodus 3:14). It is no longer just one, but not two either. —ID 176–78

The Importance of Good Theology

Brothers and sisters, I believe that behind every mistaken understanding of reality there is always a mistaken understanding of God. If you draw close to someone who is in a violent or fearful state, you will likely discover that his or her operative image of God (usually largely unconscious) is inadequate, distorted, or even toxic. That's why good theology is still important.

I believe the ultimate purpose of theology is to clarify the central, foundational doctrine of the loving nature of the One at the center of it all, whom many of us call "God."

For Christians, this became "Trinity," a word not even found in the Bible. Yet it has emerged in the deepest levels of orthodox theology as the best way to describe the "shape" of God, and therefore, finally a study of the very shape and pattern of everything else created in this divine image (Genesis 1:26–27).

God has done only one constant thing since the beginning of time: God has always, forever, and without hesitation loved "the Son"—and yes, you can equally and fittingly use "the Daughter"—understood in this sense as *creation, the material universe, you and me*. The quality of the relationship toward the other is the point, not gender or even species.

This flow of love goes full circle. The "Son" also creates the "Father" precisely *as Father*—as any parent can attest. A parent is not truly a parent until the child returns the flow. Watch the joy and tears on a mother's or father's face when their little one first says "Mama!" or "Dada!"

The Trinity has tremendous practical, pastoral, and political implications. We do not have time for anything less than loving! Fear will never build a "new creation" (Galatians 6:15); threat is an entirely worn out and false story line. The lowest level of motivation is guilt, shame, reward, and punishment; it has not moved us anywhere close to a civilization of love.

The Trinity beautifully undoes all negativity by a *totally* positive movement that never reverses its direction. God is *always* giving, even in those moments when *we* experience the inaccessibility of love as if it were divine anger.

When you find yourself drawing these conclusions, look deeply inside yourself and you will probably find that *you* are angry and projecting your anger onto God. This very human pattern is illustrated throughout the Bible, as the text reflects both the growth and resistance of the human soul. I call it three steps forward and two steps back. References to the "wrath" of God are an example of the two steps back. But the whole text moves slowly and inexorably toward inclusivity, mercy, unconditional love, and forgiveness.

I do not believe there is any wrath in God whatsoever—it's theologically impossible when God is Trinity.
—DDEMT discs 1–3 and DD 137, 139–40, 166–67

A Relational Universe

If a relational Creator started this whole thing, then there has to be a "DNA connection," as it were, between the One who creates and what is created. One of the many wonderful things that scientists are discovering as they compare their observations through microscopes with those through telescopes is that the pattern of the neutrons, protons, and electrons in atoms is similar to the pattern of planets, stars, and galaxies: all appear to be in orbit around and in relationship with everything else. There *is* a similarity between the perceived two ends of the universe, the Creator and all the creatures, just as Christians should have expected.

The energy in the universe is not in the planets, nor in the atomic particles, but very surprisingly in *the relationship between them*. It's not in the cells of organisms but in the way the cells feed and give feedback to one another through semi-permeable membranes. The energy is not in any precise definition or in the partly arbitrary names of the three persons of the Trinity as much as in *the relationship between the Three*! This is where all the power for infinite renewal is at work: in loving relationship.

In other words, it is an entirely relational universe. If, at any time, we try to stop this flow moving *through* us, *with* us, and *in* us, we fall into the true state of sin—and it is truly a *state* more than a momentary behavior. It is telling that the first destabilization of the foundational structure of the atom (in New Mexico in July 1945) created the atomic bomb. With supreme irony, the test site is still called "Trinity" as Robert Oppenheimer named it.

The divine flow either flows both in and out, or it is not flowing at all. The "trap doors" at either end must be kept open in order to both receive and let go, which is the work of all true spirituality. The Law of Flow is simple, and Jesus states it in many formulations such as "Happy are the merciful; they shall have mercy shown to them" (Matthew 5:7). Or as we cleverly put it, "What goes around comes around." We are conduits.

—DD 55–56, 71–72

The Power of Love

I think it's foolish to presume we can understand Jesus if we don't first of all understand Trinity. We will continually misinterpret and misuse Jesus if we don't first participate in the circle dance of mutuality and communion within which he participated. We instead make Jesus into "Christ the King," a title he rejected in his lifetime (see John 18:37), and we operate as if God's interest in creation or humanity only began 2,000 years ago.

Humans are more comfortable with a divine monarch at the top of pyramidal reality. So we quickly made the one who described himself as "meek and humble of heart" (Matthew 11:29) into an imperial God, both in the West (Rome) and in the East (Constantinople). This isn't the naked, self-emptying Jesus on the cross. This isn't a vulnerable, relational one, who knows how to be a brother to all creation. The Greek Zeus became the Latin *Deus*; and we no longer knew Jesus in any meaningful sense that the soul could naturally relate to (which was the main point of the Incarnation!).

Circles are much more threatening than pyramids are, at least to empires, the wealthy, or any patriarchal system. What if we actually surrendered to the inner Trinitarian flow and let it be our primary teacher? Even our notion of society, politics, and authority—which is still top-down and outside-in—would utterly change. "The grace of the Lord Jesus Christ, and the love of God, and the fellowship of the Holy Spirit" (2 Corinthians 13:13) should be our circular and all-inclusive ecology. From the very beginning of Creation, we see this pattern: God the Father, Christ the Word, and the Holy Spirit as a mighty wind (see Genesis 1:1–3).

Trinity shows that God's power is not domination, threat, or coercion. If the Father does not dominate the Son, and the Son does not dominate the Holy Spirit, and the Spirit does not dominate the Father or the Son, then there's *no domination in God.* All divine power is shared power and the letting go of autonomous power.

There's no seeking of *power over* in the Trinity, but only *power with*—a giving away, a sharing, a letting go, and thus an infinity of trust and mutuality. This should have changed all Christian relationships: in marriage, in culture, and even in international relations. Isaiah tried to teach such servanthood to Israel in the classic four "servant songs."[6] He was training them in being "light to all nations" (Isaiah 42:6, 49:6), but Hebrew history preceded what Christianity repeated: we both preferred kings, wars, and empires instead of suffering servanthood or leveling love.

We all already have all the power (*dynamis*) we need both within us and between us—in fact, Jesus assures us that we are already *"clothed"* in it "from on high" (see Luke 24:49)!

—SG disc 5 and DD 95–96

---

6. See Isaiah 42:1–9, 49:1–13, 50:4–9, 52:13–53:12.

2

1957–1985:
We Love God by Loving Others

"Love one another as I have loved you."
—John 13:34

> [T]he real meaning of our life is to develop people who
> really love God and who radiate love, not in a sense that
> they feel a great deal of love, but that they simply are
> people full of love who keep the fires of love burning
> in the world. For that they have to be . . . fully them-
> selves—real people.   —Thomas Merton

> To love as Jesus loves, we must be connected to the
> Source of love.   —Richard Rohr

FRANCISCAN EDUCATION

*Richard left home at age fourteen to join the Franciscans. As he
sees now, "I did this for all kinds of mixed motives, although at
the time I thought it was for 'God Alone,' which was my secret
motto." He entered St. Francis Seminary in Mount Healthy,
Ohio, a northern suburb of Cincinnati. Richard describes it as
"a lovely, idyllic place that I still return to in dreams even though
it was quite strict, and the priests were more disciplinarians than
friends or father figures."*

It was a "minor seminary," a secondary boarding school for teenage boys who were interested in becoming priests, prior to taking vows. Richard surmises that sending boys away at the height of adolescence was a tactic to reign in their hormones, to prevent them from meeting a girl and falling in love. Many very young men gave over their identity to the Franciscans or to the Roman Catholic Church, perhaps unconsciously letting the institution become their "wife" and their identity. This may explain why many bishops protected pedophile priests to avoid betraying the church they had "married."

Richard feels that entering seminary at such an early age worked for him and for other priests who had actually experienced the reality of God's love for them personally, but not for many others. He has worked with quite a few men who did not have the charism, or free gift, of celibacy. When celibacy is merely mandated, many become very wounded through repressing their sexuality and, as Richard says, "it all eventually backfires. Willpower does not work for long."

Intimacy Is Self-Disclosure

Intimacy is another word for trustful, tender, and risky self-disclosure. None of us can go there without letting down our walls, manifesting our deeper self to another, and allowing the flow to happen. Often such vulnerability evokes and allows a similar vulnerability from the other side. Such was the divine hope in the humble self-revelation of God in the human body of Jesus. My mind stumbles to even imagine it or think it could be true. Yet Christians dare to claim this reality.

Such human intimacy is somewhat rare and very hard for all of us, but particularly for men and for all who deem themselves to be important people, that is, those who are trained to protect their boundaries, to take the offensive, and to be afraid of weakness or neediness. God seems to have begun thawing this glacial barrier by coming precisely in male form as Jesus, who then exposes maleness itself as also naked, needy, and vulnerable. That is mind-blowing, heart-exploding, and surely impossible!

Thus, the transmission of the secret, the inner mystery of God, continues in space and time primarily through what Jesus calls again and again "the little ones" and "the poor in spirit," which he himself became.

I think that many men, celibate men even more, are very afraid of intimacy, of baring their deepest identity to another human or even to God. Yet people who risk intimacy are invariably happier and much more real people. They seem to have lots of "handles" that allow others to hold onto them and that allow them to hold onto themselves. People who avoid intimacy are imprisoned in a small and circumscribed world. *Intimacy is the only gateway into the temple of human or divine love.*

Healthy sexuality creates an obvious and ideal container for true intimacy, at least now and then. Unfortunately, the physical act of sex, which is meant to be a moment of embodied and experienced intimacy, is often not intimate at all. Both healthy celibacy and sexual encounter demand deep and true intimacy, yet celibacy and sex can also be the most effective avoidance of the same. You can be intimate and vulnerable with others without intercourse. In fact, platonic relationship is the most common form of human closeness and joy.

I believe vulnerable intimacy is the entrance into and the lynchpin between all human and divine love. It does not matter which comes first; it is just important that we pass through this gate of fear and find what lives inside us—and on the other side of the gate.

Intimate love is the true temple that we all desire. This longing seems to be hardwired into our beings in spite of our survival instincts. You have to want to love and to be loved very badly or you will never go to this strange temple and find your True Self. So God obliges and creates you in just that way, with a bottomless and endless need to be loved and to love.   —ID 168, 171–74

THE PRE–VATICAN II GOD

Richard shared that as a teenager he feared a punitive God because that's what the church taught before Vatican II, and many still prefer a disciplinary God. He calls it "learned help-lessness and taught fear." Here God is a kind of Santa Claus figure "making a list and checking it twice" within a counting and measuring system where everything is based on fear of God, purgatory, hell, or church sanctions and shaming. His high school seminary was based in legalistic and ritualistic Catholicism. Richard reflects, "A punitive notion of God and justice doesn't get you anywhere, which is why I've always preached so strongly against it."

Mercy before Judgment

When Pope Francis threw open the Door of Mercy in Rome, signifying the start of the "Year of Mercy" on December 8, 2015, he said, "How much wrong we do to God and his grace when we speak of sins being punished by his judgment before we speak of their being forgiven by his mercy. We have to put mercy before judgment, and in any event, God's judgment will always be in the light of his mercy"—which is infinite![1]

We don't know what to do with "infinity," because *it* does something with us. Our human minds can't conceptualize, comprehend, or control the "infinite." This explains why our counting and calculating minds fall back on a manageable notion like judgment. In fact, we seem to prefer it. In most sermons I've heard, when speaking about mercy the preacher quickly adds: "But of course God's mercy must always be tempered by God's judgment!" Judgment is too often the final word, and so it remains in our memories, which naturally turn toward fear. Unfortunately, the most common view of God's judgment is retributive justice, which appeals to the ego, rather than restorative justice, which brings true transformation.

---

1. Pope Francis, as quoted by Gerard O'Connell, "Pope Francis Opens Holy Door says: 'We Have to Put Mercy before Judgment,'" December 8, 2015, http://americamagazine.org/content/dispatches/pope-francis-opens-holy-door-says-we-have-put-mercy-judgment.

God's freely given grace is a humiliation to the ego because free gifts say nothing about me. Only the soul can understand grace. The ego does not know how to receive things freely or without logic. It likes to be worthy and needs to understand in order to accept things as true. The ego prefers a worldview of scarcity or *quid pro quo*, where only the clever can win. That problem, and its overcoming, is at the very center of the Gospel plot line. It has always been overcome from God's side. The only problem is getting us in on the process! That very inclusion of us is God's humility, graciousness, and love. Only inside an economy of grace can we see that God wants free and willing partners. An economy of merit cannot process free love or free anything. "Not servants, but friends" (John 15:15) is God's plan. Yet to this day, most Christians seem to prefer being servants. Divine friendship is just too much to imagine.

If we're honest, culture forms us much more than the Gospel. It seems we have kept the basic storyline of human history in place rather than allow the Gospel to reframe and redirect the story. Except for those who have experienced grace at their core, Christianity has not created "a new mind" (Romans 12:2) or a "new self" (Ephesians 4:23–24) that is significantly different than the cultures it inhabits. The old, tired, win/lose scenario seems to be in our cultural hard drive, whereas the experience of grace at the core of reality—which is much more imaginative and installs new win/win programs in our psyche—has been neglected and unrecognized by most of Christianity.

Up to now, Christianity has largely imitated culture instead of transforming it. Reward/punishment and good guys versus bad guys, have been the plot lines of most novels, plays, operas, movies, and wars. This is the only way that a dualistic mind, unrenewed by prayer and grace, can perceive reality. It is almost impossible to switch this mind during a short sermon or service on a Sunday morning. As long as we remain inside of a dualistic, win/lose script, Christianity will continue to appeal to low-level and vindictive moralisms and myths and never rise to the mystical banquet that Jesus offered us. The spiritual path and

life itself will be mere duty instead of delight, "jars of purification" instead of 150 gallons of intoxicating wine at the end of
the party (John 2:6–10). We will focus on maintaining order by
sanctified violence instead of moving toward a higher order of
love and healing—the heart of the Gospel.

—TTM and TH 156–57, 159, 177

THINKING WITHOUT THINKING

*Richard sees his teenage self as "a pious Catholic, wanting to be
a perfect little seminarian. For many, the seminary was a career
move that got you the total adulation of your family. We lived in
Catholic ghettos at the time, and in that small world there was
no downside to becoming a priest. It was nothing but praise and
'Isn't he wonderful?' Talk about feeding the ego! It was almost
anti-initiation. Rather than taking us down a few notches, as
men's rites of passage are intended to do, it built our towering
ego. Some, I'm sad to say, built their tower hiding behind God.
That's a really dangerous disguise. Then God ends up being your
cover for your own egocentricity, which looks like virtue and
heroic sacrifice to others. I only know this because I did it myself
and have experienced both clerical and white privilege."*

*Nevertheless, Richard believes he did receive "the best of
educations, the best of discipline and internalization of values. I
think I learned how to live with a prayer of quiet and developed
an inner life. We had a monthly day of recollection where we
had to keep silent a whole day. We weren't actually taught what
to do with our minds, however. Our novice master just told us,
as Francisco de Osuna said, 'pensar sin pensar,' to think without
thinking—and we did the best we could on our knees in silence
early each morning. If you learn how to live in a gracious silence,
not an enforced one (which it was at the beginning), you learn
to discern your inner world. You have time to see what's really
going on inside yourself. And that is a great gift."*

*Richard was also introduced to contemplation through
Thomas Merton. At the minor seminary's library, he was drawn*

to Merton's book, The Sign of Jonas. *Even before Merton was well known, Richard could tell that he was a major wisdom figure.*

Paradox and Mercy

Thomas Merton (1915–1968) was born in France and lived most of his adult life as a Trappist (Cistercian) monk at the Abbey of Our Lady of Gethsemani in Kentucky. He died tragically in Bangkok of accidental electrocution due to faulty wiring. Merton has been a primary teacher and inspiration to me and is one of the most significant American Catholics of the twentieth century. His whole life is a parable and a paradox, as are all of our lives. Merton wrote in his preface to *A Thomas Merton Reader*, "I have had to accept the fact that my life is almost totally paradoxical. I have also had to learn gradually to get along without apologizing for the fact, even to myself. . . . It is in the paradox itself, the paradox which was and still is a source of insecurity, that I have come to find the greatest security."

I'm convinced that is the very meaning of faith. Faith is agreeing to live without full resolution. Both the Hebrew Scriptures and the Christian Scriptures make that very clear. We are often called to walk in darkness, where God leads us to that next step which is usually not clear, predictable, or controllable by the rational mind.

"I have become convinced," Merton goes on to write, "that the very contradictions in my life are in some ways signs of God's mercy to me: if only because someone so complicated and so prone to confusion and self-defeat could hardly survive for long without special mercy."[2]

Merton had an uncanny ability to describe his inner life with God for the rest of us, and to apply that inner life in the healing of the outer world. A prayer he offered at the close of a

---

2. Thomas Merton, *A Thomas Merton Reader*, ed. Thomas P. McDonnell (New York: Doubleday, 1989), 16.

conference on East–West monastic dialogue, near the end of his
life, is representative:

> Oh God, we are one with You. You have made us one
> with You. You have taught us that if we are open to one
> another, You dwell in us. Help us to preserve this open-
> ness and to fight for it with all our hearts. Help us to
> realize that there can be no understanding where there
> is mutual rejection. Oh God, in accepting one another
> wholeheartedly, fully, completely, we accept You, and we
> thank You, and we adore You, and we love You with
> our whole being, because our being is in Your being, our
> spirit is rooted in Your spirit. Fill us then with love, and
> let us be bound together with love as we go our diverse
> ways, united in this one spirit which makes You pres-
> ent in the world, and which makes You witness to the
> ultimate reality that is love. Love has overcome. Love is
> victorious. Amen.[3]   —FU 161

NOVITIATE: DISCOVERING GRACE

*After the minor seminary, Richard's next step toward becoming
a Franciscan was a year-long novitiate in Cincinnati, Ohio.*

*He recalls: "In those days we knelt a lot. I had calluses on my
knees because we knelt so much. But it was a wonderful container that kept me in myself, in my inner world, in the silence.
Most of the day you had to keep quiet. This was a medieval
novitiate. What I mean is that it was still based on asceticism; it
was not modern spirituality. You see, at the time of the Protestant Reformation in the sixteenth century, when half of Europe
left the Catholic Church, we reacted by going into a siege mentality, trying to preserve everything the way we thought it was
before. The Church pretty much stopped maturing as a whole.*

---

3. Thomas Merton, *The Asian Journal of Thomas Merton*, ed. Patrick
Hart, James Laughlin, and Naomi Burton Stone (New York: New Directions Publishing, 1975); 318–19.

We were too divided into parts. Before Vatican II, the Catholic Church was still law-based, disconnected from experience, and not incarnational. It all circled around priests and their ministrations.

"*I was nineteen years old and trying to be the most fervent student possible: on time, clean, reverent, and respectful, like a Boy Scout. 'Yes, Father. No, Father. Whatever you want, Father.' I knew how to be a good son. I really did. I'd had such a good father, so I didn't have the usual opposition toward authority figures. But I was still going crazy with trying to be perfect. In time, I discovered it was* my *definition of perfection, so I could not take it too seriously. Everyone creates their own definition of perfection that they try to live up to and then they experience the illusion that they're either perfectly wonderful or completely inadequate.*"

Richard shares an especially powerful God experience he had in the novitiate:

"*It was somewhere in the middle of the year. I was kneeling in the choir alone in the novitiate house on Colerain Avenue. Suddenly, I felt chains fly in all directions. The Scripture that I had read that day was from Philippians 3: 'What I once considered an asset, now I consider a liability. The law that I thought was going to save me, now is my curse' (my paraphrase).*

"*Suddenly I knew that God's love did not depend on me following all these laws and mandates or being worthy. I knew I wasn't worthy, and yet here I was experiencing absolute grace and absolute acceptance. The whole system I'd grown up with had implied that God will love you* if *you change. That day I realized God's love* enables and energizes *us to change.*

"*I had that boyhood secret discovered in front of the Christmas tree: that I'd been taken over to another world, which was really this world as it truly is. I'd realized, 'My God, this is what everybody is living inside of, and they don't see it!' Now once again in the novitiate, I somehow knew that I was good, God is good, life is good. And I didn't have to achieve that goodness by any performance whatsoever. At that point, I was like a good Lutheran: saved by grace. Grace was everything!*

"In one moment, I got the Gospel! And I knew it had nothing to do with legalism, priestcraft, or punitiveness. I hadn't studied theology yet, so I had no intellectual foundation by which to justify it, but I just knew that everything was grace. In charismatic or Pentecostal language, I would call that my baptism in the Spirit. I was very free after that.

"I can't say that in the intervening years I've always believed this on a daily basis. Just like the biblical writers and the saints, I would get it and then lose it for a while. Sometimes I would let irritations, resentments, and annoyances eat me alive for weeks and would not be able to live in the state of grace and inner freedom. Or I'd get caught up in the drama of life—even good and exciting things—and wouldn't have time for God's unconditional love. Love was still and always flowing through me, but I wasn't resting in it or consciously enjoying it. Even now there's a temptation to think I have to earn God's love. There are still those inner tapes that say, 'I'm a bad boy,' or 'I am not worthy enough or good enough.' And that's where I continue to grow in love and faith—by not believing those negative voices and trusting grace's absolute givenness."

The Law and Grace

The Apostle Paul's letters to the Romans and Galatians are a *tour de force* on the pure meaning of grace and the serious limitations of morality and religion to lead you to God. Paul even calls the law a curse (Galatians 3:13). No wonder he has been called a "moral anarchist" by people who are still seeking any well-disguised path of self-realization. But it seems Christianity has paid little heed to Paul's revolutionary message, or even to Jesus who says six times in a row, "The law says, but I say!" (Matthew 5:21–45). Both Jesus and Paul knew that *rules and requirements were just to get you seriously engaged with the need for grace and mercy; they were never an end in themselves* (see Romans 7:7).

"If you keep the law, the law will keep you," we students were told on the first day in the seminary. As earnest young men anxious to succeed, we replied, "Yes, Father!" We knew how to survive in any closed system. I'm afraid we spent so much time in that world that it became the whole agenda. Canon Law was quoted much more often to us than the Sermon on the Mount before the reforms of Vatican II, and nowadays the young priests are being taught in much the same way as I was. A strong emphasis on law and order makes for a sane boarding school, or an organized anything, for that matter. I really get that. It probably made it much easier for the professors to get a good night's sleep with one hundred twenty young men next door. But it isn't anywhere close to the Gospel. The Gospel was not made to help organizations run smoothly. The full Gospel actually creates necessary dilemmas for the soul much more than resolving the organizational problems of institutions. Fortunately, the Gospel is also a profound remedy for any need to rebel or be an iconoclast.

We are justified not by good works, but by faith in an Infinite Mercy that we call grace. It has nothing to do with past performance or future plans for an eternal nest egg. All it requires is *a deep act of confidence in a loving God*. It is so hard to believe that this imperfect, insignificant creature that I am could somehow bear the eternal mystery. God can only grow bigger as we grow smaller, as John the Baptist put it (John 3:30). If we try to grow bigger by any criteria except divine mercy itself, we only grow in love with our own image. That is normally called narcissism.

How could God love me so unconditionally, we all ask? This was Paul's struggle as well, and it led him to his cataclysmic conclusion: God loved Paul in his unworthiness, "while he was yet a sinner," as he puts it (Romans 5:8). Therefore, he did not have to waste the rest of his life trying to become worthy or to prove his worthiness to himself or to others.

The only people who change, who are transformed, are people who feel safe, who feel their dignity, and who feel loved.

When you feel loved, when you feel safe, and when you know your dignity, you just keep growing! That's what loving people do for one another—offer safe relationships in which we can change. This kind of love is far from sentimental; it has real power. In general, you need a judicious combination of safety and necessary conflict to keep moving forward in life.

Paul has fallen in love with a God who has loved him "for nothing." For the rest of his life, Paul is happy to give God all the credit and he stops trying to validate himself by any means whatsoever. This creates a very different kind of person, someone who is utterly free. Paul knows that "the gift far outweighed the fall" (Romans 5:15), and he lives inside the gift all his remaining days. He never looks back to law or religion for his self-validation, but becomes the ultimate reformer of all self-serving religion.   —SPMM and GTP disc 7

The Soul's Objective Union with God

The Genesis story of the Judeo–Christian Tradition is really quite extraordinary. It says that we originate from free and overflowing love. This flow will be rediscovered and re-experienced by various imperfect people throughout the Jewish and Christian Scriptures. This sets us on a positive and hopeful foundation, which cannot be overstated. Yet we must also say that it never gained full traction in the life of many believers, either Jewish or Christian. Such utter gratuity was just too good to be true. Further, we could not control or manipulate this love; and anything humans cannot control, we do not engage with or enjoy. The Bible as a whole illustrates through various stories humanity's *objective unity with God, the total gratuity of that love, and unfortunately, our resistance to such an "impossibility."*

I find that many Christians still have no knowledge of the soul's objective union with God (see 1 John 3:2; 2 Peter 1:4), which all mystics rejoice in or they would not be mystics. Even ministers often fight me on this, quoting Augustine's "original sin," Calvin's "total depravity," or dear Luther's "humans are like piles of manure, covered over by Christ." I am sure they all meant well, but they also dug a pit so deep that many could never climb out or allow themselves to be lifted out. What a shame, literally! Such a negative starting point will not be very effective in creating loving or responsive people.

How do you ever undo such foundational damnation? Grace can only be trusted by an equally graceful human nature. Our work is merely to till the fertile soil, knowing that the Indwelling Spirit has already been planted within, the One who "teaches you all things and reminds you of all things" (John 14:26). Many Christians have tried to pile a positive theology of salvation on top of a very negative anthropology of the human person, and it just does not work. Such traditions produce few mystics and universal lovers. The human self-image is too damaged and distorted from the beginning.

The word *sin* has so many unhelpful connotations that it's very problematic today. For most of us "sin" does not mean what it really is: the illusion of separateness from God and from our original identity, our True Self. Most people think of sin as little naughty behaviors or any personal moral "stain" we suffer by reason of our "bad" thoughts, words, or deeds. Paul makes clear that sin is mostly a state, a corporate "principality" and "power," an entrapment, or what many would now call an addiction. Jesus seems to primarily see it as a blindness that traps us in self-destructive behaviors and hard-heartedness. Thus, he is always healing blind people and challenging people who see themselves as superior to others.

What we call sins are usually more *symptoms* of sin and not an inner negativity itself. What we call sins often have more to do with stupidity and ignorance than actual malice. Disconnected people *will* surely do stupid things and even become malicious, but they did not start there. They began in union, but disunion became their experienced lie and defense. Anything that is cut off festers and fumes and attacks, while often hoping to regain acceptance. The primary meaning of sin is to live outside "the garden," or in the smoldering garbage dump of Gehenna, below and outside the city walls of Jerusalem—the standing biblical images of hell or separation from God's reality (Genesis 3:23–24; Isaiah 66:24; Mark 9:47–48). Sin is primarily living outside of union; it is a state of separation, when the part poses as the Whole. It's the loss of any inner experience of who you are in God.

You can't accomplish or work up to union with God, because you've already got it. "Before the world began you were chosen, chosen in Christ to live through love in God's presence" (Ephesians 1:4). You cannot ever become worthy by yourself; you can only reconnect to your Infinite Source. The biblical revelation is about awakening, not accomplishing. It is about realization, not performance. *You cannot get there; you can only be there.* That foundational Being-in-God is for some reason too hard to believe, too good to be true. Only the humble can receive it and surrender to it, because it affirms much more about God than it does about us. And we foolishly believe it should be "all about me"! —TH 27–30

SPIRITUALITY OF IMPERFECTION

During the year of his novitiate, Richard read the little book, A Retreat with St. Therese, *by Pere Liagre. From this point forward, Therese's teaching became foundational to Richard's spirituality: "All the seeds were there for understanding God's infinite, perfect love, and that you come to God through your mistakes and through your imperfection, not your perfection." Therese is still Richard's special patroness.*

Receiving Mercy

The French Catholic Church of Therese of Lisieux's time (1873–1897) emphasized an ideal of human perfection, which took the forms of legalism and immense self-preoccupation. Yet Therese humbly trusted her own experience and taught the spirituality of imperfection instead. Therese is one of my favorite saints, perhaps because I am an Enneagram type One. The trap for the One is a self-created perfectionism, which makes us always

dissatisfied and disappointed in just about everything, starting
with ourselves. Our inner critic is quite well-trained and practiced, and it takes years of inner work to recognize how completely this critical worldview impairs our perception and keeps
us from our natural compassion.

Therese has helped me in this process. As Brother Joseph
Schmidt writes:

> Therese shifted her focus more and more from attaining
> perfection or acquiring holiness to the attitude of the
> publican (see Luke 18:9–14): She let God's mercy *be* her
> perfection, her holiness. "I desire, in a word, to be a
> saint," she prayed, "but I feel my helplessness and I beg
> you—Oh my God!—to be Yourself my Sanctity!" [All
> true holiness is reflected, and Therese allowed herself to
> enjoy that.]
>
> "Jesus, draw me into the flames of your love," she
> wrote. "Unite me so closely with you that you live and
> act in me."[4]

These prayerful sentiments expressed her solution to the
problem of perfection. She came to a complete reversal of her
original idea of what it means to be on the path of holiness and
single-handedly undid centuries of Catholic legalism. Gospel
holiness has little to do with moral achievements or the elimina-
tion of defects (that is an ego need). It is almost entirely about
receiving God's free gift of compassion, mercy, and forgiveness.
We know God by participation in God, not by trying to please
God from afar. This alone is the authentic wholeness, holiness,
and goodness that we all seek and admire.   —O 4, no. 1: 73

Perfection: A Self-Defeating Path

The path of union is different than the path of perfection. Perfection gives the impression that by effort I can achieve wholeness

---

4. Joseph F. Schmidt, "Perfection: A Problem and a Solution," "Perfection," *Oneing* 4, no. 1 (2016): 29. Emphasis mine.

separate from God, from anyone else, or from connection to the Whole. It appeals to our individualism and our ego. It's amazing how much of Christian history sent us on a self-defeating course toward private perfection. Union is instead about forgiveness, integration, patience, and compassion. The experience of union creates a very different kind of person.

On the day of my first vows in 1962, the preacher glared at us earnest and innocent novices and quoted the line, "Thou shalt be perfect as your heavenly Father is perfect!" (Matthew 5:48). Most of the honest guys left within the first few years of seminary when they could not achieve this supposed perfection. That's sad because I think a lot of them would have been really good friars and priests, precisely because they *were* so human, humble, and honest.

[Richard says that out of his class of fifty young men entering the minor seminary, twenty-one went on to the novitiate, and only ten made final vows. Of these ten, four were ordained priests and six remained brothers.]

Many people give up on the spiritual life or religion when they see they cannot be perfect. They end up being practical agnostics or atheists, because they refuse to be hypocrites. This is classic all-or-nothing thinking, characteristic of addicts. Many formal believers keep up the forms and the words, going to church and pretending to believe; but there is no longer the inner desire, love, joy, or expectation that is usually visible in people on the path of union. Mysticism does not defeat the soul; moralism (read "perfectionism") always does. Mysticism invites humanity forward; moralism excludes and condemns itself and most others.

It is quite unfortunate that the ideal of perfection has been applied to human beings. Strictly speaking, perfection can only be attributed to the Divine. Such a false goal has turned many religious people into pretenders or deniers—very often both. It has created people who, lacking compassion, have made impossible demands on themselves and others, resulting in a tendency toward superiority, impatience, dismissiveness, and negative thinking.

In the secular sphere, it has manufactured artificial ledgers of perfection that have clearly changed from age to age, class to class, and culture to culture. Perfectionism discourages honest self-knowledge and basic humility, which are foundational to spiritual and psychological growth. It has made social tranquility a largely unachievable goal. Grandiose people cannot create peace.   —YA 375 and O 4, no. 1: 11

Love Shows Itself as Mercy

Christianity's idealizing of a kind of "perfection" seems to have emanated from Jesus' teaching on loving our enemies. His exhortation has usually been translated: "You shall be perfect as your heavenly Father is perfect" (found only in Matthew 5:48). Let's take a look at the context leading up to this statement, Matthew 5:43–48, to help us better understand that Jesus was talking about God's unconditional love as the clear goal, measure, and ideal.

> You have heard that it was said, "You shall love your neighbor and hate your enemy." But I say to you, love your enemies, and pray for those who persecute you, that you may be children of your heavenly Father, for he makes his sun shine on the bad and the good, and causes rain to fall on the just and the unjust. For if you love those who love you, what recompense will you have? Do not the tax collectors do the same? And if you greet your brothers only, what is unusual about that? Do not the pagans do the same? So be perfect, just as your heavenly Father is perfect.

The parallel text in Luke (6:36) says, "Be merciful just as your Father is merciful." "Be merciful" surely fits the context more precisely than "be perfect," since Jesus has been describing how God's love is complete and impartial: God loves "the bad and the good." Jesus is telling us to love as God loves. God's love sets the standard and the bar of love very, very high, but that does not imply we can't ever reach it. We must aim and ask for this kind of love.

In effect, most Christian groups and individuals lowered the bar of perfection by emphasizing achievable goals usually associated with embodiment (attending church on Sunday, not committing adultery, not being a thief, etc.)—goals which we could accomplish and for which we could take credit. These accomplishments only inflated our own self-image, not our love of God. Jesus never emphasized such things because they could be achieved without any foundational love of God or love of neighbor—in other words, without basic conversion of either consciousness or identity. We could achieve this limited perfection through willpower, by thinking "correctly" about it, or by agreeing with a certain moral stance. This appeals to the grandiosity of the small self.

The real moral goals of the Gospel—loving enemies, caring for the powerless, overlooking personal offenses, living simply, eschewing riches—can only be achieved *through surrender and participation*. These have often been ignored or minimized, even though they were clearly Jesus' major points. *We cannot take credit for these virtues; we can only thank God for them*: "Not to us, O Lord, not to us, but to your name give glory because of your mercy and faithfulness" (Psalm 115:1).   —O 4, no. 1: 11–12

Awakening to Mercy

Her sins, her many sins, must have been forgiven her, or she would not have shown such great love.
—Luke 7:47

Those who show mercy will have mercy shown to them.
—Matthew 5:7

For the flow to happen, there must be a full opening on both ends, receiving and giving, giving and receiving, just like the Trinity. When you do not know you need mercy and forgiveness yourself, you invariably become stingy in sharing it with others. So make sure you are always waiting with hands widely cupped under the waterfall of mercy.

We now live under the weight of so many unhealed memories—including painful woundings of every stripe, political oppression, and genocides—that we have developed penal and judicial systems that think of mercy as an affront to justice. We seem to have a craven fear of—and even hatred for—anyone outside our own kind of people. After centuries of legalistic religion, sacraments administered in a juridical fashion, and biblical fundamentalism, the very word "mercy" seems newly introduced into our vocabulary, as if it were from a language other than our own, a truly foreign concept. Mercy refuses our capitalistic calculations. Unfortunately, most religion now offers no corrective to the culture, but largely reflects cultural self-interest.

Our lack of human compassion is rather starkly revealed in most of the candidates we consider worthy of public office in the United States. I am not sure if this is as much a judgment on the politicians' delusions as it is on the spiritual and human maturity of the American electorate itself. That so many who call themselves evangelical ("Gospel") cannot see through this charade has become an embarrassment for American Christianity. Many now see our cultural Christianity really has very little to do with Jesus. Any candidate is praised and deemed worthy of high office because we think, "He speaks his mind" (when it is actually our prejudices that he is speaking aloud). Two thousand years of Jesus' teaching on compassion, love, forgiveness, and mercy (not to mention basic kindness and respect) are all but forgotten in a narcissistic rage. Western culture has become all about the self, and that is just way too small an agenda. The very self that Jesus said "must die" is now just about all that we think about!

The rejection of refugee children and families fleeing for their very lives into the richest (per capita) continent of Europe has suddenly brought our lack of basic compassion and mercy into sharp and urgent focus. The unloving, glaringly self-centered, and even cruel behavior of so many Christians, Muslims, and Jews has exposed religious hypocrisy for all the world to see.

We live in a cold time, and we must now pray for the warming of hearts and opening of minds. To use Thomas Merton's lovely invitation:

> Make ready for the Christ, Whose smile, like lightning,
> Sets free the song of everlasting glory
> That now sleeps in your paper flesh.[5]

May we grow tired of such sleeping and ask for flesh that feels, weeps, and even bleeds for the immense suffering of our world today. "If we remain silent, the very stones will cry out" (Luke 19:40). —M 6, no. 2: 1 and 3

God Is the Initiator

It seems to me Christianity has put major emphasis on us loving God. But in the mystics I consistently find an overwhelming experience of how God has loved us. This comes through all of their writings: God is the initiator, God is the doer, God is the one who seduces me. It's all about God's initiative. Then we certainly want to love back the way we have been loved. As my father St. Francis would say, "Love is not loved! Love is not loved!" I want to love back the way I have been loved. But it's not like I've got to *prove* my love for God by doing things.

The mystics experience this full body blow of the Divine loving and accepting them, and the rest of their life is about trying to verbalize and embody that. They invariably find ways to give that love back through forms of service and worship; but it's not *earning* the love, it's *returning* the love. Can you feel the difference? Returning God's love is almost a different language. It's not based in fear, but in ecstasy. —FMNG disc 7

---

5. Thomas Merton, "The Victory," in *The Collected Poems of Thomas Merton* (New York: New Directions Publishing, 1977), 115. Used with permission.

A BEAUTIFUL BOOT CAMP

Richard reminisces: "After the experience of the 'chains flying,' I flourished in the novitiate. I remember creating a little banner which I hung in my private cell that said 'God Alone' because God was just so satisfying. I was so in love with God and life; every flower made me happy, and every bush made me joyous. Nothing could keep me down. I was very, very happy for the rest of the year; so much so that I asked the novice master, Father Benno, if I could do it again. I thought, 'It doesn't get any better than this!'

"He said, 'No one wants to do this again!' He was right. It was like boot camp. It was very strict. Your head was shaved and you had to be silent. You were not allowed to leave the property for the whole year. But it didn't matter, because that was the beginning of my authentic inner spiritual life. God was becoming so real to me."

Integrating Human and Divine Love

God is always given, incarnate in every moment and present to those who know how to be present themselves. It is that simple and that difficult. To be present in prayer can be like the experience of being loved at a deep level. I hope you have felt such intimacy alone with God. I promise it is available to you. Maybe a lot of us just need to be told that this divine intimacy is what we should expect and seek. We're afraid to ask for it; we're afraid to seek it. It feels presumptuous. We can't trust that such a love exists—and for us. But it does.

Often the imagery used to illustrate the human–divine relationship is erotic, because it is the only adequate language to describe the in-depth contemplative experience. I have often wondered why God would give us such a strong and constant fascination with one another's image, form, and face. What is the connection between our human passion and knowing God? Are all relationships a school of communion?

Healthy religion, as the very word *re-ligio* ("rebinding") indicates, is the task of putting our divided realities back together
again: human and divine, male and female, heaven and earth, sin
and salvation, mistake and glory. The mystics—such as John of
the Cross, Teresa of Avila, and the author of the Song of Songs
in the Bible—are those who put it together very well. Why has
this integration, this coincidence of seeming opposites, occurred
with relative rarity in much of organized religion? It is more
common in native spiritualities, Hinduism, and among Muslim
and Catholic mystics, who move beyond fast food religion to the
Mystery itself.

One would think that of all religions, Christianity would have
most welcomed this integration. After all, Christianity is the only
religion that believes God became a living human body (John
1:14)—a full, concrete, and physical enfleshment or "Incarnation." We call this incarnation "Jesus." If the Word became flesh,
then God is saying flesh is good, just as God did at Creation
(Genesis 1:31). Yet sometimes other religious traditions seem to
bow before this mystery better than Christians do.

—TH 16 and EB 135–38

The Magic and Mystery of Intimacy

It seems that Israel's God, YHWH, who is uncovering and expos-
ing the Divine Self in the Bible, soon desires not just images or
holy writings, but even *persons* with whom God can be in very
concrete and intimate relationship—quite literally friends, partners, and companions. Jesus then became the representation of
one walking on this earth who fully accepted and lived out of
that divine friendship. In fact, he never seemed to doubt it. That
must be at the core of our imitation of Jesus, how we become
"partners in his great triumph" (2 Corinthians 2:14). Such
healed people will naturally heal others, just by being "healed"
from the great lie of separation.

In calling forth freedom, consciousness, and love, God is actually empowering a certain kind of equality and dignity between

God and humanity, as strange and impossible as that might sound. Yet love is only possible if there is some degree of likeness and equality between two parties. Jesus *became* that likeness, equality, and dignity so we could begin to imagine it as possible for ourselves too.

One way to read the entire Bible is to note the *gradual unveiling of our faces* (2 Corinthians 3:18)—the gradual creating of personhood from infants, to teenage love, to infatuation, to adult intimacy, to mature and peaceful union. We are tempted to avoid the deeper risk of intimacy every step of the way. But biblical spirituality has the potential of creating people who can both receive and give out of love, a love that is both risky and free. If you are afraid of intimate interface, you will never allow this or know its softening power. You will stop the process before it even begins and never know how it works its transformation on the heart, mind, and body. If human eyes are too threatening for you, start with a stone, work up to plants and trees, animals will be easier, and probably only then are you ready for humans, and finally for the divine gaze.

Some people start with the divine gaze and move down the "Great Chain of Being" to swallows, sunflowers, and stones. But in either case, the great chain that connects us all is always and only love. Connecting more and more of the links of the chain is the supreme work of all true spirituality. A single link is never the full chain.   —TH 53–54

TEILHARD'S INFLUENCE

Richard was a freshman at Duns Scotus when a senior, Friar Max, introduced him to the writings of the Jesuit mystic and paleontologist Pierre Teilhard de Chardin (1881–1955). There was a monitum *(warning) against Teilhard at the time, but Richard was fascinated by him. "Teilhard highly influenced me. I signed my letters with his phrase 'Christ ever greater' for many years, and I spoke of 'Christic Magic' on my ordination card in 1970. Teilhard Christified the whole universe for me with contemporary language that respected science."*

The Shape of the Universe Is Love

In the beginning God says, "Let *us* make humanity in our own image, in the likeness of ourselves" (Genesis 1:26). The use of the plural pronoun here seems to be an amazing, deep time intuition of what some would later call the Trinity—the revelation of the nature of God as community, as relationship itself, a Mystery of perfect giving and perfect receiving, both within God and outside of God. "Reality as communion" became the template and pattern for our entire universe, from atoms to galaxies. The first philosophical problem of "the one and the many" was already overcome in God; and we found ourselves to be both monotheists and Trinitarians at the same time. It is one participatory universe of many diverse things in love with one another.

Physicists, molecular biologists, astronomers, and other scientists are often more attuned to this universal pattern than many Christian believers. Teilhard de Chardin said it well: "The structural shape of the universe is love."

According to Genesis 1:26, God isn't looking for servants, slaves, or contestants to jump correctly through some arbitrary hoops. God simply wants mirroring images of God to live on this earth and to make the divine visible. That is, of course, the way love works. *It always overflows, reproduces, and multiplies itself.* The experience of election, belovedness, and chosenness is the typical beginning of this re-imaging process. Then "we, with our unveiled faces gradually receive the brightness of the Lord, and we grow brighter and brighter as we are turned into the image that we reflect" (2 Corinthians 3:18). We must first surrender to the image within ourselves before we will then naturally pass it on.

Henceforth, all our moral behavior is simply "the imitation of God." First observe what God is doing all the time and everywhere, and then do the same thing (Ephesians 5:1). And what does God do? God does what God is: Love. The logic is then quite different than the retributive justice storyline most of us were given. Henceforth, it is not "those who do it right go to heaven later," but "those who receive and reflect me are in heaven now." This is God's unimaginable *restorative* justice. God does not love you *if and when* you change. God loves you *so that you can* change. That is the true storyline of the Gospel.

—TH 35–36

KEEPING GOD AND PEOPLE FREE

Studying the philosophy of the Franciscan John Duns Scotus (1266–1308) for four years had a profound effect on Richard. "Duns Scotus gave me foundational permission to broaden out, because he said that what good theology does is maintain two freedoms: It keeps people free for God and it keeps God free for people. The harder task is actually the second, because what religion tends to do is tell God whom God can love and whom God is not allowed to love.

"Love cannot happen except in the realm of freedom. When you have unfree people, you don't have love—you have obligation, you have codependency, you have obedience to law. When freedom is gone, love is gone and growth is gone."

Incarnation Instead of Atonement

Franciscans never believed that "blood atonement" was required for God to love us. Our teacher, John Duns Scotus, said Christ was Plan A from the very beginning (Colossians 1:15–20; Ephesians 1:3–14). Christ wasn't a mere Plan B after the first humans sinned, which is the way most people seem to understand the significance of the death and resurrection of Jesus. The Great Mystery of Incarnation could not be a mere mop-up exercise, a problem-solving technique, or dependent on human beings messing up.

Duns Scotus taught that the Enfleshment of God had to proceed from God's perfect love and God's absolute freedom (John 1:1–18), rather than from any mistake of ours. Did God intend no meaning or purpose for Creation during the first 13.8 billion years? Was it all just empty, waiting for sinful humans to set the only real drama into motion? Did the sun, moon, and galaxies have no divine significance? The fish, the birds, the animals were just waiting for humans to appear? Was there no Divine Blueprint ("Logos") from the beginning? Surely this is the extreme hubris and anthropocentrism of the human species!

The substitutionary atonement "theories" (and that's all they are) seem to imply that the Eternal Christ's epiphany in Jesus is a mere afterthought when the first plan did not work out. I know there are many temple metaphors of atonement, satisfaction, ransom, "paying the price," and "opening the gates"; but do know they are just that—metaphors of transformation and transitioning, rooted in the sacrificial system. Too many Christians understood these in a transactional way instead of a transformational way.

How and why would God need a "blood sacrifice" before God could love what God had created? Is God that needy, unfree, unloving, rule-bound, and unable to forgive? Once you say it, you see it creates a nonsensical theological notion that is very hard to defend. Many rightly or wrongly wondered, "What will God ask of *me* if God demands violent blood sacrifice from God's only Son?" Unfortunately, many people are already programmed to believe in punishment as the shape of the universe, particularly if they had a rage-aholic or abusive parent. A violent theory of redemption legitimated punitive and violent problem solving all the way down—from papacy to parenting. There eventually emerged a disconnect between the founding story of necessary punishment and Jesus' message of love and nonviolence. If God uses and needs violence to attain God's purposes, maybe Jesus did not really mean what he said in the Sermon on the Mount (Matthew 5), and violent means are really good and necessary. Thus, we have our violent history.

In Franciscan parlance, *Jesus did not come to change the mind of God about humanity; Jesus came to change the mind of humanity about God.* This grounds Christianity in love and freedom from the very beginning. It creates a very coherent and utterly positive spirituality which draws people toward lives of inner depth, prayer, reconciliation, healing, and even universal "at-one-ment," instead of mere sacrificial atonement. Nothing *changed* on Calvary, but *everything was revealed as God's suffering love*—so that *we* could change! (Please read that again.)

Jesus was precisely the "once and for all" (Hebrews 7:27) sacrifice given to reveal the lie and absurdity of the very notion and necessity of "sacrificial" religion itself. Heroic sacrifices to earn God's love are over! That's much of the point of Hebrews 10 if you are willing to read it with new eyes. But we perpetuated such regressive and sacrificial patterns by making God the Father into the Chief Sacrificer, and Jesus into the necessary victim. Is that the only reason to love Jesus?

This perspective allowed us to ignore Jesus' lifestyle and preaching, because all we really needed Jesus for was the last three days or three hours of his life. This is no exaggeration. The irony is that Jesus undoes, undercuts, and defeats the sacrificial game. Jesus came so we would stop counting, measuring, deserving, judging, and punishing, which many Christians are very well trained in—because they believe that is the way God operates too. This is no small thing. It makes the abundant world of grace largely inaccessible—which is, of course, the whole point.

It is and has always been about love from the very beginning.
—FM disc 3 and TH 200–202

DRAWN INEXORABLY TOWARD LOVE

Looking back from the second half of life, Richard reflects, "I can see that I thought I was being generous and giving my life away by being celibate, but now I know it was all just building the container for my small self. I think God mercifully protects us and uses everything—seeming good and bad—for God's purposes. Growing up in a more conservative paradigm was probably a good thing for me. It gave me some ideals to strive for, some boundaries to respect, some clarity and structure for the explosions of thought that would emerge in the last third of the twentieth century.

"I can remember the day I took my final vows in 1965. We had to lie on the floor, and I really thought, 'I am giving my life totally to God and God is all that matters.' I truly desired that. But did I actually know how to do that? There I was, dressed in my Franciscan robe in a heroic posture of surrender, with my family there admiring my self-sacrifice. I did mean to give my life over completely to God, but in many ways, I didn't know what that meant or how to do it. How could I? Perhaps you experienced something similar on your wedding day. As much as you believed you were committed to sharing your life with your partner forever, little did you know the renewed surrender and trust that would be required again and again.

"I wouldn't say that celibacy is the higher or best spiritual path, but it might be the easiest. Without a family, I've had the freedom to study, pray, and spend time in solitude, which has allowed me to understand and synthesize some things that others—parents and those with work responsibilities—may not have time to do. Living alone in my 'hermitage' the last couple decades has given me a valid reason to decline social invitations and limit distractions. I've had to face my own loneliness and phoniness. At the same time, the path of celibacy hasn't pushed me to really love concrete, particular people. It's easy to be nice to someone for a day or a weekend when I travel to give talks.

"Most of us need a committed partner. Some celibate priests seem to have a hard time growing up because they do not find anything they love more than themselves, to focus their dedication, commitment, and surrender. For a number of my peers, I don't think celibacy achieved its purpose of building a deep container and leading them to greater love. It can be a place to either go deep or a place to hide from intimacy and surrender.

"There is no perfect path; there is no right way to God and love. Thankfully God uses everything to lead us inexorably toward love. In my own life, I have to say that not having one incarnate love partner truly does evoke or reveal a deep aloneness in me that drives me toward prayer, desire, and God."

The Purpose of the Law

The language of the first half of life and the language of the second half of life are almost two different vocabularies, known only to those who have been in both of them. The advantage of those on the further journey is that they can still remember and respect the first language and task. *They have transcended but also included all that went before.* In fact, if you cannot include and integrate the common-sense lessons of the first half of life, I doubt if you have moved to the second. Never throw out the baby with the bathwater. People who know how to creatively break the rules also know why the rules are there in the first place. Jesus doesn't throw out the law. He just goes further with it. Often it takes an initial reliance on some outer authority to send us on the path toward our own inner authority. This is what Paul is saying in Romans and Galatians. Paul brilliantly holds the law and freedom together. It's never either/or thinking for him, although Paul is often read that way.

We must love and use the law not for its own sake, but for the sake of getting us started on the journey. What is the law's goal? What is it leading us toward? Paul says, "The law was our babysitter until the Christ came, and then we could be legiti-mated by faith" (see Galatians 3:24). It's a daring line. We must learn the first half of life's lessons and internalize them before moving on to the second half of life.

The point is not to get rid of the law, nor is it to glibly obey the law. The purpose of the law is to make us struggle with it long enough so that we can find its real purpose: love. It's in the struggle that we learn. Ask yourself, "What is the message in this for me? Why do I continually have difficulty following this law? Where is this desire or addiction coming from? What is it telling me about the nature of my soul?" The point is to bring aware-ness to the struggle, to let it teach you, and to let it lead you to a new place of deeper and more expansive love.

A growing discrimination between means and ends is the lit-mus test of whether you are moving in the right direction. All the world religions at the mature levels say similar things. For some reason, religious people tend to confuse the means with the actual goal. In the beginning, you tend to think that God really cares about your exact posture, the day of the week for public prayer, the authorship and wording of your prayers, and other such things. Once your life has become a constant communion, you know that all the techniques, formulas, sacraments, and practices were just a dress rehearsal for the real thing—life itself—which can actually become a constant intentional prayer. Your conscious and loving existence gives glory to God.

As Thomas Merton put it, it's all "mercy within mercy within mercy." It's not what you do for God; it's what God has done for you. You switch from trying to love God to just letting God love you. And it's at that point you fall in love with God. Up to now, you haven't really loved God; you've largely been afraid of God. You've been trying to prove yourself to God. Finally, perfect love casts out all fear. As John says, "In love there can be no fear. Fear is driven out by perfect love. To fear is to still expect punishment. Anyone who is still afraid is still imperfect in the ways of love" (see 1 John 4:18).

—FU xxvii–xxix, xxxiv; STHL disc 1; TMT; AC disc 1

You Are the "Imago Dei"

Searching for and rediscovering the True Self is the *fundamentum*, the essential task that will gradually open us to receiving love from and giving love to God, others, and ourselves. Grace builds on nature; it does not avoid or destroy nature. You are created in the image of God from the very beginning (Genesis 1:26–27).

You (and every other created thing) begin with your unique divine DNA, an inner destiny as it were, an absolute core that knows the truth about you, a true believer tucked away in the cellar of your being, an *imago Dei* that begs to be allowed, to be fulfilled, and to show itself. "You were chosen in Christ before the world was made—to stand before God in love—marked out

beforehand as fully adopted sons and daughters" (Ephesians
1:4–5). This is your True Self. Historically, it was often called
"the soul."

Jesus revealed and accepted a paradox in his entire being:
human and divine are not separate, but one, his life shouted! I
wonder why we so resist our destiny? For most of us, this seems
just too good and too dangerous to be true. There is so much
contrary evidence! Many clergy fight me on this, even though it
is quite constant in the Tradition. Is it because we are afraid to
bear the burden of divinity? As Marianne Williamson says: "Our
deepest fear is that we are powerful beyond measure." I would
say *that it is precisely the divine part of you that is great enough,
deep enough, gracious enough to fully accept the human part
of you. If you are merely human, you will tend to reject your
embarrassingly limited humanity.* Think on that!

Maybe we realize subconsciously that if we really recognized
our True Self—which is the Divine Indwelling, the Holy Spirit
within us—if we really believed that we are temples of God (see
1 Corinthians 3:16, 6:19; 2 Corinthians 6:16), then we would
have to live up to it. I am certainly afraid to own—and fully draw
upon—that kind of dignity, deep freedom, and infinite love.

Paradoxically, immense humility, not arrogance, characterizes
someone who lives in this True Self. You simultaneously know
you are a son or daughter of God, but you also know that you
didn't earn it and you are not worthy of it. You know it's entirely
a gift (see Ephesians 2:8–9 and throughout the Pauline writings).
All you can do is thank Somebody Else, occasionally weep with
joy, and kneel without any hesitation.

The single and true purpose of mature religion is to lead you
to ever new experiences of your True Self. If religion does not do
this, it is junk religion. Every Sacrament, every Bible story, every
church service, every sermon, every hymn, every bit of priesthood, ministry, or liturgy is for one purpose: to allow you to
experience your True Self—who you are in God and who God
is in you—and to live a generous life from that Infinite Source.

—TSFS disc 1 and ID 17

THE SECOND VATICAN COUNCIL

Richard recalls the years of the Second Vatican Council as an exciting period. "At that time, Detroit was really the most progressive diocese in the United States. Cardinal Dearden was out in front in terms of implementing the changes coming from Vatican II. We Franciscans sang at one of the first English Masses in the U.S. We were in tears after only hearing the Mass in Latin for our entire lives."

Vatican II ended in 1965. In 1966, Richard received his bachelor's degree in Philosophy. He was then sent to St. Leonard College in Centerville, Ohio, to study theology for "four very happy years, when I fell in love with theology and the new open Church." During Vatican II, the Franciscan Province of Cincinnati had sent their best and brightest to study in Europe and to absorb the history of theology. Richard was the beneficiary of these young professors who brought back the "fire, the excitement, the process, the give and take" of that pivotal time in the Church. "All I can do," he says, "is thank God for all of this!"

"I remember my systematics professor, Father Cyrin, saying to us, 'I want to make you so comfortable with the sources of Scripture and Tradition that you can theologize for yourself. Then you won't need to just quote Church documents and Fathers of the Church, but you can theologize for yourself.' Little did I know how that would form my life. That's why I can do what I do today!"

One of the most significant things Richard learned from the history of theology was the effect of "the great compromise" the church made in the years following AD 313 when the church aligned with the Roman emperor and "suddenly things like the Sermon on the Mount and Jesus telling us to turn the other cheek made no sense."

Richard reflects, "All of the mainline churches, Protestant too, I'm afraid, have basically bought into what I will call 'imperial religion.' It's top-down religion where we (the clerics) have the

*answers and we give you these answers. It's not about journey
or growth. It's belief-based Christianity, not experience-based.
I want to make that point strongly because that's where the
Pentecostals have brought in a new experiential element for the
Christianity we enjoy today." (We will see how the Pentecostal
movement intersected Richard's life shortly.)*

The View from the Bottom

In almost all of history, the vast majority of people understood
the view from the bottom due to their own life circumstance.
Most of the people who have ever lived on this planet have been
oppressed and poor. But their history was seldom written except
in the Bible (until very recently in such books as Howard Zinn's
A People's History of the United States). Only in modern times
and wealthy countries do we find the strange phenomenon of
masses of people having an establishment mentality.

This relatively new thing called "the middle class" gives
many of us just enough comfort not to have to feel the pinch or
worry about injustice for ourselves. Many of us in the Northern Hemisphere have a view from the top even though we are
nowhere near the top ourselves. The mass of people can normally be bought off by just giving them "bread and circuses," as
the Romans said. Many Americans can afford to be politically
illiterate, hardly vote, and be terribly naive about money, war,
and power. One wonders how soon this is going to catch up
with us.

Only by solidarity with other people's suffering can comfortable people be converted. Otherwise we are disconnected from
the cross—of the world, of others, of Jesus, and finally of our
own necessary participation in the great mystery of dying and
rising. In the early Christian Scriptures, or the "New" Testament,
we clearly see that it's mostly the lame, the poor, the blind, the
prostitutes, the drunkards, the tax collectors, the sinners—those
on the bottom and the outside—that really hear Jesus' teaching and get the point and respond to him. It's the leaders and

insiders (the priests, scribes, Pharisees, teachers of the law, and Roman leaders) who crucify him. That is evident in the text.

How did we miss such a core point about how power coalesces and corrupts, no matter who has it? Once Christians were the empowered group, we kept this obvious point from hitting home by blaming the Jews, then heretics, then sinners. But arrogant power is always the problem, not the Jews or any other scapegoated group. When any racial, gender, or economic group has all the power it does the same thing. Catholics would have crucified Jesus too if he had critiqued the Catholic Church the way he did his own religion.

After Jesus' death and resurrection, the first Christians go "underground." They are the persecuted ones, meeting in secrecy in the catacombs. During this time, we see a lot of good interpretation of the Scriptures, with a liberationist worldview (i.e., a view from the bottom). The Church was largely of the poor and for the poor.

The turning point, at which the Church moved from the bottom to the top, is the year AD 313 when Emperor Constantine supposedly did the Church a great favor by beginning to make Christianity the established religion of the Holy Roman Empire. That's how the Apostolic Church became Roman Catholicism. As the Church's interests became linked with imperial world views, our perspective changed from the view from the bottom and powerlessness (the persecuted, the outsiders) to the view from the top where we were now the ultimate insiders (with power, money, status, and control). Emperors convened (and controlled?) most of the early Councils of the Church, not bishops or popes. The Council in 325 was held at the Emperor's villa in a suburb of Constantinople called Nicea, where the highly abstract Nicene Creed was composed, in which the words love, justice, and peacemaking are never used once. The Nicene Creed is a far cry from the "creeds" spoken by Jesus three centuries before. What began as a teaching all about love became more about power.   —SL and GCCA

EDUCATION IN PHILOSOPHY
AND SCRIPTURE

Richard's education differed from that of most diocesan priests who were primarily taught Scholasticism, especially Thomas Aquinas. The Franciscan approach included the entire history of philosophy, as we see reflected in Richard's emphasis on the Perennial Philosophy. He was taught not only theological conclusions but the process of coming to those ideas over the centuries, not only from a Catholic perspective but from that of Calvin, Luther, and other mainline reformers.

Richard says, "We were taught how they disagreed with the Catholic Church, the good points they were making, and what we might question them about. We also learned the dark parts of the Church's history, the corruption of popes and the self-serving, greedy nature of medieval Catholicism that manipulated laity to pay 'indulgences.'"

Richard's favorite area of study was Scripture: "I fell in love with Scripture, I really did. To me it was God's self-disclosure of love for us. I'll be honest. I think my little mind was looking for validation for my intuitions. I was always an intuitive, and because of my early religious experiences, my intuitions preceded my theology. I do think, by the grace of God, that by and large my intuitions were on a rather good tangent. I devoured Scripture and systematic theology because they gave me the tools for understanding and validating my intuitions. Now I knew they were not just my ideas."

Of course, the argument could be made that "like knows like" and "how you see is what you see," two of Richard's frequent teachings. Richard intuited a loving God and a benevolent universe, so he was able to "connect the dots" and see how the Bible shows the same thing.

"I remember finding certain passages that would send me into ecstasy for days. Like when David tells YHWH he's going to build YHWH a house (2 Samuel 7). And YHWH turns it around and says, 'David, you don't need to build me a house; I am *going to build you a house!' Oh, I lived on that particular story because, for me, it was the theme of grace solidified. And now all these years later, I feel like here it is!" Richard says, referring to what God has done with his life. "It was all true! All I had to do was be open and give my little 'yes' to being used."*

Scripture as God's Self-Disclosure

Only those who truly know their need for the Beloved know how to receive the gift of the Beloved without misusing such love. A mutually admitted emptiness is the ultimate safety net for all love, and in the Scriptures, even God is presented as somehow "needing" us, and even "jealous" for our love (Exodus 20:5, 34:14). Basically, love works only inside humility. My father, St. Francis, fell in love with the "humility" of God, a word that most of us would not even think could apply to God.

Fullness in a person cannot permit love because there are no openings, no give-and-take, and no deep hunger. It is like trying to attach two inflated balloons to one another. Human vulnerability gives the soul an immense head start on its travels—maybe the only start for any true spiritual journey. Thus, the Risen Christ starts us off by revealing the human wounds of God, God's solidarity with human suffering. God begins with self-disclosure from the divine side, which ideally leads to self-disclosure from our side.

The Bible first opened up for me in the 1960s when the Second Vatican Council said that divine revelation was not God disclosing ideas about God but actually God disclosing Godself. Scripture and religion itself became not mere doctrines or moralisms for me, but love-making, an actual mutual exchange of being and intimacy. —ID 166–68

Retributive Justice and Restorative Justice in the Scriptures

In my almost fifty years as a priest, I have found that one of the best things we can do to remove people's ingrained inability to experience grace and mercy is to first clear away their false and damaging image of God. Tracing God's love throughout the Judeo–Christian Scriptures is one of the most important methods I use.

Poor theology has led most people to view God as a sometimes-benevolent Santa Claus or as an unforgiving tyrant who is going to burn us in hell for all eternity if we don't love him. (Who would love, or even trust, a god like that?) Psychologically, humans tend to operate out of a worldview of fear and scarcity rather than trust and abundance. This stingy, calculating worldview makes both grace and mercy unimaginable and difficult to experience.

Let me expand on our secular and limited definition of justice, which for most people is merely retributive justice. When people on the news say, "We want justice!" they normally mean that bad deeds should be punished or that they want vengeance. Our judicial, legal, and penal systems are almost entirely based on this idea of retributive justice. Retributive justice seems to be the best our dualistic world can do. This much bad deserves this much punishment; this much good deserves this much reward. The rational, logical, tit for tat, quid pro quo system makes sense to most of us. It does hold civil society together.

I certainly recognize there are many early passages in the Bible that present God as punitive and retributive, but you must stay with the text—and observe how we gradually let God grow up. God does not change as much as our knowledge of God evolves. Mere divine retribution leads to an ego-satisfying and eventually unworkable image of God which situates us inside of a very unsafe and dangerous universe. Both Jesus and Paul observed the human tendency toward retribution and spoke strongly about the limitations of the law.

The biblical notion of justice, beginning in the Hebrew Scriptures with the Jewish prophets—especially Moses, Isaiah, Jeremiah, Ezekiel, and Hosea—is quite different. If we read carefully and honestly, we will see that God's justice is *restorative*. In each case, after the prophet chastises the Israelites for their transgressions against YHWH, the prophet continues by saying, in effect, "And here's what YHWH will do for you: God will now love you more than ever! God will love you into wholeness. God will pour upon you a gratuitous, unbelievable, unaccountable, irrefutable love that you will finally be unable to resist."

God "punishes" us by loving us more! How else could divine love be supreme and victorious? Check out this theme for yourself: Read such passages as Isaiah 29:13–24, Hosea 6:1–6, Ezekiel 16 (especially verses 59–63), and so many of the Psalms. God's justice is fully successful when God can legitimate and validate human beings in their original and total identity! God wins by making sure we win—just as any loving human parent does. The little "time outs" and discipline along the way are simply to keep us awake and growing.

Love is the only thing that transforms the human heart. In the Gospels, we see Jesus fully revealing this divine wisdom. Love takes the shape and symbolism of healing and radical forgiveness—which is just about all that Jesus does. Jesus, who represents God, usually transforms people at the moments when they most hate themselves, when they most want to punish themselves or feel shame and guilt. Look at Jesus' interaction with the tax collector Zacchaeus (Luke 19:1–10). He doesn't belittle or punish Zacchaeus; instead, Jesus goes to his home, shares a meal with him, and treats him like a friend. Zacchaeus' heart is opened and transformed.

As Isaiah says of God, "My thoughts are not your thoughts, nor are your ways my ways" (Isaiah 55:8). Yet I am afraid we largely pulled God down into "our thoughts." We think fear, anger, divine intimidation, threat, and punishment are going to lead people to love. Show me where that has worked. You cannot lead people to the highest level of motivation by teaching them the lowest. God always and forever models the highest, and our task is merely to "imitate God" (Ephesians 5:1).

—TTM and H September 6, 2015

A Toxic Image of God

One mistaken image of God that keeps us from receiving grace is the idea that God is a cruel tyrant. People who have been raised in an atmosphere of threats of punishment and promises of reward are programmed to operate with this cheap image of God. They need deep healing, because they are actually attached to a punitive notion of God. Many experienced this foundational frame for reality as children, and it is hard to let go. It gives a kind of sick coherence to their world.

Unfortunately, it's much easier to organize people around fear and hatred than around love. Most people who want to hold onto power view God as vindictive and punitive. Powerful people actually *prefer* this worldview, because it validates their use of intimidation. Both Catholicism and Protestantism have used the threat of eternal hellfire to form Christians. Threat of hellfire "works" because it appeals to the lowest level of consciousness, where we all start.

Much of Christian history has manifested a very different god than the one Jesus revealed and represented. Jesus tells us to love our enemies, but this "cultural" god sure doesn't. Jesus tells us to forgive "seventy times seven" times, but this god doesn't. Instead, this god burns people for all eternity. The mystical, transformative journey cannot take place until this image is undone. Why would you want to spend even an hour in silence, solitude, or intimacy with such a god?

It's true that there are some troubling passages of Scripture; even Jesus used dualistic and judgmental statements. He knew that clear-headed, dualistic thinking must precede non-dual or mystical thinking. Jesus was particularly emphatic about issues people normally want to avoid, especially social justice teachings. He uses dualistic examples to make his points absolutely clear; otherwise, it's far too easy to avoid issues of justice for the poor and inclusion of the outsider.

It seems to me that in Matthew 25, when Jesus appears to make threats of "eternal punishment," he is making strong, contrasting statements about issues of ultimate significance, calling the listener to a decision. The trouble with this passage is that we focus on the threat more than on Jesus' positive promise of "eternal life." Jesus presents the teaching first in a dualistic manner. When pressed, he explains it in a non-dual way that encourages universal compassion: "Whatever you did for one of these least brothers and sisters of mine, you did for me" (Matthew 25:40). Non-dual thinkers can see that he is creating a moral equivalence between what we do to the least of the brothers and sisters and what we do to Christ.

In his book, *Inventing Hell*, Jon Sweeney points out that our Christian notion of hell largely comes from several unfortunate metaphors in Matthew's Gospel. Hell is not found in the Pentateuch (the first five books of the Bible), the Gospel of John, or in Paul's letters. The words *Sheol* and *Gehenna* are used in Matthew, but they have nothing to do with our later medieval notion of eternal punishment. Sheol is simply the place of the dead, a sort of limbo where humans await the final judgment when God will finally win. Gehenna was both the garbage dump outside of Jerusalem (the Valley of Hinnom) and an early Jewish metaphor for evil (Isaiah 66:24). The idea of hell as we most commonly view it came much more from Dante's *Divine Comedy* than the Bible. Dante's *Purgatorio* and *Inferno* are brilliant Italian poetry, but horrible Christian theology. Dante's view of God is largely nonbiblical.

Pope Benedict XVI explains his understanding of the curious phrase in the middle of the Apostles' Creed: "[Jesus] descended into hell." In *Introduction to Christianity*, Benedict says that if Jesus went to hell, that means there is no hell—because Jesus and hell cannot coexist. Once Jesus got there, the whole game of punishment was over, as it were. One of the most popular icons in the Eastern Orthodox Church shows Jesus with his legs spread, bridging the abyss of hell, pulling people out of the darkness. This is called "the icon of icons" in the East because it shows the highest level of contemplative perspective and the essence of the Good News.   —TTM; FM disc 3; TH 162

Love Is the Horse, Morality the Cart

Most of us think and act as if God is a God of retribution and even eternal punishment. But the Bible, Jesus, and the mystics of all the world religions reveal that God is infinite love, which really changes everything. Most religious people have put the cart before the horse by imagining that we can earn God's love by some kind of moral behavior. Whereas, according to the saints and mystics, God's love must be experienced first—and then our moral behavior is merely an outflowing from our contact with that Infinite Source. Love is the powerful horse; morality is then the beautiful cart that it pulls, not the other way around.

Love is not just the basis on which we build everything, but it's also the energy with which we proceed, and it's the final goal toward which we tend. Love has two lovely daughters called Grace and Mercy. Like identical twins, they are often indistinguishable: Grace is the inner freedom to be merciful. Mercy is grace in action. And both are the children of Love.

To operate inside of this always new and open-ended field, is to live in a truly new era—where evil has no chance to fester, grow, or triumph. Your failures are just another occasion and opportunity to learn and practice love, even toward yourself. You deserve mercy too.   —CC; FM disc 4; FF

Implanted Desire

The idea of grace first develops in the Hebrew Scriptures through the concept of election, or chosenness, and is finally called "covenant love" because it becomes a mutual giving and receiving. This love is always initiated from YHWH's side toward the people of Israel, and they gradually—very gradually—learn to trust it and respond in kind, just like we do. The Bible shows a relentless movement toward the actual possibility of intimacy and divine union between Creator and creatures. For this to happen, there needs to be some degree of compatibility, likeness, or even "sameness" between the two parties. In other words, there has to be a little bit of God in us that wants to find itself. (Yes, read that again!)

We see the message of implanted grace most clearly in Jesus. He is able to fully recognize that he is one with God. Jesus seems to know that it is the God part of him which does the deep knowing, loving, and serving. He seems able to fully trust his deepest identity and never doubts it, which is probably the unique character of his divine sonship. We doubt, deny, and reject our sonship and daughterhood much of the time. Humans find it hard to believe in things *we* did not choose or create *ourselves.* Such unaccountable gratuity is precisely the meaning of grace and also why we are afraid to trust it. "I am not the source," the ego says, "so it cannot be happening." Yes, it is God in you that always seeks and knows God; like always knows like. We are made for one another from the beginning (Ephesians 1:4–6). Maybe the ultimate grace is to fully know that it is entirely grace to begin with! It is already a grace to recognize that it is grace.

In Deuteronomy, God says to Israel, "If YHWH set his heart on you and chose you, it was not because you were greater than other peoples. In fact, you were the least of all the peoples. It was for love of you and to keep the covenant that he swore to your fathers and mothers that YHWH has brought you out with his mighty hand and redeemed you from the house of slavery" (7:7–8).

This passage and the continuation of this same pattern throughout Scripture emerges as the supreme theme of grace, which is concretely taught by Paul. In fact, I would call it the theme of themes. God does not choose to love the Israelites, anybody else, or us today because we are good. God loves us from a completely free, deliberate, and arbitrary choice. This recognition is the engine that drives the entire divine drama. Without it, we have nothing but sterile requirements and rituals. From the very beginning, receiving God's love has never been a "worthiness contest." This is very hard for almost everyone to accept. It is finally a surrendering and never a full understanding. The proud will seldom submit "until they are brought down from their thrones," as Mary put it (Luke 1:52). It just does not compute inside our binary, judging, competing, and comparing brains.

The older I get, the more I am sure that God does all the giving and we do all of the receiving. God is always and forever the initiator in my life, and I am, on occasion, the half-hearted respondent. That's just true! My mustard seed of a response seems to be more than enough for a humble God, even though the mustard seed is "the tiniest of all the seeds" (Matthew 13:32).

Yes, God is both very humble and very patient, if everything we see about the universe is true. God makes use of everything that we offer and seems most grateful for the smallest bit of connection or response from our side. Otherwise it would not be a covenant (mostly unilateral), but a coercion. God "does not want slaves but friends" (John 15:15). And it only gets better: God even creates the desire within us to do the desiring for love and for God. So all we need to do is to keep praying for the desire to desire, especially on those many days when the well feels dry, and prayer feels ordinary or boring.   —TH 163–64

Reading Scripture with the Mind of Christ

Looking at which Scripture passages Jesus emphasizes (remember, the Hebrew Bible was his only Bible!) shows he clearly understands how to connect the "three steps forward" dots that confirm the God he has met, knows, loves, and trusts. At the same time, Jesus ignores or openly contradicts the many "two steps backward" texts. He never quotes the book of Numbers, for example, which is rather ritualistic and legalistic. He never quotes Joshua or Judges, which are full of sanctified violence. Basically, Jesus doesn't quote from his own Scriptures when they are punitive, imperialistic, classist, or exclusionary. In fact, he teaches the opposite.

Jesus does not mention the list of twenty-eight "thou shall nots" in Leviticus 18 through 20, but chooses instead to echo the rare positive quote of Leviticus 19:18: "You must love your neighbor as yourself." The longest single passage he quotes is from Isaiah 61 (in Luke 4:18–19): "The Spirit of the Lord has been given to me. He has anointed me to bring good news to the poor, to proclaim liberty to captives, and to the blind new sight, to set the downtrodden free, and to proclaim a year of favor from the Lord." But Jesus quotes selectively; he appears to have deliberately omitted the last line—"and the day of vengeance of our God" (Isaiah 61:2)—because he does not believe in a God of vengeance.

Jesus knows how to connect the dots and find out where the text is truly heading, beyond the low-level consciousness of a particular moment, fear, or circumstance. He knows there is a bigger arc to the story: one that always reveals a God who is compassionate, nonviolent, and inclusive of outsiders. He knows how to "thin slice" the text, to find the overall pattern based on small windows of insight. He learned from Ezekiel, for example, that God's justice is restorative and not retributive.

We can only safely read Scripture—it is a dangerous book—if we are somehow sharing in the divine gaze of love. A life of prayer helps you develop a third eye that can read between the lines and find the golden thread which is moving toward inclusivity, mercy, and justice. I am sure that is what Paul means when he teaches that we must "know spiritual things in a spiritual way" (1 Corinthians 2:13). Any "pre-existing condition" of a hardened heart, a predisposition to judgment, fear of God, and any need to win or prove yourself right will corrupt and distort the most inspired and inspiring of Scriptures—just as they pollute every human conversation and relationship. Hateful people will find hateful verses to confirm their obsession with death. Loving people will find loving verses to call them into an even greater love of life. And both kinds of verses are in the Bible!

—HTJ

THINKING OUTSIDE THE BOX

Richard says that throughout his education with the Franciscans, he was basically a "B" student. He did not perform very well on tests because "I did not usually remember exactly what the professors had taught, but I gave them my thoughts on what they had taught. How arrogant of me!"

Richard was ordained as a deacon in 1969. His first assignment was to spend six months in New Mexico, working with the Acoma Indians, a pueblo people west of Albuquerque. Here Richard fell in love with the multi-cultural and beautiful "Land of Enchantment." The second six months as a deacon were spent at a black parish in Dayton, Ohio, called Resurrection Church. Richard reflects that in both churches, "I was able to speak to non-establishment audiences who could know and listen 'outside of the box.' What a gift that was to get me started!"

Richard still feels like he's in the "kindergarten" of contemplation. A consistent contemplative practice helps him see how and when he is unloving, when his mind is running riot with judgment, fear, anger, and feeling hurt. Seminary didn't give any training in what Richard calls "emotional sobriety," and he believes that's why many of his contemporaries left the priesthood. They were not taught how to love their neighbor, members of their community, the poor, or even themselves. As Richard says, "When they left the safe nest of seminary where everything was controlled and conformity was enforced, everything fell apart. Suddenly you made your final vows or you were ordained and had more and more freedom and encountered more and more diverse people—women, children, and people who weren't Franciscans, Catholic, white, or middle class."

"We were thrown into a world of diversity and I think we had no ability, no training to really deal with our emotional life and our aberrant monkey mind. Many left cynical and disillusioned, feeling that everything we had been taught didn't work in the real world. That's what drove me toward contemplation. For me it was the only way to find my ground, my center, my truth and peace in a world that was no longer uniform and contrived. Without the contemplative mind, no amount of talking about love can maintain inner freedom, peace, and compassion."

Learning to See

Those of us who are white have a very hard time seeing that we constantly receive special treatment just because of the color of our skin. This is called "white privilege," and it is invisible to us because it's part of our culture's very structure. Since we do not consciously have racist attitudes or overtly racist behavior, we kindly judge ourselves to be open minded, egalitarian, and therefore surely not racist. Because we have never been on the other side, we largely do not recognize the structural access we enjoy, the trust we think we deserve, and the assumption that we always belong. All this we take for granted. Only the outsider can spot these attitudes in us.

I would have never seen my own white privilege if I had not been forced outside of my dominant white culture by travel, by working in the jail (a disproportionate number of people of color are incarcerated), by hearing stories from counselees, and frankly, by making a complete fool of myself in so many social settings—most of which I had the freedom to avoid! And so, recognition was slow in coming. I am not only white, but I am male, overeducated, clergy (from *cleros*, the separated ones), a Catholic celibate, healthy, able-bodied, and American. I profited from white privilege on so many fronts that I had to misread the situation many, many times before I began to feel what others feel and see what others could clearly see. Many must have just rolled their eyes and hopefully forgiven me! Education about white privilege is the best doorway to help those of us who think we are not racists to recognize that structurally and often unconsciously we still are. Our easy advancement was too often at the cost of others not advancing at all.

Power never surrenders without a fight. If your entire life has been to live unquestioned in your position of power—a power that was culturally given to you, but you think you earned—there is almost no way you will give it up without major failure, suffering, humiliation, or defeat. The trouble is we cannot program that. All we can do is stop shoring up our power by our de facto idolization of money, possessions, power positions, superficial entertainment, the idolization of celebrities and athletes, and the war economy. All of these depend on our common enthrallment with being on top. As long as we really want to be on top and would do the same privileged things if we could get there, there will never be an actual love of equality, true freedom, or the Gospel. This challenges all of us to change and not just those folks who temporarily are "on the top."

Jesus' basic justice agenda was simple living, humility, and love of neighbor. We all have to live this way ourselves. From that position, God can do God's work rather easily.   —RRWP

We Are All One in Love

I believe it's especially important for those of us who are comfortable and privileged—whether we are white, financially secure, male, or have some other social "advantage"—to nurture a contemplative mind. Only through the eyes of the Divine Witness can we learn to see that to which we are mostly blind. Only when we are listening from the True Self, not the protective ego, can we hear the truth about ourselves and the unjust systems in which we participate.

Those of us who are well off and at ease have the "luxury" of feeling despair. It's easy to look around at our dysfunctional politics, homophobia, endemic racism, the unbalanced distribution of wealth, and climate change and become overwhelmed . . . and then disengaged. But those who are oppressed or connected intimately with systemic suffering have the greatest capacity—and sense the most urgency—for hope and for compassion.

From my own experience, I know I need a contemplative practice to rewire my mind. Some form of the prayer of quiet is necessary to touch me at the unconscious level, the level where deep and lasting transformation occurs. From my place of prayer, I am able to understand more clearly what is mine to do and have the courage to do it.

Unitive consciousness—the awareness that we are all one in Love—lays a solid foundation for social critique and acts of justice. I hope you will let God show you how to think and live in new ways, ways that meet the very real needs of our time on this planet. —M 6, no. 2 insert

THE HOLY SPIRIT

Finally, the big day came for Richard's ordination to the priesthood. He points out that Francis of Assisi originally did not want Franciscans to be priests. Francis wanted them to be "friars of the minor order" or "little brothers." The initials after the names of Franciscans, O.F.M., stand for "Order of Friars Minor" or "Ordo Fratrum Minorum." Francis had moved from upper Assisi, where the up-and-coming merchant class lived, to lower Assisi where the poor lived. He then moved lower still to the leper colony outside of Assisi. Francis did not want his followers to become priests because he didn't want them to be part of the establishment. But it was not long after he died that Franciscans began ordaining and relaxed their rules on poverty. "I wonder if the two are not related," Richard observes.

Richard describes his ordination: "It was 1970 and we were still in the great, free years after Vatican II; and Rome said, 'Let the boys go home to their parishes to be ordained. Let everybody see what an ordination is like.'

"So I went home to my little parish in Kansas, and my family of course was very excited. I had hippie vestments on, covered with colors and flowers. My mother said, 'Are you sure you want to wear that?'

"I said, 'Oh, yes!' I'd probably be embarrassed to wear it now, but that was 1970. I even had long hair!

"So there's the beautiful, pompous ordination ceremony, and then the receiving line in the vestibule of the church. My mom and dad are on each side of me, and my brother and sisters are there. Everybody's coming by and congratulating me, and I'm feeling very important and holy.

"Then this woman stops in front of me. She says, 'You're going to be used by the Holy Spirit.'

"I say, 'Thank you very much.' I was thinking, 'Yes, I'm a priest now. I'll be used by the Holy Spirit.'

"She replies, 'Do you know what happened on this spot in 1900, 70 years ago exactly?'

The woman proceeded to tell Richard that Charles Parham's Bible School had gathered in this very spot, asking for a renewal of the charisma of the Holy Spirit. Andreas Ebert and Pat Brockman recount:

> *A "neo-Pentecostal" breakthrough occurred, bursting forth among them with exuberant joy and the gift of tongues. The woman told Richard then that his ordination seventy years later, at this very place, was a promise and sign that God's Spirit would now return to the old churches and that he would be an instrument in this movement.[6]*

Finally, the woman moved along. "I really thought she was overly excited," Richard says. "I paid no attention to her whatsoever. It was only years later that my mother reminded me of this exchange." It seems the woman's words were prophetic: During the first retreat Richard led, a group of teenage boys began singing in tongues (as we'll see later). Through Richard's ongoing preaching and writing, many would say that God's Spirit of Love has renewed Christianity and given new life to ancient Tradition.

God's Spirit Is Universal and Inherent

I love St. Paul! What a basis he gives for loving all others as Christ has loved us. Paul offers a theological and solid foundation for human dignity and human flourishing that is inherent, universal, and indestructible by any evaluation, whether it be race, religion, gender, nationality, class, education, or social position. We now believe the reason that this one man enjoyed

---

6. Andreas Ebert and Pat Brockman, *Richard Rohr: Illuminations of His Life and Work* (New York: Crossroad Publishing, 1993), xii–xiii.

such immense success in such a short time is that he gave human dignity back to a world that had largely lost it. One more god in Greece and Asia Minor would have meant little, but when Paul told shamed populations they were temples of the divine, this made hearts burn with desire and hope.

The Acts account of Pentecost goes out of its way to emphasize that people from all over the world heard the Galileans speaking in the pilgrims' individual languages after the descent of heavenly fire and wind (see Acts 2:1–11). At least seventeen nations or groups are listed and "about three thousand persons" (Acts 2:41) were baptized and received the Holy Spirit that day. The theological message is clear: God loves everyone! God's love and favor is both totally democratic and unmerited. It was meant to be the end of all exclusive and elitist religion. But it did not last long; by the year AD 313, Christianity began aligning with empires and emperors in both Constantinople and Rome.

One of the reasons Paul's teachings had so much influence in Asia Minor was that he restored human dignity at a time when perhaps four out of five people were slaves, women were considered the property of men, temple prostitution was a form of worship, and oppression and injustice toward the poor and the outsider were the universal norm. The "civilized" world was not yet aware that human rights existed. Into this corrupt and corrupting empire Paul shouts, "One and the same Spirit was given to us all to drink!" (1 Corinthians 12:13). He utterly levels the playing field: "You, all of you, are sons and daughters of God in Christ Jesus . . . where there is no distinction between male or female, Greek or Jew, slave or free, but all of you are one in Christ Jesus" (Galatians 3:26–28).

This is quite amazing, considering the divided world at the time! In Paul's estimation, the old world was forever gone and a new world was born. This was surely impossible and frightening to some people, but utterly attractive and hopeful to the majority who had no dignity whatsoever. Who does not want to be told they are worthy and good? Who does not want their social shame taken away? No longer was the human body a cheap thing, degraded by slavery, or sexual, verbal, and physical abuse. Paul is saying, "You are the very temple of God." Scholars now believe this is Paul's supreme and organizing idea. Such an unexpected affirmation of human dignity began to turn the whole Roman Empire around.

Paul's teaching on sexuality (1 Corinthians 6:15–20) is not the moralistic message that many of us have come to expect from Christianity. Paul is just saying that your body has dignity, so preserve it and defend it. We would now call this a healthy sense of boundaries and identity. At a time when a woman had no sexual protection, this was revolutionary. A woman could now claim her own autonomy and refuse to give her body away to any man who wanted it. A man could start respecting and being responsible with his own body. This is a positive and dignifying message, not a finger-shaking, moralistic one.   —UIG

THE BIRTH OF THE NEW JERUSALEM COMMUNITY

After his ordination, Richard was asked to teach at Roger Bacon High School in Cincinnati. Though it wasn't his first choice, Richard found himself loving it. "I lived to walk into the classroom every day. We played 'Jesus Christ, Superstar' and danced to it. All the other teachers complained about how loud it was. But the boys loved me and I loved them. Of course, I looked like a kid then; I was only twenty-seven myself."

It went so well, that the next year Richard was assigned to be in charge of the youth retreat program for the Archdiocese of Cincinnati. For most of the very first retreat, November 7–9, 1971, Richard thought all the boys—"a bunch of jocks"—were just tolerating him. But as Richard finished preaching on the story of the prodigal son, "a perfect story of how Jesus saw God," the macho boys began to cry. "These guys, who were usually so afraid to touch one another because someone might think they were gay, were all putting their arms around one another!

"I moved back; I didn't know what to do with this. You'd think I'd be grateful that one of my sermons worked! And then

they began singing in tongues. I'd never heard anyone speaking in tongues before. My mouth fell open. What did this mean? I'd never heard anything so beautiful, and no one was orchestrating it!

"I endured it for about ten or fifteen minutes. Although I was delighting in it, I was also scared. I didn't know what to do, I didn't know how to join in; so I just watched. Finally, I broke in and said, 'Guys, I'll put the pizzas in the oven next door. Come over in twenty-five minutes.' No one paid a bit of attention to me. I put those pizzas in the oven. Twenty-five minutes later, I took them out and there were no boys. I couldn't understand why they were not on time!

"I'll never forget walking back across the parking lot into the chapel and opening the doors. Now they were all kneeling around the high altar of St. Anthony's Church, still singing in tongues. They never left the church the whole night.

"The priest came in the next morning. He got upset with me. He had to step over all these boys who were sleeping around the high altar. You'd think we'd be happy, wouldn't you? I said, 'I'll get them out, Father, I'll get them out. I'm sure they were just praying too long.' Actually, they were!"

That was the birth of the New Jerusalem Community. "The next Friday, all these boys brought their girlfriends and it grew quickly by word of mouth. The girls were singing in tongues too. The next month they brought their parents and grandparents. It mainly remained a youth community, though."

For Richard, a downside was that he began to be treated like a "demigod." "All these parents with troubled kids were sending them to our prayer meetings so they'd get 'saved,' or 'slain in the Spirit' as the Pentecostals say. It did happen to a lot of them. But I swear to you, I was just watching; I wasn't orchestrating it. They all thought I had some magic. But it wasn't me, and it wasn't about me. It was about Life and Love.

"Eventually I began to sing in tongues. Paul says it's a gift of the Spirit; maybe the least of the gifts, but nevertheless a gift. All I can say is it must be like when you first see your lover naked

and you're like ah, ah, ah—you're at a loss for words. That's
what singing in tongues is like. It's like having experiences that
are just too good to be true, larger than life, and you move into
incoherent babbling. When you stop resisting the experience and
just allow it, you may receive the gift of tongues. It doesn't sur-
prise me that when you have an experience of being taken on the
other side and you know that God is real and God is love and
God is in you and you have nothing to be afraid of, you would
start singing in tongues."

You Belong

I believe that we have no real access to *who we fully are* except
in God. Only when we rest in God can we find the safety, the
spaciousness, and the scary freedom to be *who* we are, *all* that
we are, and *much more* than we think we are. Only when we live
and see through God's eyes can "everything belong." All other
systems exclude, expel, punish, and protect to find identity for
their members in some kind of ideological perfection or purity.
The contaminating element always has to be searched out, isolated, and often punished. This wasted effort keeps us from the
centrally important task of love and union.

When God looks at us, God can only see "Christ" in us. Yet
it's hard—*for us*—to be naked and vulnerable and allow ourselves to be seen so deeply. It is hard to simply receive God's loving and all-accepting gaze. We feel unworthy and ashamed. The
very essence of all faith is to trust the gaze and then complete the
circuit of mutual friendship.

When you go to your place of prayer, don't try to think too
much or manufacture feelings or sensations. Don't worry about
what words you should say or what posture you should take.
It's not about you or what you do. Simply allow Love to look at
you—and trust what God sees! God just keeps looking at you
and loving you *center to center*. Hinduism called this *darshan,*
the practice of going to the temple—not to see the deity, but to
allow yourself to be fully and lovingly seen. This reversal is the
triumph and victory of grace.   —EB 26; EL 167; HDWG disc 3

The Sacrament of the Present Moment

Only unitive, non-dual consciousness can open our hearts, minds, and bodies to actually experience God. Ultimate Reality cannot be seen with any dualistic operation of the mind, where we divide the field of the moment and eliminate anything mysterious, confusing, unfamiliar, or outside our comfort zone. Dualistic thinking is highly controlled and limited seeing. It protects the status quo and allows the ego to feel like it's in control. This way of filtering reality is the opposite of naked presence to Presence.

We learn the dualistic pattern of thinking at an early age, and it helps us survive and succeed in practical ways. But it can get us only so far. That's why all religions at the more mature levels have discovered another "software" for processing the really big questions like death, love, infinity, suffering, and God. Many of us call this access "contemplation" or "prayer." It is a non-dualistic way of seeing the moment.

Non-dual knowing is living in the naked now, the "sacrament of the present moment." This consciousness will teach us how to actually experience our experiences, whether good, bad, or ugly, and how to let them transform us. Words by themselves will invariably divide and judge the moment; pure presence lets it be what it is, as it is. Words and thoughts are invariably dualistic; but pure experience is always non-dualistic.

As long as you can deal with life as a set of universal abstractions, you can pretend that the binary system is true. But once you deal with concrete reality—with yourself, with someone you love, with actual moments—you find that reality is always a mixture of good and bad, dark and light, life and death. Reality requires more a both/and approach than either/or differentiation. The non-dual mind is open to everything. It is capable of listening to the other, to the body, to the heart, to all the senses. It begins with a radical *yes* to each moment.

When you can be present in this way, you will know the Real Presence. I promise you this is true. You will still need and use

your dualistic mind, but now it is in service to the greater whole
rather than just the small self.   —NN 12, 50, 56, 74 and NWS disc 1

THE GOOD NEWS

*During our interviews, Richard shared how important good
friends have been to him throughout his life. One of these
friends was a Glenmary sister called Gus who helped Richard
lead youth retreats in Cincinnati. In her book,* The New Children *(no longer in print), Sister Gus shares a sermon Richard
gave during that period:*

> *The Word of the Lord does not make sense to human
> minds. It only makes sense in the living of it. The Word
> of the Lord is a dangerous Word because it demands
> everything. . . . You must come to the point where you
> know that you need a Savior, a Lover. You have to come
> to that state of littleness to know that you need Jesus.
> Jesus is saying, "Turn around. There's a whole world
> you don't even know is there."*
>
> *If you haven't taken the Word seriously, you don't
> know what you're missing. But you have to want it. . . .
> Love lays down its life. You give that person you love
> power over you. Love asks everything, but we don't
> want to give everything so we run from it and kill it. . . .*
>
> *Once you're in the Spirit, the Lord becomes so real
> to you. That's the gift of the Spirit. . . . It's the Christian
> adventure, that Jesus joy that fills every moment, every
> event of your life.*

*In a closing prayer, Richard said, "Expect everything from God.
Ask everything from God. Open up your heart and allow the
Lord to love you. . . . Father, we praise You and thank You for
hearing our prayer—the prayers we have spoken and those in
our hearts. You know the needs of each one here. Just fill those
needs, Father. Let it be to your glory. We ask this in the all-
powerful name of Your Son, Jesus, our brother and redeemer."*

[*Of course, today Richard would balance "all-powerful" with "all-vulnerable."*]

Sister Gus writes: "*Richard speaks of the Good News like it is—simple, radical, challenging. Guaranteed to make you uncomfortable because you realize how your own hang-ups get in the way of the Good News. . . . Richard had enough of Christ in him to waken the comfortable conservatives from their lethargy.*"[7]

Richard's teaching has broadened over the years (from an emphasis on Jesus to the bigger picture of the Trinity and the Universal Christ), lengthened (from asking God to meet individuals' needs to including concern for the world as a whole), and deepened (from an emphasis on that "Jesus joy" to the full paschal mystery of suffering, death, and resurrection). But some things remain the same, especially his focus on God's love and grace.

God Is Eternally Giving Away God

> *It is by grace that you are saved, through faith, not by anything of your own, but by a pure gift from God, and not by anything you have achieved. Nobody can claim the credit. You are God's work of art.*   —Ephesians 2:8

> *By grace you notice, nothing to do with good deeds, or grace would not be grace at all.*   —Romans 11:6

> *Happy are those servants whom the master finds awake. I tell you he will put on an apron, sit them down at table, and wait on them.*   —Luke 12:37

I think grace, arising from God's limitless love, is the central theme of the entire Bible. It is the divine Unmerited Generosity that is everywhere available, totally given, usually undetected as such, and often even undesired. This grace was defined even in the old Baltimore Catechism as "that which confers on our souls

---

7. Sister Gus, *The New Children* (New Kensington, PA: Whitaker House, 1975), 52, 168–69.

a new life, that is, a sharing in the life of God." We always knew it on paper, but much less in experience and conviction.

In the parable of the watchful servants (Luke 12:35–40), God is actually presented as *waiting on us*—in the middle of the night! In fact, we see God as both our personal servant inside our house and the *divine burglar* who has to "break through the walls of our house." That's really quite extraordinary and not our usual image of God. It shows how much God—the "Hound of Heaven," as Francis Thompson says—wants to get to us and how unrelenting is the work of grace.

Unless and until you understand the biblical concept of God's unmerited favor, God's unaccountable love, most of the biblical text cannot be interpreted or tied together in any positive way. It is, without doubt, the key and the code to everything transformative in the Bible. People who have not experienced the radical character of grace will always misinterpret the meanings and major direction of the Bible. The Bible will become a burden, obligation, and weapon more than a gift.

Grace cannot be understood by any ledger of merits and demerits. It cannot be held to patterns of buying, losing, earning, achieving, or manipulating, which is where, unfortunately, most of us live our lives. Grace is, quite literally, "for the taking." It is God eternally giving away God—for nothing—except the giving itself. I believe grace is the life energy that makes flowers bloom, animals lovingly raise their young, babies smile, and the planets remain in their orbits—for no good reason whatsoever—except love alone.   —TH 155–56

THE MOVEMENT GROWS

In 1973, there were about 1,200 young people attending Friday night services. Richard would preach for an hour, mostly on Scripture. Soon, Sr. Pat Brockman, an Ursuline nun, suggested recording Richard's series of lectures on Scripture and selling the cassettes. Richard didn't think anyone would buy them. Audio cassette tapes were just becoming popular and widespread.

"But Sister Pat asked me to pray about it for a day and then we'd ask God what to do. So we met the next day and opened the Bible. I put my finger on the verse 'The sower went out to sow the seed' (Mark 4:3). Really! That sounded sort of like making tapes. So we did. For years I was introduced as 'the tape priest.' Now my friends say I don't have a single untaped thought! It is sort of embarrassing. I guess Sister Pat was right. People really wanted to learn the Scriptures. Those first twelve tapes were called The Great Themes of Scripture. They went all over the world, especially to Catholic missionaries. I began receiving invitations to travel and give retreats in other countries, and my education was thus expanded."

My Hope and My Vocation

I try to follow the Franciscan call and strategy to bring great truths and scholarship to the common person and the ordinary Christian, so everyone can profit and grow from them. Just as bad theology has been used for purposes of slavery and oppression, good theology—made available in simple form to the masses—offers much needed liberation to both individuals and society. That is my hope and vocation.   —EL 179

A New Experience

The biblical revelation is inviting us into a new experience and a new way of seeing. Evolved human consciousness seems to be more ready to accept the divine invitation, but have no doubt, the Gospel is a major paradigm shift, and there will always be "an equal and opposite reaction" and resistance to such things as simplicity, nonviolence, restorative justice, and inclusivity.

A major problem is that theologians and the Church have presented the Bible as a collection of mental ideas about which we can be right or wrong. This traps us in a dualistic and argumentative mind, which is a pretty pathetic pathway to Great Truth. Many people don't expect from the Bible anything good or anything really new, which is how we translate the very word

"Gospel"—good news. So we first of all need mature people who can read texts with wider eyes, and not just people who want quick and easy answers by which they can affirm their ideas and self-made identities. The marvelous anthology of books and letters called the Bible is for the sake of *a love-affair between God and the soul*, not to create an organizational plan for any particular religion. The Gospel is about our transformation into God (*theosis*) rather than mere intellectual assurance or "small-self" coziness. It is more a revolution in consciousness than a business model for the buying and selling of God as a product.

Some scholars, interestingly enough, have said that Jesus came to end religion. That's not as bad as it might sound. Archaic religion was usually an attempt to assure people that nothing new or surprising would happen, and that the gods could be controlled. Most people want their lives and history to be entirely predictable and controllable, and the best way to do that is to try to manipulate the gods. Low-level religion basically teaches humans what spiritual buttons to push to supposedly keep our lives and God predictable. This kind of religion initially appeals to our lowest levels of egocentric motivation (security and group status) instead of moving us to our highest (generosity and trust). Jesus had a hard job cut out for him!

For most of human history, God was not a likable, much less lovable, character. That's why every "theophany" (an event where God breaks through into the human realm) in the Bible begins with the same words: "Do not be afraid." People have too often been afraid of God—and afraid of themselves as a result. When God appeared on the scene, most people did not see it as good news, but as bad news with fearful questions arising: Who has to die now? Who needs to be punished? By and large, before the biblical revelation, most of humanity did not expect love, much less intimate love, from God. Even today, most humans feel that any notion of a Divine Lover is quite distant, arbitrary, and surely impossible to enjoy or expect.

This fear-based pattern is so ingrained in our hardwiring that in the two thousand years since the Incarnation of God in Jesus

Christ, not much has really changed—except in a rather small percentage of humanity which is still growing toward a critical mass (Romans 8:28–30). In my experience, most people still fear or try to control God instead of learning to trust and return the love of a very loving God. When one party has all the power—which is most people's very definition of God—all you can do is fear and try to control.

The only way this can be changed is for God, from God's side, to change the power equation and invite us into a world of mutuality and vulnerability. Our living image of that power change is Jesus! In him, God took the initiative to overcome our fear and our need to manipulate God and made intimate Divine relationship possible. We can trace the thread of God's loving-kindness throughout Scripture—which is simultaneously a history of humanity's resistance, denial, and rejection of that very loving-kindness, reaching its climax in the crucifixion of Jesus. This movement both forward and backward is the story line of the whole Bible.   —TH 7–10 and NGTS disc 1

COMMUNITY LIFE

The New Jerusalem Community became a small phenomenon. Cardinal Bernardin, then Archbishop of Cincinnati, offered Richard an old school and convent in Winton Place, a neighborhood where Procter & Gamble had built homes for their workers. The community members rebuilt the houses, and eight to ten people shared each home. At the height of the movement in the late 1970s, there were 440 people living in the New Jerusalem Community, many in fourteen households of mixed ages and genders. They tried to emulate the Early Church as described in Acts 2. Some of the members held full-time jobs; they'd bring home their paychecks to share. Others offered internal ministry, including a Saturday co-op (where food was sold in bulk), a guest ministry, and a maintenance ministry for all the houses they had rebuilt. Some members were freed to walk the streets and minister to those they met. Visitors came from all over the world to learn from the model of community God had created there.

"It really was quite wonderful," Richard reminisces. "I would call 1973–1979 the 'golden period' when I would have to pinch myself each day to believe what I was seeing all around me. And believe me, that was all I did—watch! I did not create the movement, but watched it grow and tried to keep out of the way. Fr. John Quigley, a fellow Franciscan, came to help me, and he had much more practical and organizational skills than I did. We are still soul mates to this day. Soon some Jesuit scholastics also came to work with us and live in our households. What gifts they all were!"

Community as the Body of Christ

The template of all reality is Trinity: "Let *us* create humanity in *our* own image," the creation story says (Genesis 1:26). God is essentially shared life, life in relationship. *In the beginning is relationship*, we might say. Within the Trinity, Father, Son, and Spirit perfectly love and are perfectly loved. We come to know who God is through exchanges of mutual knowing and loving.

God's basic method of communicating Godself is not the "saved" individual, the rightly informed believer, or even personal careers in ministry, but the journey and bonding process that God initiates in community: in marriages, families, tribes, nations, events, scientists, and churches who are seeking to participate in God's love, maybe without even consciously knowing it.

The Body of Christ is our Christian metaphor for this bonding. It seems to be God's strategy and God's leaven inside the dough of creation. It is both the medium and the message. It is both the beginning and the goal: "May they all be one . . . so the world may believe it was you who sent me . . . that they may be one as we are one, with me in them and you in me" (see John 17:21, 23).

Thomas Merton writes, "The Christian is not merely 'alone with the Alone' in the Neoplatonic sense, but he is One with all his 'brothers [and sisters] in Christ.' His inner self is, in fact, inseparable from Christ and hence it is in a mysterious and unique way inseparable from all the other 'I's' who live in Christ, so that they all form one 'Mystical Person,' which is 'Christ.'"[8]

There is no other form for the Christian life except a common one. Until and unless Christ is experienced as a living relationship between people, the Gospel remains largely an abstraction. Until Christ is passed on personally through faithfulness and forgiveness, through concrete bonds of union, I doubt whether he is passed on by words, sermons, institutions, or ideas.

—NOG 49–51

Embodiment

While Paul's writing includes philosophical and poetic passages, it's not esoteric. Paul's teaching is incarnational. He sees that the Gospel message must have concrete embodiment. Concrete embodiment is Jesus' idea of church, too. Jesus' first vision of church is "two or three gathered in my name" (Matthew 18:20). This is why he insists that the message be communicated not by the lone evangelist but sends the Twelve out "two by two" (Mark 6:7). The individual is not a fitting communicator of the core message, and I am not either. (I am blessed to be part of a supportive Franciscan community that gives me the structural freedom to teach and write. The Center for Action and Contemplation helps bring my messages to readers and listeners. I certainly could not do it alone!)

During Paul's lifetime, the church was not yet an institution or structural grouping of common practices and beliefs. The church was *a living organism* that communicated the Gospel through *relationships*. This fits with Paul's understanding of Christ as what we might call an energy field, something inside of which you live and in which you participate organically.

---

8. Thomas Merton, *The Inner Experience: Notes on Contemplation* (San Francisco: Harper San Francisco, 2003), 22.

Paul's brilliant metaphor for this living, organic, concrete embodiment is the Body of Christ: "For as in one body we have many parts, and all the parts do not have the same function, so we, though many, are one body in Christ and individually parts of one another. Since we have gifts that differ according to the grace given to us, let us exercise them" (Romans 12:4–6). At the heart of this body, providing the energy that enlivens the community is "the love of God that has been poured out into our hearts through the Holy Spirit" (Romans 5:5).

This Spirit is itself the foundational energy of the universe, the Ground of all Being. Union is not just pious rambling or pretty poetry, but the concrete work of God in love-making. Paul writes, "Now you in your togetherness are Christ's Body" (1 Corinthians 12:27). In our connectedness with this luminous web, this vibrational state of love, we are participating in the embodiment of God.

Paul's communities are the audiovisual aids he can point to, giving credibility to his statements about new life. To people who ask, "Why should we believe there's a new life?" Paul can say, "Look at these people. They're different. They've been changed." As Jesus said, "This is how all will know that you are my disciples, if you have love for one another" (John 13:35).

For Jesus, such teachings as forgiveness, healing, and justice are the clear evidence of a shared life. When we do not see this happening, religion is "all in the head." Peacemaking, forgiveness, and reconciliation are not some kind of ticket to heaven later. They are the price of peoplehood—the signature of heaven—now.   —GTP disc 9 and NOG 51

Community as Alternative Consciousness

If the Trinity reveals that God is relationship itself, then the goal of the spiritual journey is to discover and move toward connectedness on ever new levels. The contemplative mind enjoys union on all levels. We may begin by making little connections with other people and with nature and animals, then grow into deeper connectedness with people. Finally, we can experience full connectedness as union with God. Remember, *how you do anything is how you do everything*. Without connectedness and communion, we don't exist fully as our truest selves. Becoming who we really are is a matter of learning how to become more and more deeply connected. No one can possibly go to heaven alone—or it would not be heaven.

Of course, we won't become vulnerable enough to connect unless we learn to trust over and over again. Einstein is said to have claimed this to be the most important question: "Is the universe a friendly place or not?" The spiritual experience is about trusting that when you stop holding yourself, Inherent Goodness will still uphold you. Many of us call that God, but you don't have to. It is the trusting that is important. When you fall into such Primal Love, you realize that everything is foundationally okay. Unfortunately, this is often absent in our secular world today.

Foundational love gives us hope and allows us to trust "what is" as the jumping-off point toward working together for "what can be." The life, death, and resurrection of Jesus shows us what's fully possible. God will always bring yet more life and wholeness out of seeming chaos and death. In the words of Timothy Gorringe and Rosie Beckham, "Faith in the resurrection is the ground on which Christians hope for a *different* future, a transition to a society less destructive, more peaceful and more whole. Living in this hope grounds the Christian ethic of resistance and calls *ekklesia* to live as a 'contrast community' to society."[9]

Building such communities in contrast to the surrounding society of emperor-worship was precisely Paul's missionary strategy. Small communities of Jesus' followers would make the message believable: Jesus is Lord (rather than Caesar is Lord); sharing abundance and living in simplicity (rather than hoarding wealth); nonviolence and suffering (rather than aligning with

---

9. Timothy Gorringe and Rose Beckham, *Transition Movement for Churches* (London: Canterbury Press, 2013), 79.

power). Paul was very practical. He taught that our faith must take form in a living, loving group of people. Community was everything for him.

Paul seems to think, and I agree with him, that corporate evil can only be confronted or overcome with corporate good. He knows that the love-transformed individual can do little against what he calls "the powers and the principalities." Today we might call powers and principalities our collective cultural moods or mass consciousness or institutions considered "too big to fail." We are mostly oblivious to this because we take all these things as normative and absolutely needed. It is the "absolutely" that gets us into our blindness and idolatry. Because we share in this collective evil, it doesn't look like evil. For instance, I've never once heard a sermon against the tenth commandment, "You shall not covet your neighbor's goods," because in our culture that's the only game in town. It is called capitalism.

The individual is largely helpless and harmless standing against the system. Paul believes cultural blind spots can only be overcome by a group of people affirming and supporting one another in an alternative consciousness. Thankfully, we're seeing many people, religious and secular, from all around the world, coming together to form alternative systems for sharing resources, living simply, and imagining a sustainable future.

—NOG 51; CCC; GTP disc 9

The Meaning of Community

Living in community means living in such a way that others can access me and influence my life and that I can get "out of myself" and serve the lives of others. Community is a world where brotherliness and sisterliness are possible. By community, I don't mean primarily a special kind of structure, but a network of relationships. On the whole, we live in a society that's built not on community and cooperation, but on competition.

—S 65

NINE FACES OF LOVE

One of the tools for strengthening community that Richard taught the members of New Jerusalem was the Enneagram.[10] *He first learned the Enneagram in 1973 from his Jesuit spiritual director, Father Jim O'Brien. He recalls it as a powerful "confrontation with my shadow. I was driving back to New Jerusalem after seeing my spiritual director at Xavier University in Cincinnati. I can still almost picture the place on the street where it hit me: My God, I am a One! It was like a Damascus Road experience where the scales fell from my eyes and I saw that what I had thought were my virtues—my hard work ethic, righteous idealism, perfectionism, and chosen celibacy—were also my worst traps. It was my earliest direct teaching of non-dual thinking, even though we didn't use that word then. The Enneagram shows us that our gift is our sin and our sin is our gift and you can't have one without the other.*

"It just gave me such clarity of language and perception about why I was the way I was: why I expected so much of myself and other people, and why I had a hard time letting go of my expectations for supposed perfection. When I saw that was all 'One' compulsiveness, it helped me begin to have a lot more patience and compassion with myself and with others. That's how the Enneagram can help us become more loving. It still works with me to this day. The only people who do not believe the Enneagram is 'true' are those who do not know it. There's the first flash of One resentment, judgment, or anger because something's not 'perfect'; but the second minute I can usually see through it or

---

10. In this book we offer a brief overview of the Enneagram and an introduction to Richard's own type, the One. See the Appendix for a short description of each type. To learn more, see Richard's book, *The Enneagram: A Christian Perspective* (New York: Crossroad Publishing, 2011). Richard also recommends Don Richard Riso and Russ Hudson's book, *The Wisdom of the Enneagram: The Complete Guide to Psychological and Spiritual Growth* (New York: Bantam, 1999).

beyond it. That's just tremendous freedom from the trap of nursing resentment or anger toward myself or anything else.

"In terms of the journey of learning how to love, the Enneagram was extremely helpful in allowing me to see my own set of blinders, my own compulsiveness, my own obsessions. I was able to take myself less seriously and to be more compassionate with others because I knew they were in a box just as constricted as my own, just with a different shape to it. The Enneagram teaches that there are two sides to everything, and you can't really love if you just think of anything or anyone as all good or all bad. Our gifts carry our 'sin' and our sin can often deliver our greatest gifts of love and compassion. The Enneagram reveals nine different faces of divine and human love."

Knowing Ourselves

The Enneagram is a dynamic system for self-knowledge and spiritual transformation. It is a wonderful tool that can help us see and let go of the false self—which masks the image of God within us—and allow us to live from our True Self—the unique manifestation of Love that God intends us to be. It seems we are most defended against that which we most deeply know to be true, our original blessing. This ontological belovedness and okayness is hard to trust because this true mirroring has invariably been distorted, denied, or even betrayed. The Enneagram serves as a very helpful mirror to reveal our egoic habits that keep our authentic self from thriving.

Although the Enneagram is an ancient tool, with roots in the Desert Fathers and Mothers, it was neglected for centuries. I first learned about the Enneagram from the Jesuits who brought it to America during the early 1970s. The Jesuits discovered this tool for their gift of spiritual direction. It is used in "the reading of souls" to help people rediscover who they are in God. When used in conjunction with a regular practice of contemplative prayer, the Enneagram can be powerfully transformative. It can open us to deeper and deeper levels of understanding and insight, love and grace.

The Enneagram describes nine different personalities, each of which covers a broad spectrum from "immature" to "mature," or "compulsive" to "redeemed." It is more about recognizing "energies" than it is about describing precise traits. People who know the Enneagram in a superficial way think it's about putting people into boxes, but its real goal is to let people out of their self-created boxes. It makes us aware of our *root sin,* our *passion,* our particular *trap* or *blindness* that prevents us from experiencing reality holistically and honestly. These passions were called the seven "capital sins" by Pope Gregory the Great in the sixth century, although predictably he missed the most common ones in Western civilization, which are *fear* and *deceit.* You can't see as sin what you have idealized as virtue.

Freedom from our habitual trap comes through some in-depth experience of Love, be it a sudden overflowing, hitting the bottom and being lifted up, or the gradual opening through contemplative practice. At some point many people wake up and begin to realize, however tenuously, their own True Self, a one-of-a-kind reflection of God's love in the world. There's a part of us that has always been in union with God. Gradually we learn more and more to trust our deepest soul and draw our life from that Source. We learn how to live more consistently from this true identity of original blessing, who we are in God and who we will be through eternity. Then we know that any notion of heaven is not just later, but has begun here and now.

—ECP xvii–xviii, 29, 40; EG disc 1; and ETSJ disc 4

REALITY AS PARADOX

Richard reflects upon how the Enneagram has helped him see himself truly: "When my One-ness became obvious to me, I was in a daze of humiliating recognitions. 'My God, I became a Franciscan for the wrong reason, I became celibate for the wrong reason, I became a priest for the wrong reason. Oh God, did I do anything right?' I realized that I wasn't right at all. [And being right is especially important to a One.] My very best efforts stemmed from mixed motives, to make myself look good or to feel good about myself. I wasn't loving God; I was loving Richard! This insight was an initial and substantial death to my false self and helped me understand what the false self is. It also set me on a course that has become one of my central themes: the understanding of reality as paradox, reality as a seeming contradiction that in a bigger frame is not a contradiction at all. Non-dual thinking became a phrase I commonly use to teach contemplation."

Type One: The Need to Be Perfect

All of us begin life in union with God, as our True Self, totally in Love. Each Enneagram type has a uniquely gifted way of being connected with the Real. It reveals our original "soul space."

Our Enneagram *passions* or *sins* come from the suffering and agitation caused by the perception that we've been torn from the womb of Love. The ego creates a false self, trying to recreate the original positive soul experience. Eventually, as Russ Hudson says, "The healing of the passion comes through turning back toward the grace. Allowing grace to work us over a long period develops our virtue."[11] Thus, the issues of the false self are only resolved by experiencing our forgotten but real connection with God.

Understanding the Enneagram has helped me to understand and have compassion for myself and others. It helps me see when I am acting out of my false self and makes it easier to accept myself and return to my True Self.

I am an Enneagram type One, a reformer. Ones need to be perfect, and for Ones this means feeling that they are right and good. Ones are idealists, motivated and driven by the longing for a true, just, and moral world. Somewhere in their childhood, they experienced the world as beautiful and perfect. And it's no

---

11. Russ Hudson, *The Enneagram as a Tool for Your Spiritual Journey*, disc 2 (Albuquerque, NM: Center for Action and Contemplation, 2009), CD, DVD, MP3 download.

wonder, because their "Soul Child," or original dream of life, is the joyful Seven. I remember moments that were so wonderful, so serene, so whole, with no need to eliminate anything. God was in it and I was in it and life all made sense. Then somewhere later on I realized, "Darn it, it isn't a perfect world!" So I moved to the impossible conviction: "I'm going to find a way to make it perfect." And that became my entrapped Enneagram One position. It's the original, positive soul experience that all the types are trying to recreate, but their new agenda becomes an entrapped "false self."

Ones are often good teachers and reformers. They can spur others to work and mature and grow. The demanding, critical voices within them make it hard for Ones to live with imperfection—especially their own. "Anger" is their root sin, although they seldom get directly angry. It is more a low-level resentment because the world is not the way they know it should be! They repress their anger because they see it as something imperfect in themselves. At the same time, it energizes them to work really hard for their ideals and principles. Talk about an inner conflict! Ones are driven toward righteousness, arrogance, and perfectionism. They unfortunately believe in meritocracy: you get what you deserve, so you'd better be good and work hard. There is no free lunch! That is why the concept of grace is so foundationally important for me; it alone breaks down all this silly merit badge thinking.

In order to discover their gift, which is cheerful tranquility or serenity, Ones must first realize that they are *not* that good. They may have to "sin boldly" to see this or at least recognize that every good thing they have ever done has also involved self-interest. Then they can experience unearned grace, which finally allows them to be at peace and happy—even with imperfection.

Many integrated Ones say that three things help them: *prayer, love,* and *nature.* When I pray, I can increasingly let go of the voices of duty and responsibility and let myself drop down into God, into Love. Love is "the perfect bond," as Paul says (Colossians 3:14). That is why I have to fall in love with somebody or something every day, even if it's only a tree or the wonderful turquoise sky over New Mexico. When I don't love, the negative voices immediately get the upper hand. Finally, nature helps me discover perfection in the flux and chaos of creative evolution. *God, love, and nature are perfect precisely because they include and incorporate imperfection.* This is important! Without these three, Ones can scarcely imagine cheerful serenity and patience, but remain aggressive idealists.   —ECP 45, 49, 52–55 and EDS

EXPERIENCES IN HEALING

Richard recalls an experience from his early days in Cincinnati. A pregnant woman came to him and asked Richard to pray over her. The baby was due soon and would be born breech if not turned. Richard laid his hands on her belly and prayed. "Her belly started to move!" The baby turned and was born a couple days later. Word spread around Cincinnati: "'This priest has a gift for turning babies around.' Soon the women from around town were lining up," Richard says. Not all of the babies turned, but some did. "I quickly realized why Jesus did not want to be known as a healer. It tends to take all the attention.

"Once I prayed with a group of people in New Jerusalem over a woman whom tests had shown was carrying a baby boy with spina bifida. Shortly before he was born, tests showed he no longer had spina bifida!

"I share this because you can't engineer healing. It's not based on being more holy or faithful. Remember that sometimes Jesus healed people who didn't even ask to be healed. Some people made no mention of faith, just need and desire. Jesus took the initiative and offered his healing touch—and it was always touch, which we now call 'praying over people.' God seems to be saying that there's no way we're ever going to control how or when the flow happens. But we must not doubt that we are instruments of that flow. The Trinitarian life of God—Father, Son, and Holy Spirit—is an eternal outpouring of love. Quite simply, those who have the gifts are those who use the gifts. It has nothing to do with worthiness.

"*If you can trust that God loves you enough to use you and cares about someone who is in pain or sick, then you're not afraid to lay your hand on their forehead or arm or whatever is hurting. I have to believe that life and love flow from God through you to that person.*

"*As the Gospel writers ask, 'Can you imagine that if you pray, God would* not *give God's Holy Spirit?' (see Luke 7:5–13 and Matthew 7:7–12). The answer to every prayer is an infusion of the Holy Spirit. It's not always what you expect or want. But you can trust that there has been a very real transference of life. This gift is not just for priests or bishops or deacons. It's for every member of the Body of Christ.*

"*New Jerusalem was a charismatic community that believed in healing. And when you have a whole community that believes in healing and constantly prays together for healing, you just see it happen much more often. That's one of the experiences that attracted me to the idea of Love and the Holy Spirit as a force field.*"

The Loving Inner Witness

We each carry a certain amount of pain from our very birth. If that pain is not healed and transformed, it actually increases as we grow older, and we transmit it to people around us. We can become violent in our attitudes, gestures, words, and actions.

We must nip this process in the bud by acknowledging and owning our own pain, rather than projecting it elsewhere. For myself, I can't pretend to be loving when inside I'm not, when I know I've thought cruel, judgmental, and harsh thoughts about others. At the moment the thought arises, I have to catch myself and hand over the annoyance or anger to God. Contemplative practice helps me develop this capacity to watch myself and to connect with my loving Inner Witness. Let me explain why this is important.

If you can simply observe the negative pattern in yourself, you have already begun to separate from it. The watcher is now over here, observing yourself thinking that thought—over there. Unless you can become the watcher, you'll almost always identify with your feelings. They feel like real and objective truth.

Most people I know are *overly* identified with their own thoughts and feelings. They don't really have feelings; their feelings have them. That may be what earlier Christians meant by being "possessed" by a demon. That's why so many of Jesus' miracles are the exorcism of devils. Most people don't take that literally anymore, but the devil is still a powerful metaphor, which demands that you take it quite seriously. Everyone has a few devils. I know I'm "possessed" at least once or twice a day, even if just for a few minutes!

There are all kinds of demons—in other words, there are lots of times when you cannot *not* think a certain way. When you see certain people, you get afraid. When you see other people, you get angry. For example, numerous studies show that many white people have an implicit, unacknowledged fear of black men. Most of us are not explicitly racist, but many of us have an implicit and totally denied racial bias. This is why all healing and prayer must descend into the unconscious where the lies we've believed are hidden in our wounds.

During contemplation, forgotten painful experiences may arise. In such cases, it helps to meet with a spiritual director or therapist to process old wounds and trauma in healthy ways.

Over a lifetime of practice, contemplation gradually helps you detach from *who you think you are* and rest in your authentic identity as Love.   —MN

THE BEGINNING OF THE END

Richard shares that he was a "black sheep" of the Catholic Charismatic Pentecostal movement for two reasons: he was concerned about issues of social justice, and from the very beginning he welcomed women into leadership roles at every level. "I had thought that the Pentecostals were the new free group, and yet I soon found they were just as legalistic and clerical as we mainline Catholics were, just with different forms of legalism.

"*I was also being called a heretic in the Catholic Church. I had 'no place to lay my head' except for the support of the Franciscans and some Jesuits. The diocesan priests thought I was taking young people away from their Masses. Some people thought we were muddying the boundaries of organized religion, because we began mostly Catholic, but then people from all denominations started coming. But for some reason Archbishop Bernardin liked me. He always protected me. And the people who needed community or needed healing thought we were wonderful. Most of the people who trusted us were the little people, which helped me understand the Gospel's bias toward the bottom.*

"*Sadly, the early fervor of the New Jerusalem Community couldn't be sustained. Actually, we have no evidence that the community described in Acts 2 ever lasted beyond a few years either. This seems to be the history of radical Christian community, unless it goes the path of celibacy and monasticism. Perhaps it is just a way for God to stir the pot. Why was there so much stirring of the pot in the early 1970s? This was happening all over. Sojourners Community began around the same time in Illinois, and by the late 1970s there were seventeen groups linked together in what we called 'The Community of Communities.' Those were exciting years. Many of these movements were charismatic and almost all of us had significant ministries for the poor and the excluded in one way or another. We were no longer fully at home in our historic Christian denominations.*"

A Learning Experience

Many communities that evolved during the 1970s and '80s failed, I believe, because they talked, met, and worried themselves to death. After years of in-house and seemingly cyclical conversations, many movers and shakers decided to move on. Usually they later admitted that community was an excellent school of growth, character, and conversion. But it was often not a permanent "home" for many reasons.

It's all too easy to project unrealistic expectations on our community. No group can meet all our needs as individuals—

parenting, marriage, therapy, and emotional, mental, and physical well-being. The human psyche needs space and healthy boundaries. Even in marriage, you cannot meet most of your partner's needs; in the end, you still remain a profound mystery to one another. Expectations of false and impossible intimacy make practical community very difficult, and sometimes even counterproductive. The thousands of disillusioned and alienated former community members are a judgment not only on the limits of their communities but also on our own narcissistic expectations. But imperfect community can still be a good school!

—NOG 14–15

DIFFERENT AND UNITED

During his years at New Jerusalem, due to the popularity of his Great Themes of Scriptures cassettes, Richard began receiving invitations to speak all over the world. He spoke in Africa, Asia, the Philippines, and the Caribbean. "I became aware that there's a much bigger world than the United States of America, and there's a much bigger church than the Roman Catholic Church, and there are many ways of looking at reality and at God. It helped me see you can be different and still be united. In fact, that's the doctrine of the Trinity. That's the very shape of God: different and united."

Richard emphasizes: "It's all a school of love. The whole thing called life is a school of love to pull us out of our egocentricity, our natural 'I'm the reference point, I'm the grand normal. Why isn't everybody like me?' That kind of egocentricity has to be undercut radically and dramatically. And it's clear to me that Christianity has not been doing it very well up to now." He came to see how white, patriarchal, wealthy, and Eurocentric most of Catholicism was, even though the church in the Southern Hemisphere was full of vitality.

The Delight of Diversity

One of the most wonderful things I find in the classic naming of God as Father, Son, and Holy Spirit is its affirmation that

there is an *intrinsic plurality* to goodness. Goodness isn't sameness. Goodness, to be goodness, needs contrast and tension, not
perfect uniformity. If Father, Son, and Holy Spirit are all God
yet clearly different, and we embrace this differentiation, resisting the temptation to blend them into some kind of amorphous
blob, then there are at least three shapes to the foundational
goodness, truth, and beauty of things.

God's goal, it seems to me, is the same as in creation. It is the
making of persons, not the making of a uniform mob, which
means there is clear diversity and a kind of open-endedness in
all of nature. In other words, heaven is precisely not uniformity.
The diversity of heaven was never something I considered in my
earlier years. I thought we were all handed the same white robe
and standard-issue harp, assigned to an identical cloud for all
eternity. But how does Jesus himself deconstruct this big-box,
strip-mall, McHeaven franchise? He tells us: "In my Father's
house are many mansions" (John 14:2).

Even in the eternal nature of things, you're somehow *you*
in your you-ness, on the path that God is leading *you,* on the
journey *you* are going through, with the burdens that *you* are
bearing. All of these are combining to create the precise alchemy
of *your* soul, *your* holiness, and *your* response. In the eternal
scheme of things, you discover that all God wants from you is
you.

It feels so insignificant, and yet this is the liberating secret: I
am precisely the gift God wants—in my full and humble surrender to my ordinariness—which ironically is my eternal specialness. *All I can give back to God is who I really and fully am!*
That is all God wants. Yet this seems so boring and pedestrian
to us, if we want to be high flyers.

The Trinity reveals a pattern of perfect freedom whereby each
of the Three Persons allows the other Two to be fully themselves
and remains in full given-ness toward each of them, while still
allowing, protecting, and honoring itself *as itself,* and forever
emptying itself of itself to make room for the other Two. *We
now have a full definition of the shape of Divine and also human
Love.*   —DD 61–63

From Disconnection to Connection

I'm convinced that beneath the ugly manifestations of our present evils—political corruption, ecological devastation, warring against one another, hating each other based on race, gender, religion, or sexual orientation—the greatest dis-ease facing humanity right now is our profound and painful sense of disconnection. We feel disconnected from God, certainly, but also from ourselves (our bodies), from each other, and from our world.

Yet many are discovering that the gift of the Trinity—and our practical, felt experience of this gift—offers a grounded reconnection with God, with self, with others, and with our world that all religion and spirituality, and arguably, even politics, are aiming for, but which conventional religion, spirituality, and politics fail to access.

Trinity represents the overcoming of the foundational philosophical problem called "the One and the Many." How things are both utterly connected and yet distinct is invariably the question of the serious seeker. In the paradigm of Trinity, we have three autonomous "Persons," as we call them, who are nevertheless in perfect communion. It is a new definition of unity and a protection of diversity too, which offers us a template for everything else. We must hold the tension between distinct individuals and absolute communion. That's the only way we'll survive in this world, it seems to me.

Trinity is all about relationship and connection. We know the Trinity through experiencing the flow itself, which dissolves our sense of disconnection. The principle of one is lonely; the principle of two is oppositional and moves you toward preference and exclusion; the principle of three is inherently moving, dynamic, and generative.

God is not a being among other beings, but rather the Ground of Being itself which then flows through all beings. As Paul says to the intellectuals in Athens, this God "is not far from us, but is the one in whom we live and move and have our being" (Acts 17:27–28). The God whom Jesus reveals is presented as unhindered dialogue, a positive and inclusive flow, and a water-wheel of outpouring love that never stops! St. Bonaventure would later call God a "fountain fullness" of love.

Our sense of disconnection is only an illusion. Nothing human can stop the flow of divine love; we cannot undo the eternal pattern even by our worst sin. God is always winning, and God's love will win. Love does not lose, nor does God lose. Nothing can stop the relentless outpouring force that is the divine dance.
—DDEMT discs 2–3 and DD 39–40, 42–43

A School of Relationship

We all fear and avoid intimacy, it seems. It is too powerful and demands that we also "have faces," that is, self-confidence, identity, dignity, and a certain courage to accept our own unique face. Once we accept and love ourselves, we must be willing to share this daring intimacy with another. The brilliant title of C. S. Lewis' book, *Till We Have Faces*, suggests how central this is; the archetypal myth of Cupid and Psyche reveals the human and divine longing for face-to-face intimacy.

At first the individual is not ready for presence. We settle for tribal customs, laws, and occupations as our identity. Most individuals cannot contain or sustain trust and love by themselves. So God starts by giving the whole group a sense of dignity and identity. YHWH creates "a chosen people": "You will be my people and I will be your God," God says to Israel (Jeremiah 32:38). Only the *Whole* can carry the weight of glory and the burden of sin. Western individualism is a large part of the ineffectiveness of most contemporary Christianity.

It seems the experiences of specialness and of sinfulness are both too heavy to be carried by an individual. One will disbelieve them or abuse them, either through self-hatred or by ego-inflation and conceit. It is almost impossible for a person to stand before the face of God in a perfect balance between extreme humility and perfect dignity. So God begins with a people "consecrated as God's very own" (Deuteronomy 14:2). The group holds the Mystery which the individual cannot carry. This eventually becomes the very meaning of "church" or the Body of Christ. Membership in the sacred group should and can become the gateway to *personal encounter and inner experience*, though too often it is a substitute for it.

We could say that the original blueprint for everything that exists is relationship. John's word for that was *Logos* (John 1:1). In other words, the first blueprint for reality was relationality. It is all of one piece. How we relate to God reveals how we eventually relate to just about everything else. And how we relate to the world of "the ten thousand things" is how we are actively relating to God, whether we know it or not (1 John 4:20). How we do anything is how we do everything!

Thus, we must read the whole Bible as a school of relationship. The Bible is slowly making humanity capable of living inside of what Charles Williams called co-inherence. All creation is in the end drawn and seduced into the Great Co-inherence. "I shall return to take you with me, so that where I am you also may be too," Jesus clearly says (John 14:3). Salvation is giving us a face capable of receiving the dignity of the divine embrace, and then daring to think that we could love God back—and that God would enjoy this, or even care about it.

—TH 56–57

LESSONS FOR THE EGO

Richard realizes that he, himself, probably helped dismantle the New Jerusalem Community. He vividly remembers coming back from his first trip to Latin America in 1977. He had been in Peru and was deeply touched by the poverty and the little boys begging, "sticking their noses up against the window of the restaurant in Cusco while I'm sitting there, probably eating crème brûlée. And I'm supposed to be a Franciscan! It just tore me apart.

"So the next Sunday, I gave a climactic (for the community) sermon on social justice. The New Jerusalem Community was at

its height. We were strong and united. Everybody was imitating us, admiring us, loving us. And I, the supposed founder, came in and threw a hand grenade right in the middle of it, saying, 'We're just creating a little country club here of people who are comfortable and love one another. But do you know most of the world is starving? Most of the world is suffering.' I'm sure I probably overdid it in my righteous, judgmental, perfectionistic style. And the more I traveled to developing countries and then told the community about it, the more I tore my own community apart. I did not yet know how to teach in a contemplative way.

"When you make an intentional community an end in itself, it becomes idolatry. We had to live up to this image of 'we are the perfect New Jerusalem.' Even the name gives that away. Of course, that name was also my heroic idea!" [New Jerusalem is described in Revelation as "the holy city coming down out of heaven from God" (21:2, 10).]

"I'm afraid New Jerusalem had become self-preoccupied with maintaining, perpetuating, and preserving itself. So much time was spent defining membership: Who's in and who's out? What are our rules and requirements for belonging? The women were demanding equal say on everything, which is absolutely right. But that upset some of the men who still thought it was a patriarchal church. We certainly always had a good contingent of LGBTQ people in the community; and I never had any problem with that, but others did. Believe me, I can be patient now with any church, including the Roman Catholic Church, because I saw what happened to my own community in a very short time. Once you institutionalize, a whole new set of issues immediately locks into place."

Richard says that New Jerusalem was "my school. I was being educated in how to deal with emotions, how to deal with people who don't like you, people who tell lies about you, people who try to destroy you or undo the work that you thought you did. There was a lot of pride in me that had to be cut down more than a few notches. As you know, those are not easy lessons for the ego to take, especially when you are considered 'The Founder.'"

Unworkable Programs for Happiness

I've come to realize that I have a great need for approval and esteem, for people telling me how wonderful I am. I'd gotten so much approval as a kid and growing up. And after being on stage all these years and having people applaud, I'm afraid the ego comes to expect that. When someone criticizes me, well my false self feels "How dare you? Don't you know I'm an internationally known speaker?" Of course, what has been offended is my life-long, reinforced need for approval, affection, and esteem. It's my ordinary program for happiness and I just can't understand anybody who would not think I'm wonderful! But thank God, I began to see it, and I get enough hate mail and angry letters to make me know it's an "unworkable program for happiness," as Thomas Keating would say.

You see, my program for happiness is almost entirely dependent upon outside events and other people. I rely on people around me to give me affirming cues and feedback. But as long as I'm dependent on the approval of others, I have no center or ground of being. My identity is unstable, and I'll be defeated every day by folks who don't like me. The same is true for the other two "unworkable programs for happiness": the need for power and control, and the need for survival and security. They all work from the outside-in instead of from the inside-out.

This is why contemplative practice is so important. My "Inner Witness" helps me rediscover the true Source of my identity— Infinite Love.   —ES

Already in Union

> For I am convinced that neither death, nor life, nor angels, nor principalities, nor things present, nor things to come, nor powers, nor height, nor depth, nor any other created thing, will be able to separate us from the love of God, which is in Christ Jesus our Lord.
> —Romans 8:38–39, NASB

We are already in union with God! There is an absolute, eternal union between God and the soul of everything. At the deepest level, you and I are "hidden with Christ in God" (Colossians 3:3) and "the whole creation . . . is being brought into the same glorious freedom as the children of God" (Romans 8:21). The problem is that Western religion has not taught us this. Our ego over-emphasizes our individuality and separateness from God and others. We limited God's redemption to the human species—and not very many individuals within that species!

Daily contemplative prayer helps you rediscover your inherent union and learn how to abide in Presence, trusting that you are already good and safe in God. You don't have to worry about your little private, separate, insecure self. I am one with you and you are one with your neighbor and your neighbor is one with God. That's the Gospel! That's the whole point of communion or Eucharist; we partake of the bread and the wine until it convinces us that *we are in communion*. It seems easier for God to convince bread and wine of its identity than to convince us.

You're not here to save your soul. That's already been done once and for all—in Christ, through Christ, with Christ, and as Christ (see Ephesians 1:3–14). By God's love, mercy, and grace, we are already the Body of Christ: the one universal body that has existed since the beginning of time. You and I are here for just a few decades, dancing on the stage of life, perhaps taking our autonomous self far too seriously. That little and clearly imperfect self just cannot believe it could be a child of God. I hope the Gospel frees you to live inside of a life that is larger than you and cannot be taken from you. It is the very life of God which cannot be destroyed.

As Thomas Merton wrote in his journal, "We are already one. But we imagine that we are not. And what we have to recover is our original unity. *What we have to be is what we are.*"[12]

—H September 13, 2015 and ES

---

12. Thomas Merton, *The Asian Journal of Thomas Merton*, ed. Patrick Hart, James Laughlin, and Naomi Burton Stone (New York: New Directions Publishing, 1975), 308. Emphasis mine.

SPEAKING TRUTH TO POWER

Richard participated in several protests in the 1980s, particularly against nuclear arms. On Pentecost Sunday in 1983, he was arrested in Washington, DC, and his mother saw him on the national news, walking down the Capitol building steps in handcuffs, wearing his Franciscan habit. Richard tells us, "I was arrested for kneeling and praying in the rotunda. I was thrown in jail for one night, but there was nothing heroic about it. We all felt famous because we were in jail with famous people. We talked and sang all night."

Richard shares similar experiences in Cincinnati and at the Nevada Test Site. Protestors were typically arrested, detained for a short time, and then released. "We really didn't suffer. It certainly fed my ego," he says. While Richard believes these gestures of solidarity and protest are important, and it's good that someone does them, after a while he realized it was not his calling. In his case, there were too many ego pay-offs.

"I don't think most people feel called to activism; I myself don't. I had to finally say that it was not what I was called to do. It was humiliating to admit, and I lost the trust and admiration of some friends and supporters. But as we come to know our soul gift more clearly, we almost always have to let go of some 'gifts' so we can do our one or two things with integrity, instead of being driven by 'the tyranny of the urgent.'

"My calling was more to be a teacher and also to keep going deeper with the inner experience. If I had focused on activism, I don't think I could have taught as well and would have been drawn in many other directions and into drama. I remember being at some protests in Cincinnati where the energy of other protesters was oppositional, angry, and self-righteous—much different than what I would now call 'third force' energy. During the Center for Action and Contemplation's early years when we protested at the gates of the national nuclear labs in New Mexico, we always carried positive signs with meaningful questions like 'Do you really want to give your life to building bombs? Is

this your contribution to the world?' I know people who left their jobs there because of our signs. Rather than accuse them, we would invite people to wrestle with what they were doing. It was very effective."

Ahimsa: Love Is Your Nature

> *Before you speak of peace, you must first have it in your heart.*
> —St. Francis of Assisi[13]

Christianity seems to have forgotten Jesus' teachings on nonviolence. We've relegated visions of a peaceful kingdom to a far distant heaven, hardly believing Jesus could have meant we should turn the other cheek here and now. It took Gandhi, a Hindu, to help us apply Jesus' peace-making in very practical ways. As Gandhi said, "It is a first-class human tragedy that people of the earth who claim to believe in the message of Jesus, whom they describe as the Prince of Peace, show little of that belief in actual practice."[14] Martin Luther King, Jr., drawing from Gandhi's work, brought nonviolence to the forefront of civil rights in the 1960s.

Nonviolence training has understandably emphasized largely external methods or ways of acting and resisting. These are important and necessary, but we must go even deeper. Unless those methods finally reflect inner attitudes, they will not make a lasting difference. We all have to admit that our secret inner attitudes are often cruel, attacking, judgmental, and harsh. The ego seems to find its energy precisely by having something to oppose, fix, or change. When the mind can judge something to be inferior, we feel superior. We must recognize our constant tendency

---

13. Paraphrase of Francis of Assisi, *Opuscoli di S. Francesco d'Assisi*, ed. Fr. Bernardo da Fivizzano (Firenze Tip. della SS. Concezione di R. Ricci: 1880), 272.

14. Mahatma Gandhi, *Truth Is God*, ed. R. K. Prabhu (Ahmedabad, India: Navajivan Publishing House, 1955), 145.

toward negating reality, resisting it, opposing it, and attacking it on the level of our mind. This is the universal addiction.

Authentic spirituality is always first about *you*—about allowing your own heart and mind to be changed. It's about getting your own *who* right. *Who* is it that is doing the perceiving? Is it your illusory, separate, false self; or is it your True Self, who you are in God?

As Thomas Keating says:

> We're all like localized vibrations of the infinite goodness of God's presence. So love is our very nature. Love is our first, middle, and last name. Love is all; not [love as] sentimentality, but love that is self-forgetful and free of self-interest.
>
> This is also marvelously exemplified in Gandhi's life and work. He never tried to win anything. He just tried to show love; and that's what *ahimsa* really means. It's not just a negative. Nonviolence doesn't capture its meaning. It means to show love tirelessly, no matter what happens. That's the meaning of turning the other cheek. Once in a while you have to defend somebody, but it means you're always willing to suffer first for the cause—that is to say, for communion with your enemies. If you overcome your enemies, you've failed. If you make your enemies your partners, God has succeeded.[15]
>
> —MN and HOV discs 2 and 5

A Nonviolent Gospel

Jesus' teachings seem to have been understood rather clearly during the first few hundred years after his death and resurrection. Values like nonparticipation in war, simple living, and love of enemies were common among his early followers. For example, the *Didache,* written around AD 90, calls readers to

---

15. Thomas Keating, *Healing Our Violence through the Journey of Centering Prayer*, disc 5 (Cincinnati, OH: Franciscan Media: 2002), CD.

"share all things with your brother; and do not say that they are your own. For if you are sharers in what is imperishable, how much more in things which perish?"[16] At this time, Christianity was countercultural, untouched by empire, rationalization, and compromise.

However, when the imperial edict of AD 313 began elevating Christianity to a privileged position in the Roman Empire, the church increasingly accepted, and even defended, the dominant social order, especially concerning war, money, and class. Morality became individualized and largely sexual. Formal Christianity slowly lost its free and alternative vantage point, which is probably why what we now call "religious life" began and flourished after 313. People went to the edges of the church and took vows of poverty, living in satellites that became "little churches," without ever formally leaving the big Church.

If you look at texts in the hundred years preceding 313, it was unthinkable that a Christian would fight in the army. The army was killing Christians; Christians were being persecuted. By the year 400, the entire army had become Christian, and Christians were killing the "pagans." In a two-hundred-year period, we went from being complete outsiders to directing the inside! Once you are inside, you have to defend your power and your privilege.

It is during this transition that people like St. Anthony of the Desert, John Cassian, Evagrius Ponticus, and the early monks went off to Egypt, Syria, and the deserts of Palestine. They critiqued the self-protective, privileged lifestyle of mainline Christianity by utterly leaving it! Soon they learned and taught a different way of seeing called "contemplation." From that point through the modern period, most governments assumed that Christian monks and priests could not, or should not, wage war or kill others.

Why this split between two brands of Christianity? Why were some expected to take the Sermon on the Mount seriously, while

---

16. *Didache: The Teaching of the Twelve Apostles*, chap. 4.8.

the rest were exempt? Even as recently as the Vietnam War, laity could kill, while the clergy could not. As a Franciscan, I received an immediate draft deferment in the 1960s. When the Gospel is heard and understood at its deepest level, Christians cannot and will not kill or wage war.   —DSS 47–51

Jesus Reveals the Lie of Scapegoating

If your ego is still in charge, you will find a disposable person or group on which to project your problems. People who haven't come to at least a minimal awareness of their own dark side will always find someone else to hate or fear. Hatred holds a group together much more quickly and easily than love and inclusivity, I am sorry to say. Rene Girard developed a sociological, literary, and philosophical explanation for how and why the pattern of scapegoating is so prevalent in every culture.[17]

In Leviticus 16 we see the brilliant ritualization of what we now call scapegoating, and we should indeed feel sorry for the demonized goat. On the Day of Atonement, a priest laid hands on an "escaping" goat, placing all the sins of the Jewish people from the previous year onto the animal. Then the goat was beaten with reeds and thorns, and driven out into the desert. And the people went home rejoicing, just as European Christians did after burning a supposed heretic at the stake or white Americans did after the lynching of black men. Whenever the "sinner" is excluded, our ego is delighted and feels relieved and safe. It sort of works, but only for a while. Usually the illusion only deepens and becomes catatonic, blind, and repetitive—because of course, scapegoating did not really work to eliminate the evil in the first place.

Jesus came to radically undo this illusory scapegoat mechanism, which is found in every culture in some form. *He became the scapegoat to reveal the universal lie of scapegoating.* Note

---

17. Richard highly recommends James Alison's exploration of Rene Girard's work, particularly Alison's series of studies, *Jesus: The Forgiving Victim*, http://www.forgivingvictim.com/.

that John the Baptist said, "Behold the Lamb of God, who takes away the *sin* [singular] of the world" (John 1:29). It seems "the sin of the world" is ignorant killing, hatred, and fear.

The Gospel is a highly subversive document. It painstakingly illustrates how the systems of both church and state (Caiaphas and Pilate) conspired to condemn Jesus. Throughout most of history, church and state have sought plausible scapegoats to carry their own shame and guilt. *Jesus became the sinned-against one to reveal the hidden nature of scapegoating* so we would forever see how wrong power can be—even religious power! (See John 16:8–11 and Romans 8:3.) Jesus says from the cross: "Father, forgive them, for they don't know what they're doing" (Luke 23:34). The scapegoat mechanism largely operates in the unconscious; people do not know what they are doing. Scape-goaters do not know they are scapegoating, but they think they are doing a "holy duty for God" (John 16:2). You see why inner work, shadow work, and honest self-knowledge are all essential to any healthy religion.

The vast majority of violence in history has been "sacred" violence. Members of ISIS probably believe they are doing God's will. The Ku Klux Klan use the cross as their symbol! With God supposedly on your side, your violence becomes necessary and even "redemptive violence." But there is no such thing as *redemptive* violence. Violence doesn't *save;* it only destroys in both short and long term.

Jesus replaced the myth of redemptive violence with the truth of redemptive suffering. He showed us how to hold the pain and let it transform us, rather than pass it on to the others around us. Spiritually speaking, no one else is your problem. You are first and foremost your own problem. There are no bad goats to expel.   —DSS 72–73 and C2016 sessions 2 and 3

Ending the Cycle of Violence

Picture yourself before the crucified Jesus; recognize that he became what you fear: nakedness, exposure, vulnerability, and failure. He became sin to free you from sin. (See 2 Corinthians

5:21.) He became what we do to one another in order to free us from the lie of punishing and scapegoating each other. He became the crucified so we would stop crucifying. He refused to transmit his pain onto others.

In your imagination, receive these words as Jesus' invitation to you from the cross:

> My beloved, I am yourself. I am your beauty. I am your goodness, which you are destroying. I am what you do to what you should love. I am what you are afraid of: your deepest and best and most naked self—your soul. Your sin largely consists in what you do to harm goodness—your own and others'. You are afraid of the good; you are afraid of me. You kill what you should love; you hate what could transform you. I am Jesus crucified. I am yourself, and I am all of humanity.

And now respond to Jesus on the cross, hanging at the center of human history, turning history around:

> Jesus, Crucified, you are my life and you are also my death. You are my beauty, you are my possibility, and you are my full self. You are everything I want, and you are everything I am afraid of. You are everything I desire, and you are everything I deny. You are my outrageously ignored and neglected soul.
>
> Jesus, your love is what I most fear. I can't let anybody love me for nothing. Intimacy with you or anyone terrifies me.
>
> I am beginning to see that I, in my own body, am an image of what is happening everywhere, and I want it to stop today. I want to stop the violence toward myself, toward the world, toward you. I don't need to ever again create any victim, even in my mind.
>
> You alone, Jesus, refused to be crucifier, even at the cost of being crucified. You never asked for sympathy.

You never played the victim or asked for vengeance. You breathed forgiveness.

We humans mistrust, murder, attack. Now I see that it is not you that humanity hates. We hate ourselves, but we mistakenly kill you. I must stop crucifying your blessed flesh on this earth and in my brothers and sisters.

Now I see that you live in me and I live in you. You are inviting me out of this endless cycle of illusion and violence. You are Jesus crucified. You are saving me. In your perfect love, you have chosen to enter into union with me, and I am slowly learning to trust that this could be true. —OT disc 1

GROWING UP

Richard often says that it can take a major defeat, loss, or failure to get us to move from the first half of life to the second half. But, he says, "I can't say New Jerusalem was a failure; it was just something I knew I needed to let go of if they—and I—were going to grow up."

"The young men and women in New Jerusalem were seventeen and eighteen and I was twenty-eight when the movement started. I had become their father figure. Now they were in their thirties. They still loved me but, like young people in ordinary families, they were grownups now, and they didn't like how much they still relied on me. They no longer needed a 'Daddy.'

"Psychiatrist C. G. Jung points out that the Father archetype is very fragile, volatile, and ambivalent; it can turn on a dime. He says our whole culture is suffering from that need for the father, and then the hatred of the father when he doesn't live up to the perfection that no one can achieve.

"That's why I hate to be put on a pedestal, because I know what's going to happen when people see how ordinary I am! A preacher, a teacher, a leader has to exert a certain kind of strength and authority so people will trust him or her. At the

*same time, I better be honest about my inability to even live up
to what I tell others is the truth. It can still be truth, even though
I can't totally live up to it. I must always be vulnerable, honest,
and humble about my own capacities and incapacities."*

Change as a Catalyst for Transformation

The word *change* normally refers to new beginnings. But transformation more often happens *not when something new begins
but when something old falls apart.* The pain of something old
falling apart—chaos—invites the soul to listen at a deeper level.
It invites and sometimes forces the soul to go to a new place
because the old place is falling apart. The mystics use many
words to describe this chaos: fire, darkness, death, emptiness,
abandonment, trial, the Evil One. Whatever it is, it does not feel
good and it does not feel like God. You will do anything to keep
the old thing from falling apart. This is when you need patience,
guidance, and the freedom to let go instead of tightening your
controls and certitudes. Perhaps Jesus is describing this phenomenon when he says, "It is a narrow gate and a hard road that
leads to life, and only a few find it" (Matthew 7:14). Not acci-
dentally, he mentions this narrow road right after teaching the
Golden Rule. Jesus knows how much letting go it takes to "treat
others as you would like them to treat you" (7:12).

Transformation usually includes a disconcerting reorienta-
tion. Change can either help people to find a new meaning, or it
can cause people to close down and turn bitter. The difference is
determined by the quality of your inner life, what we call "spirituality." Change of itself just happens; but spiritual transformation is an actual process of letting go, living in the confusing
dark space for a while, and allowing yourself to be spit up on a
new and unexpected shore. You can see why Jonah in the belly
of the whale is such an important symbol for many Jews and
Christians.

In the moments of insecurity and crisis, "shoulds" and
"oughts" don't really help; they just increase the shame, guilt,
pressure, and likelihood of backsliding. It's the deep "yeses"

that carry you through. Focusing on something you absolutely believe in, that you're committed to, will help you wait it out. Love wins over guilt any day. It is sad that we settle for the short-run effectiveness of shaming people instead of the long-term life benefits of grace-filled transformation. But we are a culture of progress and efficiency, impatient with gradual growth. God's way of restoring things interiorly is much more patient—and finally more effective. God lets Jonah run in the wrong direction, but finds a long, painful, circuitous path to get him back where he needs to be—and almost entirely in spite of himself! Looking in this rear-view mirror fills you with gratitude for God's work in your life.   —HAD 69, 81–82

A Contemplative Year

There are two spiritual disciplines that keep me honest and growing: contemplative prayer and the perspective from the bottom. Regarding the first, I was always encouraged in contemplative prayer from my early days as a Franciscan novice. But in 1985, I was freed for a year to pursue that part of my vocation. It was a major turning point. After a thirty-day solitude in Thomas Merton's hermitage in Kentucky, I spent the rest of the year at our Franciscan novitiate house in Cincinnati. (I always called that place my Holy Hill.) I took as my guide a simple phrase from the philosopher Wittgenstein: "Don't think. Just look." Father McNamara's definition of contemplation became transformative: "A long loving look at the real." The world, my own issues and hurts, all goals and desires gradually dissolved into proper perspective. God became obvious and everywhere.

You see, we do not earn or find God. We just get ourselves out of the way. We let go of illusion and the preoccupations of the false self. As the cheap scaffolding falls away, the soul stands revealed. The soul, or True Self, cannot be created or worked for. It is, and it is already. The soul is God's "I AM" continued in me. That part of me already knows, desires, and truly seeks God. That part of me knows how to pray naturally. Here "I" and God seem to be one "I." All we can do is forget the false self. Don't fight, hate, or reject it. Just observe it and let go of it. As you let go of your own "house" you will find yourself living in a place that is both "utterly different and exactly the same." Merton called it "the palace of nowhere," and Jesus called it "the Father's house." It is the only place you will ever want to live.

I am not there, but I am being urged and led in spite of myself. Someone out there—and within here—is loving me and loving through me. The days continue to be given. And I am in wonder.
—NOG 96–97

Loving as Mirror and Mask

The following is an excerpt from Richard's last sermon and letter written to New Jerusalem Community, "On the Occasion of Its 14th Birthday," in 1985.

To talk about love is to talk about what Plato calls "holy madness." Jung even refused to include love in any of his classic categories of archetype, function, or complex. It finally defied psychological description. Perhaps that is why love has so many false meanings in our minds and emotions. Perhaps that is why Jesus never defined love, but instead made it a command. You *must* love, you absolutely must enter into this unnamable mystery if you are to know God and know yourself! So let's try to come at this *mysterium tremendum* in a whole new way if possible. Perhaps we can even try to let go of our old preconceptions about love, so that we can again be taught. To get at this holy madness, I would like you to consider two images: a mirror and a mask.

First of all, love is like a *mirror*. The mirror, according to Zen masters, is without ego and without mind. If a face comes in front of it, it reflects a face. If a table comes by, it reflects a table. It shows a crooked object to be crooked and a straight object to be straight. Everything is revealed as it really is. There is no discriminating mind or self-consciousness on the part of the mirror. If something comes, the mirror reflects it; if the object moves on, the mirror lets it move on. The mirror is always *empty of itself and therefore able to receive the other.* The mirror has no pre-conditions for entry, no preconditions for acceptance. It receives and reflects back what is there, nothing more and nothing less. The mirror is the perfect lover and the perfect contemplative. It does not evaluate, judge, or act.

If we are to be a continuation of God's way of seeing, we must first of all be mirrors. We must be no-thing so that we can receive some-thing. It is probably the only way that love is ever going to happen. To love demands a rather complete transformation of consciousness, a transformation that has been the goal of all religious founders, saints, mystics, and gurus since we began to talk about love. And the transformation of consciousness is this: we must be liberated from ourselves. We really need to be saved from the tyranny of our own judgments, opinions, and feelings about everything, the "undisciplined squads of emotions" that T. S. Eliot criticizes in his poetry. We must stop believing these false *subjects* that we are that choose to *objectify* everybody and everything else in the world—including God and our own soul.

The Jewish scholar, Martin Buber, said that we have entered into I-it relationships with reality, when we were in fact created for the I-Thou relationship. The I-Thou relationship is a universal attitude of reverence and mutuality in which we encounter people, things, and events as subject to subject, knowing and being known, giving only insofar as we can also receive, taking insofar as we can also surrender. This is why the Franciscan school of theology always puts knowledge in submission to love. Yet we live in an age which is quite content to know simply for the sake of curiosity or control. In that, knowledge has become a demon in the hands of men and women without wisdom, mercy, or discernment.

We now make objects of everything and therefore understand nothing. We forgot how to know because we have not allowed ourselves to be known by God—"face to face . . . knowing as fully as I am known" (1 Corinthians 13:12). In God, our self is no longer its own center; it is now centered in God and the false individual person is transformed. There is a death of the

self-centered and self-sufficient ego, and in its place is awakened
a new and liberated self which loves and acts in the Spirit. This
person, and not just the pious or churchy person, is worthy of
being called a truly spiritual person. Now we see why the saints
without exception practiced self-denial, mortification, sacrifice,
humility, fasting, and actually prayed for experiences of failure
and rejection. Nothing, certainly not passing whims, feelings,
and needs, was going to keep them from living whole at the
Center. Their self-abnegation continually put the false self to
the test. (You see, finding God and losing the self are the same
thing.) At last they were no-things "hidden with Christ in God"
(Colossians 3:3). At last they were like the mirror, empty and
able to receive the truth.

And that brings us to the *mask*. The Latin word for mask is
persona, from which comes our word for the individual human.
The word seems to indicate that the individual manifestation is
no more than a mask of a larger reality. It may have first referred
to the large theatrical masks which the Greek actors used to
speak through to magnify their voices. Eventually it was used
by Christian philosophers and theologians to define the individual as separate from the group. Each person was a mask of
God. God was breathing and sounding through each person.
Each person was one image of a much larger truth. I come to
know my personhood only in the infinite respect of the I-Thou
relationship, that refuses to objectify or curtail. Unless I know,
love, and serve God, I will frankly never be a real person. That is
fundamental and certain.

My personhood is in direct continuity with the Divine Personhood. As Genesis says, I am created in the "image" of God
(1:26–27). My "I am" is merely a further breathing forth of
the eternal and perfect "I Am Who Am" (Exodus 3:14) of the
Creator. And all love and contemplation is a living out of that
BEING, a being that precedes and perfects all doing. I am loved,
or better, I AM LOVE, before I do anything right or wrong, worthy or unworthy, true or false. To put it philosophically, ontol-
ogy precedes morality. Unfortunately, institutional Christianity

has put all of its emphasis upon moralisms and therein lost the real power and basis of that same morality! Love is quite simply Who-We-Are-In-Christ. Love is our objective identity as sons and daughters of God. God took human flesh in Christ to teach us that identity. Baptism is the symbol and sacrament of the transformation to that original incarnate truth. And all holiness is a matter of doing the truth in love (Ephesians 4:15). If we are going to get back to the fundamentals, then we must learn to live as adult Christians, fully believing and acting out of Who-We-Already-Are-In-Christ. Sin is to live out of something else, the false self.

This transcendent Self or True Self, is awakened when Love moves us beyond our false individuality and re-founds us at the Center. Becoming a loving person is not so much a matter of growing up as perhaps growing down. *Finding God and losing the false self are the same thing.* For we live, as Jesus says, "With me in them and you in me" (John 17:23). Western religion has tended to separate and objectify God—as it does everything—with disastrous results for Christianity, prayer, and simple love of God.

What I am saying is that we have it all wrong—utterly wrong! The Bible calls it the state of sin, psychology calls it the inflated ego, philosophy calls it dualism or individualism, and Thomas Merton calls it the false life of the unreal self. And believe it or not, that is exactly where most of us live out our entire lives! No wonder we cannot obey or live the Gospel. No wonder that love has become impossible. A fiction, an illusion, a lie, is trying to enter into love and be moral.

We must return to the Center and realize that we are just a mask, a fragment, an unbelievably blessed part. From that true identity, Love can happen. Whatever we do in ministry or community will bear fruit only insofar as we live and act out of the truth of the Whole. Jesus said, "Just as a branch cannot bear fruit on its own unless it remains on the vine, so neither can you unless you remain in me" (John 15:4). Radical communion with God will finally be the deepest level of involvement with all other persons, events, and things. Today we call it solidarity or compassion.

Love alone is sufficient unto itself. It is its own end, its own merit, its own satisfaction. It seeks no cause beyond itself and needs no fruit outside of itself. Its fruit is its use. I love simply because I am love. That is my deepest identity and what I am created in and for. To love someone "in God" is to love them for their own sake and not for what they do for me or because I am psychologically healed and capable. Our transformed consciousness sees another person as another self, as one who is also loved by Christ with me, and not as an object separate from myself on which I generously bestow my Christian favors. If I have not yet loved or if love wears me out, is it partly because other people are seen as tasks or commitments or threats, instead of as extensions of my own suffering and loneliness? Are they not in truth extensions of the suffering and loneliness of God?

When I live out of this truth of the Love that I am, instead of the lie and human emotion of fear, I will at last begin to live. Love is always letting go of a fear. In modern Christian community with all of our Enneagram numbers, Myers-Briggs letters, and expert psychologizing, we have become very proficient at justifying our fears and avoiding simple love. The world will always teach us fear. Jesus will always command us to love. And when we seek the spiritual good of another, we at least forget our fears and ourselves. As Dr. Gerald Jampolsky rightly says, the only time we fully let go of our fears is when we are really serving another person.

Our deep anxiety comes from the endless burden of trying to fix ourselves by ourselves—and we unconsciously know that we are not really getting fixed! We are still shadowy and selfish. We do want to love others and we do want to be loved by God, but *we want to love and be loved for who we are autonomously, apart from God.* That is our never-ending pride and useless attempt at *self-justification.* It never works. For as long as we persist in thinking that we are lovable because of our own independent goodness, we will always be shot down by the de facto evidence to the contrary. There will always be new feelings of guilt, as we see in most middle-class Americans. But Divine love or charity has nothing to do with feelings of "liking" or natural attraction. Most of us here are not, nor need we be, one another's best friends. Our love is not based on the myth of romantic love or good feelings about one another. It is a love grounded in God that allows us to honestly desire and seek the other's spiritual growth. That is why I prefer to see the basic paradigm of Christian community as "School of the Spirit." The idea of one, big, happy family does nothing but create false expectations, softness, and needless hurts.

I need to take a real delight in myself, but precisely for who I am—as one blessed and broken member of the Great Body of Jesus. That endless delighting is the gift of contemplative prayer. It is not dependent on moods, likes or dislikes, ups or downs, or how others hurt me or respond to me. That is the mystery of "justification by faith" that Paul spends so much time explaining in Romans, Galatians, and Ephesians. Being saved from the endless need to prove and justify ourselves, we are even more legitimated by simply being Who-We-Really-Are-In-Christ. The gift is so basic, so hidden, so free and gratuitous, so absolutely unearned or worked for—that most people either miss it or create monstrous religious gymnastics to make themselves feel worthy of it!

This faith, this love, this Holy Mystery—of which we are only a small part—can only be awakened and absorbed by the silent gaze of prayer. Those who contemplate who they are in God's ecstatic love will be transformed as they look and listen and find and share. This God, like a Seductress, does not allow Herself to be known apart from love. *We know God by loving God.* And I think that it is actually more important to know that we love God than to know that God loves us; although the two movements are finally the same. At the end of our lives of faith, the sum total of all of our knowing about God is that God knows us—and God's knowing is perfect receiving—like a mirror. For some reason, that realization is enough to keep us delighting endlessly. Try it.

Brothers and Sisters in this Great Body of Jesus, you and I are both NOTHING (mirror) and EVERYTHING (mask). The journey into our nothingness is called faith. The journey into the everything is called love. And both are known in the quiet and immense joy of contemplative prayer. From that place of truth where we are "hidden with Christ in God" (Colossians 3:3) we can with full authority and dedication speak to and serve the world as the mirrors and masks of God. "For Christ plays in ten thousand places, lovely in eyes and lovely in limbs not his, to the Father through the features of men's faces," in the words of poet Gerard Manley Hopkins.[18]

At age fourteen we, the New Jerusalem Community, are being invited to return to the Center. Like all inexperienced lovers, we have been tempted to play the prostitute. We have been tempted to substitute good process for faith, investment and personal ownership for the obedience of faith, psychologisms for love, and unbothered time for contemplative prayer. If we have not yet had strong faith, if we have not yet loved well, if we have not yet begun to pray, is it because we have thought that we could do it ourselves apart from Who-We-Are-In-Christ?

We are now an adult community, ready for adult faith and love. Christ alone is our Glory. Christ alone is our Justification and Victory. Christ alone is our Founder and Cornerstone. Christ alone is our Joy and Radical Liberation. In Christ, we are both nothing and everything; in Christ, we are freed to be mirror and mask.

And let me end with a quotation from Thomas Merton who has taught me so much ever since I lived with his spirit in his hermitage:

> *Everything is mine* precisely because *everything is His.*
> If it were not His, it could never be mine. If it could not
> be mine, He would not even want it for Himself. All that

---

18. *The Major Works* (London: Oxford University Press, 2009), 51.

is His, is His very self. All that He gives me becomes, in
some way, my own self. What then is mine? He is mine.
And what is His? I am his.[19]   —NJC

DISCERNMENT

Richard often reminds us to begin with "yes" rather than "no."
"Don't say no to anything unless God has given you a bigger yes
to something else."

Love God and Do What You Want

After my sabbatical year, I found my way to the conviction that
I should open the Center for Action and Contemplation in New
Mexico to help people get thoroughly involved in the issues and
goals of social justice, to help people turn to the poor, but from
the right point of departure—because you can do the right thing
for the wrong reasons.

Contemplation is a way to hear with the Spirit and not with
the head. Contemplation is the search for a wide-open space. The
space is broad enough for the head, the heart, the feelings, the
gut, the subconscious, our memories, our intuitions, our whole
body. We need a holistic place for hearing and finding wisdom.

The effect of contemplation is authentic action; if contemplation doesn't lead to genuine action, then it remains only
navel-gazing and self-preoccupation.

But I'm convinced that if you stick with it, if you do this exercise regularly, then you will come to the inner place of compassion. In this place, you'll notice how much the suffering of
the world is your suffering and how committed you are to this
world, not cerebrally, but from the much deeper perspective of
your soul. At this point, you're indestructible, because there you
find the peace that the world cannot give. You don't need to

---

19. Excerpt from "Promethean Theology" from *The New Man* by
Thomas Merton. Copyright © 1961 by Thomas Merton. Copyright
renewed 1989 by Farrar, Straus & Giroux, Inc. Reprinted by permission of
Farrar, Straus & Giroux.

win anymore; *you just need to do what you have to do*, as naive and simplistic as that might sound. That's why Augustine could make such an outrageous statement as "love God and do what you want"! People who are living from a truly God-centered place instead of a self-centered place are dangerously free precisely because they are tethered at the Center.

But you can't solve the problem by just acting "interiorly" or from correct inner motives. I also suggest committing yourself in solidarity to a person who is different from you, for example, to an elderly person, a handicapped person, a gay person, a poor person, or a person with a mental disability. If we view reality from the standpoint of others, then we'll experience complete conversion, namely, inner *and* outer transformation. We will have "turned around," and that is the biblical meaning of *metanoia*.   —S 98–99

Discerning God's Spirit at Work in Us

Our goal consists in doing the will of God. We first have to remove our attachment to our own will so that we can recognize the difference between the two. Throughout history, many people who did horrible things were convinced that they were doing the will of God. That's why we have to find an instrument to distinguish between God and us. Paul calls this gift the discernment of spirits. We have to learn when our own spirit is at work and when the Spirit of God is at work.

The most convincing social activists in our country were and are people of prayer: men and women like Dorothy Day, Martin Luther King, Jr., Sister Simone Campbell, John Dear, and Jim Wallis. It's very important that we bring the contemplatives and the activists together in the Church. Because neither is credible without the other. Christ went into the wilderness for forty days; only after that did he begin to preach the Reign of God and to heal the sick. And along the way he kept saying to his disciples: "Come, let us withdraw and find a quiet, peaceful place" (Matthew 14:23).

This means that the Christian life must be a constant journey back and forth between the radical way inward and the radical way outward. We all begin either on one side or the other. That's why we all have to be converted to come to the place where they meet. It's the path of the true Church and the Way of Christ.

—S 100–101

Lay Leadership

As a founder of a community, one has a wonderful but in some ways negative influence: you're able to hold a community together almost in spite of yourself. By staying for fourteen years at New Jerusalem, I put off the necessity of forming a lay leadership that came from the group itself. After I left they endured many painful years. But dark times are among the best teachers. The people had to decide: What do we really want? And not just: What does Richard want? They chose some very good lay pastors. And they carried out some very loving, prophetic actions. For instance, the community's first house was placed at the disposal of refugees from Central America.   —S 52

END OF AN ERA

By the late 1980s and early 1990s most of the charismatic communities that had formed in the 1970s had died out. There is still a small and sincere New Jerusalem Community in the same location in Cincinnati, but it is much different than it appeared in the 1970s, "and that is more than okay with me," Richard says. "For many of us, New Jerusalem was a school for a time rather than something to be sustained in itself."

3

1985–2000:
We Love God by Loving Our Self

"We love because God first loved us."
—1 John 4:19

> When Israel was a child I loved him, and I called my
> son out of Egypt. . . . I myself taught Ephraim to walk,
> I took them in my arms; yet they have not understood
> that I was the one looking after them. I led them with
> reins of kindness, with leading-strings of love.
> —Hosea 11:1, 3–4, JB

MOVING ON: THE SECOND HALF OF LIFE

*In his teaching, Richard often speaks of the first half of life as
building the "container"—a healthy ego and sense of belonging
and identity in a group, career, family, or church. While this is
well and good, if one stays in this first half of life, growth and
maturity is limited. Eventually the ego, the false or separate self,
must undergo many small deaths to allow the True Self, our soul,
to guide us deeper into wisdom. We discover that the container
was ultimately meant to hold unitive, unconditional love. Protecting our separate self becomes less and less important as we
realize our oneness with God and others.*

For Richard, moving into the second half of his life began symbolically "when I got in my little blue pickup truck and moved to Albuquerque in August of 1986. I left behind what was clearly my first half of life in Kansas, Michigan, and Ohio, including my wonderful New Jerusalem experience."

Richard was forty-three when he moved to Albuquerque, which, he says, "is almost classic midlife for most people." For many there is a lot of psychological and emotional suffering during this period. Richard was no exception. "Even before I left Cincinnati, I already had a lot of what my spiritual director called 'success guilt.' My talks and recordings were getting such immense positive response, and I was being invited to give the keynote address at many major Christian and healing conferences. Add to that being treated like a demigod in Cincinnati. I knew I was not the saint people thought I was. I felt like a phony, a hypocrite. It tore me up. My public image was so inflated that it made me feel all the more like a fake."

Richard struggled with depression during this dark period: "I didn't want to get up in the mornings. I woke up with dread, thinking, 'It's twelve more hours before I get to sleep again. My God, help me!' I didn't want to keep going through the motions. It didn't make sense: The Church didn't make sense, I didn't make sense, the country didn't make sense. It all felt so stupid and silly. Mostly I felt stupid and silly, like I was an illusion. The inner demons were paralyzing. I just wanted to sleep to get away from these feelings, to get away from the self-hatred, fear, meaninglessness, and aimlessness."

"I think grace eventually leads us into some situation that we can't fix, that we can't control or even understand. That is where I was and that's when real faith begins. Up until that time, it's all preparation; it's religion more than a living spirituality."

Falling in Love

Some have called the principle of going down in order to go up a "spirituality of imperfection" or "the way of the wound." It has

been affirmed in Christianity by St. Francis of Assisi as the way
of poverty, by St. Therese of Lisieux as her Little Way, and by
Alcoholics Anonymous as the necessary first step of powerlessness. St. Paul taught this unwelcome message with his enigmatic
statement, "It is when I am weak that I am strong" (2 Corinthians 12:10). Of course, in saying that, he was merely building on
what he called the "folly" of the crucifixion of Jesus—a tragic
and absurd dying that became resurrection itself.

The transition from the first half of life to the second half of
life is itself a "falling upward." Contrary to the idea of climbing
a ladder of perfection, the way up is the way down. It is *not*
by our own willpower or moral perfection that we ascend to
higher levels of consciousness. This is completely counterintuitive! Moreover, we can't engineer enlightenment by ourselves. It
is done unto us.

You will not know for sure that this message is true until you
are on the "up" side. You will never imagine it to be true until
you have gone "down" and come out on the other side in larger
form. You must be pressured "from on high," by fate, circumstance, love, or God, because nothing in you wants to walk the
path of descent. Falling upward is a "secret" of the soul, known
not by thinking about it or proving it but only by risking it—at
least once. Those who have allowed it know it is true, but only
after the fact.

This is probably why Jesus praised faith and trust even more
than love. It takes a foundational trust to fall or to fail—and
not to fall apart. Faith alone holds you while you stand waiting
and hoping and trusting. Then, and only then, will deeper love
happen. It's no surprise that we speak of "falling" in love. I think
falling is the only way to get to authentic love. None would go
freely, if we knew ahead of time what love is going to ask of us.
Very human faith lays the necessary foundation for the ongoing
discovery of love. Have no doubt, though: *great love is always
a discovery, a revelation, a wonderful surprise, a falling into*

*"something" much bigger and deeper that is literally beyond us
and larger than us.*   —FU xxiv, xxvi–xxvii

My Own Doubts

Maybe, as many have said, the temptation has been to wave the
flag of resurrection but without going through the experience of
humiliation and loss. You can't deny the necessary, painful journeys all of us go through in the middle of life, often through family situations where we're forced to confront our own shadow.
Only by going through them can we come out the other side and
live with hope of resurrection.

I'm not saying I'm there twenty-four hours a day, but now
I can more or less be at home in the tension. I don't think this
consciousness really started being home base until my late 50s.
Most of my 40s and early 50s I struggled with doubt. So many
people were reading my books and listening to my tapes, and
then I'd go back to my room and ask myself, "What does it all
mean? Richard, do you believe what you preach? Do you live it
yourself?"

After preaching about the transformative power of love and
suffering, I'd wonder, "Have you ever *really* suffered, Richard?
Have you ever *really* loved anybody?" They told us in seminary
that we love Jesus and so we didn't have to love anybody in particular. That's far too easy.

These are the soul's deep questions. I'm just giving you mine;
you have to discover yours. There are interior "dark nights" as
John of the Cross says, where you doubt yourself, God, your
country, your religion. That's a necessary part of the journey.
Even Mother Teresa seemed to have doubts about her faith.
That's part of the human experience. Don't believe your faith
unless you've doubted it, unless you've woken up a few mornings in the middle of your life questioning, "I'm not sure I agree
with this at all. I'd like to jump ship. Staying in this church, this
relationship, this career, feels more problematic to me than leaving."   —GTP disc 7

INCOMPLETE RELATIONSHIPS

During our interviews, Richard was open to being vulnerable, something he said his role as a public speaker does not readily allow.

"Throughout my life, I can honestly say—and this is not just a cliché—that the closer I have come to the Light, the more I would see my own darkness and hypocrisy, that I only half believe what I teach. You've heard me say, 'I talk about it better than I live it.' And I'll always be grateful to God for letting me talk about it; but one reason I can talk about it is because I'm constantly losing it, not living up to it, seeing my phoniness and my false self. I'm really preaching to myself! On my best days, am I fully living in the divine light more than an hour? I hope so. But even that's enough. It's enough to know that I have at least tasted the Real world.

"As I look back, I just see the incompleteness of so many relationships. Maybe part of it is because I've met so many people on my travels for speaking engagements, and we'll spend time together and have wonderful conversations, but then I leave the next day. Or people will write me for a short period, and maybe I'll give them some advice, and we'll have a delightful exchange for a few weeks, but then it peters out.

"Not all friendships can be maintained your entire life. It may not be either person's fault. It's just that our lives go in different directions. Sometimes I've had to work through feelings of rejection, betrayal, abandonment, or hurt. I think there's always a bit of guilt or shame, asking myself, 'What did I do wrong? Should I have called him or her after we drifted apart? Or was this relationship only for a time? Have I ever really, really loved anybody?' Oh, these questions are still agonizing and accusing.

"I know it's not possible to have time for many relationships, but—and this is probably my perfectionism—I do, nevertheless, feel guilty. 'Did you live up to that relationship, Richard? Did it really mean anything to you? Do you love people, Richard; or do you just let them move in and out of your life?' So the

constant fear is that I'm not being a loving person; I'm not loving individual people. We celibates were told that if we don't
love anybody in particular, we'd be able to love everybody in
general and to love God.

"But Incarnation is always concrete. I think I can avoid the
concrete more than most people, because I am a public person,
I am a celibate person, I am allowed to have my own space. I've
been given a lot of outs that people in committed relationships
like marriage don't get.

"On the other hand, I think not having that one person to
love is what has driven me toward God. God has to be my daily
lover, because I don't have anyone else to meet that need or to
be my one love object."

The Challenge and Opportunity in Marriage

I think most people are called to marriage because we need
another person to be like a mirror for us, to reflect our best
self and our worst self. The interesting thing about a mirror is
that it doesn't change the image; it simply takes it as it is. We
all need the experience of being loved unconditionally. Without a human experience of unconditional love, which we hope
to experience in marriage or in any good friendship, it's hard
to believe in God's unconditional love. Our friend or partner
constantly holds a mirror up to us. This person shows us our
good side and our dark side and reminds us that we still hav-
en't really *learned to love*. That's what every healthy relationship does. You have fallen into an infinite mystery that assures
you, you can't live up to it. That's why Jesus gave what was
symbolically an infinite number, "seventy times seven," as the
number of times even good people will need to forgive each
other.

Thankfully, the Gospel does give us a blessed assurance that
we are operating inside of an abundant, limitless, infinite Love.
So even though we will constantly fail, failure is not the final
word. We also have hope that everything can be mended, healed,

and restored. Where the welding takes place is normally the strongest place of all on a steel bar. It's the breaking and the welding and the mending that creates the real beauty of relationship. This is the dance of intimacy: as we ask one another for forgiveness, as we confess to one another that once again we didn't do it right. Don't be surprised and don't hate yourself for it (which we all do). Darn it, I didn't love right again! How can I miss the point so many times?

I don't think success teaches us vulnerability. It's when we do it wrong that we are taught vulnerability. We finally realize we are falling ever-deeper into something that we can never live up to—a sustained vulnerability, a continual risk. It's not a vulnerability and intimacy that we need just now and then. Eventually, it becomes second nature to apologize, to admit we are wrong, to ask for forgiveness but not to hate ourselves for it.

The dynamics for divine intimacy and human intimacy are the same. I believe one is a school for the other. Most start with human intimacy and move from there to divine intimacy. But I do believe there are a few souls who start with the divine ambush first, who first learn how to be vulnerable before God. Two of those who have taught me that best are Therese of Lisieux and Julian of Norwich. Both are among my favorite mystics, and both are women. Women seem to have a readiness for romance, intimacy, mutuality, and vulnerability that has a lot to teach the Church.   —IDA disc 7 and S 85

Living the Contradictions

How do we *live* the contradictions? *Live them*—not just endure them or relieve ourselves from the tension by quickly resolving them. The times where we meet or reckon with our contradictions are often turning points, opportunities to enter into the deeper mystery of God or, alternatively, to evade the mystery of God. I'm deliberately using the word *mystery* to point to depth, an open future, immense freedom, a kind of beauty and truth that can't be fully spoken or defined.

Many mystics speak of the God-experience as simultaneously falling into an abyss and being grounded. This sounds like a contradiction, but in fact, when you allow yourself to fall into the abyss—into hiddenness, limitlessness, unknowability, a void without boundaries—you discover it's somehow a rich, supportive, embracing spaciousness where you don't have to ask (or answer) the questions of whether you're right or wrong. You're being held and so you do not need to try to "hold" yourself together. Please reflect on that.

This might be the ultimate paradox of the God-experience: "falling into the hands of the living God" (Hebrews 10:31). When you can lend yourself to it and not fight it or explain it, falling into the abyss is ironically an experience of ground, of the rock, of the foundation. This is totally counterintuitive. Your dualistic, logical mind can't get you there. It can only be known experientially. That's why the mystics use magnificent similes—none of them adequate or perfect—for this experience. "It's like. . . . It's like . . . ," they love to say.

Mystery is not something you *can't* know. Mystery is *endless knowability*. Living inside such endless knowability is finally a comfort, a foundation of ultimate support, security, unrestricted love, and eternal care. For all of us, it takes much of our life to get there; it is what we surely mean by "growing" in faith. I can't prove this to you. Each soul must learn on its own, hopefully aided by observing other faith-filled people. —HTP disc 3

Recognizing Our Need for Mercy

Struggling with one's own shadow self, facing interior conflicts and moral failures, undergoing rejection and abandonment and daily humiliations, experiencing any kind of abuse or form of limitation are all gateways into deeper consciousness and the flowering of the soul. These experiences give us a privileged window into the naked now, because impossible contradictions are staring us in the face. Much needed healing, forgiving what is, weeping over and accepting one's interior poverty and contradictions, are normally necessary experiences that invite a person into the contemplative mind. (Watch Paul do this in a classic way from the depths of Romans 7:14 to the heights of his mystic poetry in most of Romans 8.)

In facing the contradictions that we ourselves are, we become living icons of both/and. Once you can accept mercy, it is almost natural to hand it on to others (see the story of the unforgiving debtor in Matthew 18:23–35). You become a conduit of what you yourself have received. If you have never needed mercy and do not face your own inherent contradictions, you can go from youth to old age, dualistically locked inside a mechanistic universe. That, in my opinion, is the "sin against the Holy Spirit." It cannot be forgiven because there is a refusal to recognize that you even need mercy or forgiveness. You have blocked the conduit that you are. Did you ever notice the remarkable fact that in her great Magnificat Mary speaks three times of God showing her "mercy" (Luke 2:49, 54, 55)? If even the Virgin Mary, the Mother of Jesus, lives under that mercy, how much more so the rest of us?   —NN 125–26

FOUNDING THE CENTER FOR ACTION AND CONTEMPLATION

Several factors influenced Richard's decision to choose Albuquerque as the place for the Center for Action and Contemplation. He had fallen in love with New Mexico in 1969 when he was a deacon at Acoma Pueblo. He knew that there was much poverty in the state, and that it was the home of two national labs which were developing nuclear weapons. The first atomic bomb had been built in New Mexico and dropped south of Albuquerque at the Trinity Test Site on July 16, 1945. Also, the CAC would be only four hours away from the impoverished city of Juarez, Mexico. New Mexico is one of the most visibly multicultural states, and Albuquerque itself is surrounded by indigenous groups. It seemed an ideal desert environment for a "school for prophets."

An article in CAC's newsletter explains the purpose of the nonprofit:

> The name was chosen because it expressed the paradoxical nature of the Center's purpose: standing in a middle place, at the center of the cross, where opposites are held together.
>
> We believed that action and contemplation, once thought of as mutually exclusive, must be brought together or neither one would make sense. We wanted to be radical in both senses of the word, simultaneously rooted in Tradition and boldly experimental. One of the expressions of the radical nature of our work was our extensive inclusivity, bridging gaps within the spiritual and justice communities, building a rhythm of contemplative prayer and Zen meditation into our days, and even more fundamentally, believing that external behavior should be connected to and supported by inner guidance.
>
> We believed . . . that the power to be truly radical comes from trusting entirely in God's grace and that such trust is the most radical action possible. We know one thing for certain: grace has brought us to this place and grace flows in and through and among us. In our best dream, grace itself does the work; guides our hands and our hearts, motivates our choices. We continue to realize that everything is a gift.   —RG December 1999

The Contemplative Mind

What is the relation of [contemplation] to action? Simply this. He who attempts to act and do things for others or for the world without deepening his own self-understanding, freedom, integrity, and capacity to love, will not have anything to give others. He will commu-

> *nicate to them nothing but the contagion of his own*
> *obsessions, his aggressiveness, his ego-centered ambi-*
> *tions, his delusions about ends and means, his doctri-*
> *naire prejudices and ideas. There is nothing more tragic*
> *in the modern world than the misuse of power and*
> *action.*   —Thomas Merton[1]

I founded the Center for Action and Contemplation in 1987 because I saw a deep need for the integration of both action *and* contemplation. Over the years, I met many social activists who were doing excellent social analysis and advocating for crucial justice issues, but they were not working from an energy of love except in their own minds. They were still living out of their false self with the need to win, the need to look good, the attachment to a superior, politically correct self-image.

They might *have* the answer, but they are not *themselves* the answer. In fact, they are often part of the problem. That's one reason that most revolutions fail. Too many reformers self-destruct from within. For that very reason, I believe, Jesus and other great spiritual teachers first emphasize transformation of consciousness and soul. Unless that happens, there is no lasting or grounded reform or revolution. When a subjugated people rise to power, they often become as controlling and dominating as their oppressors because the same demon of power has never been exorcised in them. We need less reformation and more transformation.

The lie always comes in a new form that looks like enlightenment. We are easily allured by the next new thing, the new politically correct agenda. And then we discover it's run by unenlightened people who in fact do not love God but themselves. They do not love the truth but control. The need to be in power, to have control, and to say someone else is wrong is not enlightenment. Such unenlightened leaders do not love true freedom for everybody but freedom for their new ideas. That's been my great disappointment with many liberals. Untransformed

---

1. *Thomas Merton: Spiritual Master: Essential Writings*, ed. Lawrence Cunningham (New York: Paulist Press, 1992), 375.

liberals often lack the ability to sacrifice the self or create foundations that last. They can't let go of their own need for change and control and cannot stand still in a patient, humble way as people of deep faith often can. It is no surprise that Jesus prayed not just for fruit, but "fruit that will last" (John 15:16). Conservatives, on the other hand, idolize anything that lasts, but then stop asking the question, "Is it actually bearing any fruit?" It is the perennial battle between idealism and pragmatism.

If we are going to have truly prophetic people who go beyond the categories of liberal and conservative, we have to teach them some way to integrate their needed activism with a truly contemplative mind and heart. I'm convinced that once you learn how to look out at life from the contemplative eyes of the True Self, your politics and economics are going to change on their own. I don't need to teach you what your politics should or shouldn't be. Once you see things contemplatively, you'll begin to seek the bias from the bottom, you'll be free to embrace your shadow, and you can live at peace with those who are different. From a contemplative stance, you'll know what action is yours to do almost naturally.   —CP and EB 73–75

Alternative Consciousness

I often use this line, a paraphrase of Albert Einstein: "No problem can be solved by the same consciousness that caused it." Unfortunately, we have been trying to solve almost all our problems with the very same mind that caused them, which is the calculating or dualistic mind. This egocentric mind usually reads everything in terms of short-term effect, in terms of what's in it for me and how I can look good. As long as you read reality from that small self, you're not going to see things in any new way. All the great religions taught a different way of seeing, a different perspective. This alternative vantage point is the contemplative or non-dual mind. It is what we usually mean by *wisdom*.

The word *contemplation* has ancient roots, but for a long time it was not taught much in the Western church. Contemplation was finally rediscovered through Thomas Merton's writings in the 1950s and '60s. What is contemplation? Simply put, contemplation is entering a deeper silence and letting go of our habitual thoughts, sensations, and feelings. You may know contemplation by another name. Many religions use the word *meditation*. Christians often use the word *prayer*. But for many in the West, prayer has come to mean something functional, something you do to achieve a desired effect, which puts you back in charge. Prayers of petition aren't all bad, but they don't really lead to a new state of being or consciousness. The same old consciousness is self-centered: How can I get God to do what I want God to do? This kind of prayer allows you to remain an untransformed, egocentric person who is just trying to manipulate God.

That's one reason why religion is in such desperate straits today: it isn't really transforming people. It's merely giving people some pious and religious ways to again be in charge and in control. It's still the same small self or what Thomas Merton called the false self. Mature, authentic spirituality calls us into experiences and teachings that open us to an actual transformation of consciousness (Romans 12:2). I think some form of contemplative practice is necessary to be able to detach from your own agenda, anger, ego, and fear. We need some practice that touches our unconscious conditioning where all our wounds and defense mechanisms lie. That's the only way we can be changed at any significant or lasting level.

For a full lifestyle change, I believe we need *both* action *and* contemplation. The state of the communal soul is the state of the social order. As Jack Jezreel, founder of JustFaith puts it, "The world cannot be changed by love to become just unless we are changed by love to become whole, *but* we cannot be made whole without engaging in the work of making the world whole. Personal transformation and social transformation are one piece."[2] And as the Zen Reverend angel Kyodo williams says, "Love and justice are not two. Without inner change, there can be no outer change; without collective change, no change matters."   —CP

2. Jack Jezreel, "To Love without Exception," "Perfection," *Oneing* 4, no. 1 (2016): 52.

Becoming Pure in Heart

True religion is radical; it cuts to the root (*radix* is Latin for root). It moves us beyond our "private I" and into full reality. Jesus seems to be saying in the Sermon on the Mount (Matthew 5—7) that our inner attitudes and states are the real sources of our problems. We need to root out the problems at that level. Jesus says not only that you must not kill, but that you must not even harbor hateful anger. He clearly *begins* with the necessity of a "pure heart" (Matthew 5:8) and knows that the outer behavior will follow. Too often we force the outer, and the inner remains like a cancer.

If you walk around with hatred all day, morally you're just as much a killer as the one who pulls the trigger. You can't live that way and not be destroyed. Yet, for some reason, many Christians have thought they could think and feel hatred, negativity, and fear. The evil and genocide of World War II was the result of decades of negative and paranoid *thinking* among good German Christians.

Jesus tells us to not harbor hateful anger or call people names in our hearts like "fool" or "worthless person" (Matthew 5:22). If we're walking around all day thinking, "What an idiot he is," we're living out of death, not life. If that's what we think and feel, that's what we will be—death energy instead of life force. We cannot afford even inner disconnection from love. How we live in our hearts is our real truth.

In Matthew 5:44, Jesus insists that we love our enemies and pray for those who persecute us. For Jesus, prayer seems to be a matter of *waiting in love, returning to love, trusting that love is the unceasing stream of reality.* Prayer isn't primarily words; it's a place, an attitude, a stance. That's why Paul could say, "Pray unceasingly" (1 Thessalonians 5:17). If we think of prayer as requiring words, it is surely impossible to pray always. Once we recognize that whatever we do in conscious, loving union with Reality is prayer, we can better understand what Paul means.

—EB 80–82

Face to Face Knowing

According to the book of Exodus, "The Lord used to speak to Moses face to face, as a person speaks to a friend" (33:11). And yet the Exodus text also demonstrates how coming to the point of full *interface* is a gradual process of veiling and unveiling. God takes the initiative in this respectful relationship with Moses, inviting him into an amazing intimacy and ongoing conversation, which allows mutual self-disclosure, the pattern for all love affairs.

Moses describes this initial experience as "a blazing bush that does not burn up" (Exodus 3:2). He is caught between running forward to meet the blaze and coming no nearer and taking off his shoes (Exodus 3:4–5)—the classic response to *mysterium tremendum*. It is common for mystics, from Moses to Bonaventure, Philip Neri, and Pascal, to describe the experience of God as fire or a furnace or pure light. But during this early experience, "Moses covered his face, afraid to look back at God" (Exodus 3:6). He has to be slowly taught how to look at God. At first Moses continues to live like most of us, in his shame.

God gradually convinces Moses of God's respect, which Moses calls "favor," but not without some serious objections from Moses' side: 1) "Who am I?" 2) "Who are you?" 3) "What if they do not believe me?" 4) "I stutter." 5) "Why not send someone else?" In each case, God stays in the dialogue, answering Moses respectfully and even intimately, offering a promise of personal Presence and an ever-sustaining glimpse into who God is—Being Itself, Existence Itself, a nameless God beyond all names, a formless God previous to all forms, a liberator God who is utterly liberated. God asserts God's ultimate freedom from human attempts to capture God in concepts and words by saying, "I am who I am" (Exodus 3:14). Over the course of his story we see that Moses slowly absorbs this same daring freedom.

But for Moses to learn foundational freedom in his True Self, God has to assign Moses a specific task: create freedom *for* people who don't want it very badly, freedom *from* an oppressor who thinks he is totally in control. It is in working for outer freedom, peace, and justice in the world that we have to discover an even deeper inner freedom just to survive in the presence of so much death. Most people become cynical and angry and retreat into various ideological theories over time. Or they walk away and return to an indulgent liberal worldview. This happened with much of my own generation in the 1960s.

Again, we see the inherent connection between action and contemplation, the dialogue between the outer journey and the inner journey. Contemplation is the link to the Source of Love that allows activists to stay engaged for the long haul without burning out. Moses shows us that this marriage of action and contemplation is essential and possible.   —SB 17–19

Love in Action

The way to arrive and remain within "the force field of the Holy Spirit"—which is one way of describing consciousness—is both very simple and very hard: you've got to remain in love, with a foundational yes to every moment. You can't risk walking around with a negative, resentful, gossipy, critical mind, because then you won't be in the force field. You will not be a usable instrument. That's why Jesus *commanded* us to love. It's that urgent. It's that crucial.

Love, as contemplatives learn, can begin in the mind or can be inhibited by the mind. You may have heard this saying:

Watch your thoughts; they become words.
Watch your words; they become actions.
Watch your actions; they become habits.
Watch your habits; they become character.
Watch your character; it becomes your destiny.

Contemplation nips negativity, hatred, and violence in the bud. It begins by retraining your initial thoughts, because if you let the mind operate in a paranoid, angry, and resentful way, you aren't going to get very far. You're not going to see clearly. At the

same time, if you spend your time only in contemplation without moving toward positive engagement, you end up with what
many call spiritual constipation. I am afraid it is quite common.

—TW disc 3 and BUW 103

LEADING STRINGS OF LOVE

*Richard was formed in the years of the Second Vatican Council,
but during most of his time in the priesthood, the Roman Catholic Church has been "circling the wagons" and pulling back on
the great reforms of Vatican II. Many have appreciated Richard's
outspoken efforts to keep the windows of the Church open to
the wind of the Spirit. But others have not. In some places, Richard is not allowed to teach or invitations have been rescinded.*

*We asked why he didn't leave the Roman Catholic Church.
"I don't think it would have been good or right for me to leave
because it was the anchor, the grounding that kept me from taking myself too seriously. I am still a part of humanity, a part of
a team, and I am not a prima donna flying around the world by
myself. Instead, I belong to a concrete group. You've heard me
call that the principle of incarnation: The concrete is the way to
the universal. I believe that somewhere, somehow you need to be
rooted, your feet have to be on the ground. For most people, it
is marriage and children. If I didn't have a community or mirror
like the Franciscans, I think I would have become very inflated
and ungrounded."*

*He reaches for his worn Jerusalem Bible and turns to a favor-
ite passage in Hosea: "This is God talking: 'I took them in my
arms; yet they have not understood that I was the one looking after them. I led them with reins of kindness, with leading
strings of love. I was like someone who lifts an infant close
against his cheek; stooping down to him I gave him his food'
(Hosea 11:3–4).*

*"That text was a favorite of mine for many years because I
felt God always treated me that way. The New Jerusalem Bible
says 'I was leading them with human ties, with leading strings of*

love.' Human love taught me divine love and divine love taught me human love. It was a mutual, symbiotic experience."

When he first joined the Franciscans, Richard told God that he'd give 50 percent and he trusted God would give the other 50 percent. Gradually that equation changed. "By my forties, I felt God was giving 60 percent, and 40 percent was up to me. I knew God did most of the work. Now in my later years, it's about 98 percent God and 2 percent Richard. God is really doing it all. All I do is give my little 'yes' and try to stay out of the way! This is truthful."

Midlife was difficult for Richard, he says, "precisely because people thought I was giving 100 percent, but I knew it wasn't true. God was using me completely and undeservedly. That's why grace was the overwhelming theme of my talks. I've often said that God has allowed me to do everything wrong so God could do everything right!"

What did Richard do wrong?

"It was just that I knew I was selfish, egocentric, and narcissistic. My motives were not pure; I did good things for half-hearted motives. But then I got the credit as if I did it for perfect motives. God used me anyway. That's why I always say, 'If God waited for a perfect instrument, nothing would get done.' All we have to offer is our own imperfection. I'll bet even the Catholic saints were imperfect. We all are! This realization gave me more patience with myself and everyone else. Eventually I stopped demanding a perfect world before I could be happy, before I could love it."

A carving on Richard's bookshelf says it well: "Life doesn't have to be perfect to be wonderful."

Richard is still grateful for his Jewish therapist in Albuquerque and his Catholic spiritual director in Jemez Springs, New Mexico. During this pivotal period of growth, both men gave him the freedom to say whatever he needed to say without fear of judgment. He recalls times with each of them when he was hating himself and looked up to see them "just grinning at me." Could that be the way God looks at us? Richard often says that *whenever God looks at us, God sees God's Son, God's child, in us, and can't help but love us.*

The Meaning of Spiritual Love

> *When you regarded me*
> *Your eyes imprinted your grace in me,*
> *In this, you loved me again,*
> *And thus my eyes merited*
> *To also love what you see in me. . . .*
> *Let us go forth together to see ourselves in Your beauty.*
> —St. John of the Cross, *Spiritual Canticle*, 32, 33

When we read poetry as beautiful and profound as this verse, we can see why John of the Cross was far ahead of his time in the spiritual and psychological understanding of how love works and how true love changes us at a deep level. He consistently speaks of divine love as the template and model for all human love, and human love as the necessary school and preparation for any transcendent encounter. *If you have never experienced human love, it will be very hard for you to access God as Love. If you have never let God love you, you will not know how to love humanly in the deepest way.* Of course, grace can overcome both of these limitations.

In the inspired passage above, John describes the very process of love at its best. Here is my paraphrase:

> You give a piece of yourself *to* the other.
> You see a piece of yourself *in* the other (usually unconsciously).
> This allows the other to do the same in return.
> You do not need or demand anything back from them,
> because you know that you are both participating
> in a single, Bigger Gazing and Loving—
> one that fully satisfies and creates an immense Inner Aliveness.
> (Simply to love is its own reward.)

> *You accept being accepted—for no reason and by no criteria whatsoever!*
> This is the key that unlocks everything in me, for others, and toward God.
> So much so that we call it "salvation"!

To put it another way, what I let God see and accept in me also becomes what I can see and accept in myself. And even more, it becomes that whereby I see everything else. This is "radical grace." This is why it is crucial to allow God and at least one other person to see us in our imperfection and even in our nakedness, as we are—rather than as we ideally wish to be. It is also why we must give others this same experience of being looked upon in *their* imperfection; otherwise, they will never know the essential and utterly transformative mystery of grace. This is the glue that binds the universe of persons together.

Such utterly free and gratuitous love is the only love that validates, transforms, and changes us at the deepest levels of consciousness. It is what we all desire and what we were created for. Once you allow it for yourself, you will almost naturally become a conduit of the same for others. In fact, nothing else will attract you anymore or even make much sense.

Can you let God "look upon you in your lowliness," as Mary put it (Luke 1:47), without waiting for some future moment when you believe you are worthy? Remember the words of John of the Cross: "Love what God sees in you." Many of us never go there, because to be loved in this way is to live in the naked now, and it is indeed a naked moment.   —NN 140–42

Love Alone

We have been graced for a truly sweet surrender, if we can *radically accept being accepted—for nothing—*"or grace would not be grace at all" (Romans 11:6). As my father, St. Francis, put it, when the heart is pure, "Love responds to Love alone" and has little to do with duty, obligation, requirement, or heroic

anything. It is easy to surrender when you know that nothing
but Love and mercy is on the other side.   —BUW 27

Human Development in Scripture

It is helpful for us to know about the whole arc of life and
where it is tending and leading. Walter Brueggemann, one of
my favorite scripture scholars, brilliantly connected the development of the Hebrew Scriptures with the development of human
consciousness.[3]

Brueggemann says there are three major parts of the Hebrew
Scriptures: the Torah, the Prophets, and the Wisdom literature.
The Torah, or the first five books, corresponds to the first half of
life. This is the period in which the people of Israel were given
their identity through law, tradition, structure, certitude, group
ritual, and chosenness. As individuals, we each must begin with
some clear structure and predictability for normal healthy development (a la Maria Montessori). That's what parents are giving
their little ones—containment, security, safety, and a feeling of
specialness. Ideally, you first learn you are beloved by being mirrored in the loving gaze of your parents and those around you.
You realize you are special and life is good—and thus you feel
"safe."

The second major section of the Hebrew Scriptures is called
the Prophets. This introduces the necessary suffering, "stumbling
stones," and failures that initiate you into the second half of life.
Prophetic thinking is the capacity for healthy self-criticism, the
ability to recognize your own dark side, as the prophets did for
Israel. Without failure, suffering, and shadowboxing, most people (and most of religion) never move beyond narcissism and
tribal thinking (egoism extended to the group). This has been
most of human history up to now, which is why war has been
the norm. But healthy self-criticism helps you realize you are not

3. See Walter Brueggemann, *An Introduction to the Old Testament:
The Canon and Christian Imagination* (Louisville, KY: Westminster John
Knox Press, 2003).

that good and neither is your group. It begins to break down either/or, dualistic thinking as you realize all things are both good and bad. This makes all idolatry, and all the delusions that go with it, impossible.

My mother could give me prophetic criticism and discipline me and it didn't hurt me in the least because she gave me all the loving and kissing and holding in advance. I knew the beloved status first of all, and because of that I could take being criticized and told I wasn't the center of the world.

If the psyche moves in normal sequence, the leaven of self-criticism, added to the certainty of your own specialness, will allow you to move to the third section of the Hebrew Scriptures: the Wisdom Literature (many of the Psalms, Ecclesiastes, the Song of Songs, and the Book of Job). Here you discover the language of mystery and paradox. This is the second half of life. You are strong enough now to hold together contradictions, even in yourself, even in others. And you can do so with compassion, forgiveness, patience, and tolerance. You realize that your chosenness is for the sake of letting others know they are chosen too. You have moved from the Torah's exclusivity and "separation as holiness" to inclusivity and allowing everything to belong. We don't move toward the second half of life until we've gone through the first half and the transition period. The best sequence, therefore, is order-disorder-reorder. And you *must* go through disorder or there is no reorder! No exceptions. Paul calls this "the foolishness of the cross" (see 1 Corinthians 1:18–25).

—FU vii; TMT; STHL disc 2

LOVE IS NOT A STRAIGHT LINE

Richard reflects, "I'm a little leery of saying you cannot love others until you love yourself. I don't think it is that linear, and I have worked with too many people who use that as a perpetual ego excuse for not serving others. I know people who have basically said, 'I'm not going to do justice work until I love myself'—as though one task had to be completed before they could start the next. It's really not a straight line from point A to point B. Love is more a spiral or a dance. It's dipping into deeper acceptance of myself, deeper forgiveness of myself, and in that, finding the energy to care about someone beyond myself, whether I feel like it or not! Realizing I can indeed care about people who don't love or like me in return expands my self-worth and self-confidence. Otherwise we make people far too codependent on their own whimsical feelings."

The Weeds and the Wheat

> *Can true humility and compassion exist in our words and in our eyes unless we know we too are capable of any act?*   —St. Francis of Assisi[4]

Jesus uses a number of images that illustrate the tension between good and evil. This world is a mixture of different things, and unless you learn how to see deeply, you don't know which is which, and you don't notice that God allows both good and bad to grow in the same field (Matthew 13:24–30). Jesus instructs his listeners to "let both the weeds and wheat grow together until the harvest" (13:30). Then, at the end of time, God will decide what is wheat and what is a weed. In a certain way, Jesus is saying it is none of our business to fully figure it out. This is really quite risky of God—and it takes tremendous courage on our part to trust God and ourselves here.

We are all a mixture of weeds and wheat, and we always will be. As Martin Luther put it, we are *simul justus et peccator*. We are simultaneously saint and sinner. That's the mystery of holding weeds and wheat together in our one field of life. It takes a lot more patience, compassion, forgiveness, and love than aiming for some illusory perfection that is usually blind to its own

---

4. Daniel Ladinsky, paraphrase of Francis of Assisi, *Love Poems from God: Twelve Voices from the East and West* (New York: Penguin Compass, 2002), 37. Used with permission.

faults. Acknowledging both the wheat and weeds in us keeps us from thinking too highly of ourselves and also from dismissing ourselves as terrible.

To avoid cynicism and negativity, you have to learn to accept and forgive this mixed bag of reality that you are—and everyone else is, too. If you don't, you'll likely become a very angry person. To accept the weeds doesn't mean that you say, "It's okay to be ignorant and evil." It means you have some real wisdom about yourself. You can see your weeds and acknowledge when you are not compassionate or caring. You have to name the weed as a weed. I'm not perfect; you're not perfect; the Church is not perfect; the United States is not perfect.

If we must have perfection to be happy with ourselves, we have only two choices: We can blind ourselves to our own evil (and deny the weeds), or we can give up in discouragement (and deny the wheat). It takes uncommon humility to carry both the dark and the light side of things. The only true perfection available to humans is the honest acceptance of our imperfection. This is precisely what Divine Perfection can help us do; only God in us can love imperfect and broken things. By ourselves, we largely fail.

Learning how to love—which is our life's project—is quite simply learning to accept our messy reality. If you love anyone, then you have learned to accept them despite their faults. You see a few things you'd like to change in your partner, your children, yourself. *By the largesse of God within you, you are able to trust that the good is deeper than the bad, and usually it is well hidden.* This is probably why so many of Jesus' parables are about hiddenness, seeking, and finding.

—EB 41 and H July 20, 2014

God Sees in Wholes, We See in Parts

Both therapy and spirituality have an important place in a full life. Much therapy today is a needed way of dealing with our psychological problems. But eventually we must move from exclusively trying to solve our problems to knowing that we can never fully resolve them, but only learn from them. Sometimes, we can only forgive our imperfections and neuroses, embrace them, and even weep over them (which is not to hate them!). This is very humbling for the contemporary Promethean individual. As Jung writes, "the greatest and most important problems in life are all in a certain sense insoluble. They must be so because they express the necessary polarity inherent in every self-regulating system. They can never be solved, but only outgrown."[5]

Only an in-depth spirituality can fully accept the paradox of our flawed humanity, indwelled by God's presence, where both light and dark are allowed and used by God. This is not a capitulation to our shadow self, but an integration that brings forth what Thomas Merton called "a hidden wholeness." We grow through necessary conflicts and tensions. I don't think there is any other way. Dancing along a self-created primrose path will merely lead you to illusion and superficiality.

The movement from the purely psychological model to the full spiritual self will initially feel like a loss of power. And indeed it is for the ego! But for the True Self, it is actually the rediscovery of an authentic and original power, where human clay meets divine breath (Genesis 2:7). To succeed in the first half of life we usually have to deny our shadow and unacceptable self. This allows us to look good, but not really *be* good. The burden of the second half of life is often reclaiming what we have denied, feared, and rejected in the first half. I know it feels like backtracking, and in some ways it is. But remember, your shadow self is not your evil self; it is simply your denied and rejected self.

All sin is merely *disordered love*, which is searching for a pure and true love. God is very patient with us while we learn how to really love. As we integrate and forgive our shadow self, life gradually looks very different. Life becomes many shades of

5. Commentary by Carl Jung, in *The Secret of the Golden Flower: A Chinese Book of Life*, trans. Richard Wilhelm (New York: Mariner Books, 1962), 92.

pastel instead of just several primary colors. We finally see what
we have never dared look at before. This is the birth of compassion. The journey toward biblical faith will often feel like losing
our vision (note Paul's conversion in Acts 9) and being given by
grace a whole new pair of eyes.

The steps to maturity are necessarily immature, and we must
learn from each one of these missteps, and never hate or dismiss
them. Julian of Norwich says it so well: "God judges us according to our true essence, which [God] keeps whole and safe, inside
[Godself] always. Divine judgment reflects our Beloved's righteousness. But human judgment reflects our changeable fleshli-
ness. . . . I could not find blame and anger anywhere in God!"[6]
How different the entire history of Christianity would have been
if we had trusted that infinite love can only be accepted in finite
steps.   —EB 161–64

Twelve-Step Spirituality

Although I have never formally belonged to a Twelve Step
group, I have learned much from people who are in recovery. I
truly believe that the Twelve Step program (also known as Alcoholics Anonymous or A.A.) will go down in history as America's
greatest and unique contribution to the history of spirituality.
It represents what is good about American pragmatism. There's
something in the American psyche that becomes mistrustful and
impatient with anything that's too abstract, theoretical, or distant. Americans want a spirituality that is relevant, that changes
people, and that really makes a difference in this world. For
many people, the Twelve Steps do just that. They make the Gospel believable, practical, and even programmatic.

My first eight years in Albuquerque, beginning in the late
1980s, I lived downtown, next door to a little church where
Twelve Step meetings were held. As the members gathered right

---

6. Julian of Norwich, *The Showings of Julian of Norwich: A New
Translation,* trans. Mirabai Starr (Newburyport, MA: Hampton Roads,
2013), 111–12.

outside my back door almost every other evening, we became
friends. They invited me to join them in even their closed meetings. I felt very privileged. It was like being invited into a sacred
sanctuary of people who weren't afraid to openly admit they
were "sinners." I'd go home afterward thinking this felt more
like church than the liturgy on Sunday morning. It was as if each
person was a priest, and they were all healing one another. The
God-talk was honest and experience-based, not "belief"-based.
There was no hesitancy for each person to describe their history
of failure and recovery—or death and resurrection, if you prefer
Christian vocabulary.

Opening with "Hi, I'm Joe, and I'm an alcoholic" is a humble
and honest admission of deep need, which is what the Catholic
penitential rite, "Lord have mercy, Christ have mercy, Lord have
mercy" is supposed to be. Jesus tried to teach us that God's love
is not dependent on our "worthiness." He healed and ate with
sinners and outcasts when he was on earth. He told parables
about the Pharisee and the tax collector (Luke 18: 9–14) and the
prodigal son (Luke 15:11–32) where the one who did it wrong
ended up being right and the one who seemingly did it right
ended up being wrong. The entrance requirement for an A.A.
meeting is not worthiness, but unworthiness, not capacity, but
deep need—just as it should be.

Worthiness is not the issue; the issue is trust and surrender. As
Therese of Lisieux said, "Jesus does not demand great actions
from us but simply surrender and gratitude." Let's just resolve
this once and for all: *You're not worthy!* None of us are. Don't
even go down that worthiness road. It's a game of denial and
pretend. We're all saved by grace. We're all being loved in spite of
ourselves. A.A. had the courage to recognize that you don't come
to God by doing it right; you come to God by doing it wrong,
and then falling into an infinite mercy that you can't fall out of.
The Twelve Steps wisely calls such mercy "Your Higher Power."

But I am also going to add what only the Gospel is fully prepared to proclaim: *You're absolutely worthy of love!* Yet this has
nothing to do with any earned worthiness on your part. You see,

God does not love you because you are good. God loves you because God is good!

And thus, A.A. and the Gospel fit together like hand in glove.

—L; HDWB; ET; ATWS

MINISTRY AS JAIL CHAPLAIN

Soon after Richard moved to Albuquerque, two nuns came to him and said, "Richard, there is no priest that comes to the jail." Richard lived just down the street from the jail. "It seemed God had planted me right where I was needed. So I said yes and went there regularly for fourteen years. Almost every Sunday morning, I had Mass at the jail."

Richard has spoken of how grateful the prisoners were to hear the Good News of God's love for them in spite of their mistakes and crimes. They were open to the message because they were so hungry for it. Here Richard experienced the reality of the "bias from the bottom": those most in need of grace have a "head start" in accepting mercy.

Richard also talks about the "father wound" he found so prevalent in the jail population. "Macho" men often called him "Padrecito" when they met privately for confession. Richard believed they were hungry for a good father figure.

Once Richard was asked to counsel a young woman who had killed a woman who was eight-months pregnant, cutting her open and removing the baby. By some miracle, the baby survived.

"When I was asked to talk with her, I honestly did not want to. The story had been all over the news, and I knew I would have no natural empathy for this woman. But once she poured out her story, I couldn't hate her; nor could I wish her evil or to be in jail for the rest of her life. I felt very lucky that I got to know her personally and to see that she wasn't a monster. She at least deserved my and other people's respect. She was very disturbed and wounded herself. I think her own inner child had been destroyed. It was probably the most dramatic encounter I had at the jail. It taught me so much about the importance of

understanding and building empathy for people outside of our comfort zone."

Overcoming Contradictions

The binary, dualistic mind cannot deal with contradictions, paradox, or mystery, all of which are at the heart of religion. Sadly, a large percentage of religious people become and remain quite rigid thinkers because their religion taught them that to be faithful, obedient, and stalwart in the ways of God, they had to seek some ideal "order" instead of growing in their capacity for love. These are not bad people; they simply never learned much about living inside of paradox and mystery as the very nature of faith.

Dictionaries define a *contradiction* as two things that cannot be true at the same time. I would say it this way: a contradiction is two things that cannot be true at the same time *by your present frame of logic.* As long as you do not reframe your reality, as long as you insist on your own frame of reference, you will not be able to find the wisdom in paradox. "The kingdom of God" is Jesus' term for the bigger frame, or what we often call "the big picture" or "in the light of eternity" (*sub specie aeternitatis*). You've got to find some framework that allows you to stand back and look at the moment with the eyes of Infinite Love and Mercy. Then you'll see that many things which appear to be contradictory through logical, egocentric, dualistic thinking might not necessarily be so to a non-dual mind.

A *paradox* is a seeming contradiction that may nonetheless be true if seen in a different frame than my "rational" mind. The word comes from the Greek prefix *para* meaning "beyond" or "outside of" and the verb *dokein* meaning "to appear or to think." A paradox is beyond the normal way of thinking. Contradictions are based on logic, a set of assumptions or expectations which we take for granted. Conversion—a changed mind—allows you to call those assumptions and expectations into question. If you're still overly attached to your ego, you normally can't let go of these opinions. It takes true transformation to allow you to look at yourself from a bit of distance—with some calmness, compassion, and the humility and honesty to know that you don't know.

In truth, we are all living paradoxes. No one or no thing is totally good or totally bad. Look at Paul, for example. He was a persecutor of Jesus' followers, maybe even a murderer, all in the name of being a good Pharisee. Suddenly, on the road to Damascus, he meets Christ, and the strict line between good and bad, evil and virtue, dissolves. In that moment, the contradictions have been overcome in him.

—HTU; NN 36–37; NWS discs 1–2

Following Jesus

We should not be surprised or scandalized by the sinful and the tragic. Do what you can to *be* peace and to *do* justice, but never expect or demand perfection on this earth. It usually leads to a false moral outrage, a negative identity, intolerance, paranoia, and self-serving crusades against "the contaminating element," instead of "becoming a new creation" ourselves (Galatians 6:15).

We must resist all utopian ideologies and heroic idealisms that are not tempered by patience and taught by all that is broken, flawed, sinful, and poor. Jesus is an utter *realist* and does not exclude the problem from the solution. Work for win/win situations. Mistrust all win/lose dichotomies.

Following Jesus is not a "salvation scheme" or a means of creating social order (which appears to be what most folks want religion for), as much as it is *a vocation to share the fate of God for the life of the world.* Some people are overly invested in religious ceremonies, rituals, and rules that are all about who's in and who's out. Jesus did not come to create a spiritual elite or an exclusionary system. He invited people to "follow" him by personally bearing the mystery of human death and resurrection. Of itself, this task does not feel "religious," which is why it demands such faith to trust it.

Those who agree *to carry and love what God loves*, both the good and the bad of human history, and to pay the price for its reconciliation within themselves—these are the followers of Jesus. They are the leaven, the salt, the remnant, the mustard seed that God can use to transform the world. The cross is the dramatic image of what it takes to be such a *usable* one for God.

—EB 179–80

FACING DEATH

In May of 1991, Richard was surprised to find he had malignant melanoma on his right leg. Later, in the Center for Action and Contemplation's newsletter, Richard looked back on that experience and admitted his initial response was pretty much denial. He poured himself into leading a men's retreat in the mountains, "preaching to 112 men about wounds and heroes." Richard writes, "After all, hadn't I tried to live my life as if I were going to die tomorrow? That was my immediate cavalier reaction, but I probably still thought I was immortal and necessary to this struggling earth. Isn't that what they mean by 'hubris' in Greek tragedy?"

Upon returning home and meeting with an oncologist, "It all became real. My God, I may die! The word had spread, friends and relatives began to call, I got on the phone to cancel upcoming speaking engagements, flowers arrived. So this is how it feels to wind things up. The love felt so good; the sky and the whole world took on a nostalgic and fleeting tone; God seemed inside my skin but silent too."

The surgery was a success; a CAT-scan showed that the cancer was gone. "Just as I was learning to say 'yes' and 'thy will be done,' and two-score and eight years seemed like enough gratuity, my life was given back to me! Now I still hobble around a bit, the emotions of new death/new life upon me, the smile of nature, time, and friends seems wondrous. I hope I can hear the messages: listen to your body, slow down, live in the precious now, love all that is. How can I not believe in the Incarnation of God in the compassion of so many, in my new wound, in a pattern of discovery, waiting, and healing that all feels like mercy?"

—RG 4, no. 4

The Two Hands of God

We cannot avoid the Paschal Mystery. At the middle of our Eucharist, we stop and proclaim the mystery of our faith. Not a mystery, but *the* mystery. "Christ has died, Christ is risen, Christ will come again." That's it. The paschal mystery. In the East, they call this the yin and yang. Jungian psychology calls it darkness and light. It's a statement about the mystery of life: that life is full of death and pain, it's unjust, absurd, dishonest, doesn't work, requires hard choices and arduous effort. That's "Christ has died." And the other side of the mystery is that life is full of joy, beauty, humor, and love. That's "Christ is risen."

Just recently [this was in 1991] I found a cancerous mole on my leg. The first prognosis was two to six months to live. "Christ died." After the surgery, my house looked like a florist shop as many of my friends and relatives showed me the unconditional love they feel for me. "Christ is risen." It would take the rest of my life to enjoy and savor the love I've been shown in the past few weeks. Always, always, in life there's this paschal mystery, there's joy and pain interwoven, richness and poverty, darkness and light, all together.

I feel as though I've just had direct experience in my body of the two hands of God, both the left hand, the painful mystery, and the right hand, the warm generous lover who gives me everything I need. My prayer is showing me that finally I am beginning to trust those two hands of God. When I was facing the big issues of life and death and whether I really believed in the resurrection I've been preaching all my life, I noticed that God was always with me, there was always this connection. I couldn't have kicked God out of the room. The issues were too big and vital.

When I look back over my life, I see the two hands of God leading me to where I am right now. At the time, I may not have seen it; but looking back I do. Now by the grace of God I believe I can trust the future because those two hands have upheld me so well in my past.　　　　—NOG 113–14, 117–18

Two Paths of Transformation

Two universal and prime paths of transformation have been available to every human being God has created since Adam and Eve and the Stone Age: great love and great suffering. These are offered to all; they level the playing fields of all the world religions. Only love and suffering are strong enough to break down our usual ego defenses, crush our dualistic thinking, and open us up to Mystery. In my experience, they like nothing else exert the mysterious chemistry that can transmute us from a fear-based life into a love-based life. No surprise that the Christian icon of redemption is a man offering love from a crucified position.

Love and suffering are part of most human lives. Without doubt, *they are the primary spiritual teachers* more than any Bible, church, minister, sacrament, or theologian. Wouldn't it make sense for God to make divine truth so available? If the love of God is as perfect and victorious as we believe, wouldn't it offer every human equal and universal access to the Divine as love and suffering do? This is what Paul seemed to be saying in his brilliant sermon on the Acropolis: "All can seek the Deity, feeling their way toward and succeeding in finding God. For God is not far from any of us, since it is in God that we live and move and have our being" (Acts 17:27–28). What a brilliant and needed piece of theology to this day.

Love is what we long for and were created for—in fact, love is what we *are* as an outpouring from God—but suffering often seems to be our opening to that need, that desire, and that identity. Love and suffering are the main portals that break us open into breadth, depth, and communion. Almost without exception, great spiritual teachers will always have strong direct guidance about love and suffering. If you never allow yourself to experience love or suffering, you will not know the essentials. You'll try to work it all out in your head, but your mind alone can't get you there. You must "love with your whole heart, your whole soul, your whole mind, and your whole strength" (Mark 12:30), or it does not appear to be love at all. That's how love works and why it leads to giving up control, which is my simple definition of suffering: *whenever you are not in control.*

When you are inside of great love and great suffering, you have a much stronger possibility of surrendering your ego controls and opening to the whole field of life—frankly, because you do not have much choice now: you are being led. Great love makes you willing to risk everything, holding nothing back. The feeling of fusion or acceptance by another or with the Other, at least temporarily, overcomes your terrible sense of aloneness, separateness, and fear. The ecstasy of this union makes you let down your barriers and *see things inside of a new kind of wholeness and happiness for a while.*

No wonder people run toward love. At least for a while, one's seeing is much broader, more adventuresome, and less defensive. But love cannot be sustained at this honeymoon level for long. To sustain this wondrous open heart long-term, and to remain permanently "in love," something else is needed—some level of mysticism, whether nature-based, consciousness-based, or God-based.

Great suffering opens you in a different way. Here, things happen *against your will*—which is what makes it suffering. And over time, you can learn to give up your defended state, again because you have no choice. *The situation is what it is,* although we will invariably go through the stages of denial, anger, bargaining, resignation, and (hopefully) acceptance. The suffering might feel wrong, terminal, absurd, unjust, impossible, physically painful, or just outside of your comfort zone. We must have a proper attitude toward suffering, because many things every day leave us out of control—even something as benign as a long stoplight. Remember that *if you do not transform your pain, you will surely transmit it to those around you and even to the next generation.*

Suffering, of course, can lead you in one of two directions: It can make you very bitter and close you down, or it can make you wise, compassionate, and utterly open, either because your heart has been softened, or perhaps because suffering makes you feel like you have nothing more to lose. It often takes you to the edge of your inner resources where you "fall into the hands of the living God" (Hebrews 10:31), even against your will. We must all pray for the grace of this second path of softening and opening. My personal opinion is that this is the very meaning of the phrase "deliver us from evil" in the Our Father (Lord's Prayer). We aren't asking to avoid suffering. It is as if we were praying, "When the big trials come, God, hold on to me, and don't let me turn bitter or blaming," an evil that leads to so many other evils.   —NN 122–25

Solidarity with Suffering

The outer poverty, injustice, and absurdity we see when we look around us mirrors our own inner poverty, injustice, and absurdity. The poor man or woman outside is an invitation to the poor man or woman inside. As you learn compassion and sympathy for the brokenness of things, when you encounter the visible icon of the painful mystery in "the little ones," then you'll learn compassion and sympathy for your own "little one," the brokenness within yourself.

Each time I was recovering from cancer, I had to sit with my own broken absurdity as I've done with others at the jail or hospital or sick bed. The suffering person's poverty is visible and extraverted; mine is invisible and interior, but just as real. I think that's why Jesus said we have to recognize Christ in the least of our brothers and sisters. It was for *our* redemption, *our* liberation, *our* healing—not just to "help" others and pad our spiritual resume.

When we see it over there, we become freed in here, and we also become less judgmental. I can't hate the person on welfare when I realize I'm on God's welfare. It all becomes one truth; the inner and the outer reflect one another. As compassion and sympathy flow out of us to any marginalized person, wounds are bandaged—both theirs and ours.

The church has tried to resolve all theological dilemmas with analysis and academic thinking. It just doesn't work. It produces a faith that isn't real, that has no passion in it, no power to compel—just endless theological distinctions and books and articles while the world goes by and says, who cares? This wouldn't have happened if we'd kept Jesus' counsel to stay close to the poor. The poor keep us close to the Gospels, to the important questions and issues, the Christ-child within and without.

In many ways, I think we have become a Leviticus church more than an Exodus church. When the clergy and ceremony take over and fail to keep that solidarity with the poor, then the Book of Leviticus is dominant. We become overly concerned with laws and liturgies, structure, ceremony and vestment, with what goes on inside the church building.

The Exodus church, on the other hand, is in touch with the poor, hearing their cry. It is the church on the streets, encountering the outer world, liberating people from slavery, offering healing and justice. The Exodus church reveals a much more gutsy God than that of Leviticus. I'm very fortunate that my travels have often taken me out to that Exodus church. I've met wonderful Catholics who are in the trenches listening to the poor. They've been formed by the Tradition, and they know what they know, and love what they love, and are living it out. It's encouraging to see more and more of this kind of church. However, I do believe and accept that it will always be a remnant, a minority—just as in Exodus.   —NOG 108–10

A BIAS FROM THE BOTTOM

Richard often speaks about the importance of staying close to the bottom—in touch with people who are marginalized, oppressed, or poor. For twenty-five years, the Center for Action and Contemplation took interns across the U.S./Mexico border to Juarez, a city infamous for violence and poverty. "Of all CAC's programs, I think this had one of the strongest impacts. Participants came back knowing something by standing on the other side that they could not know in any other way. They had a changed perspective."

Changing Sides

> *God chose things the world considers foolish in order*
> *to shame those who think they are wise. And he chose*
> *things that are powerless to shame those who are pow-*
> *erful.*   —1 Corinthians 1:27, NLT

In all honesty, once it was on top and fully part of the establishment, the Church was a bit embarrassed by the powerless one,
Jesus. We had to make his obvious defeat into a glorious victory
that had nothing to do with defeat—his or ours. Let's face it,
we feel more comfortable with power than with powerlessness.
Who wants to be like Jesus on the cross, the very icon of powerlessness? It just doesn't look like a way of influence, a way of
access, a way that's going to make any difference in the world.

We Christians are such a strange religion! We worship this
naked, bleeding loser, crucified outside the walls of Jerusalem,
but we always want to be winners, powerful, and on top ourselves . . . at least until we learn to love the little things and the
so-called little people, and then we often see they are not little at
all, but better images of the soul.

Yes, those with mental and physical disabilities, minority
groups, LGBTQ folks, refugees, prisoners, those with addictions—anyone who's "failed" in our nicely constructed social or
economic success system—can be our best teachers in the ways
of the Gospel. They represent what we are most afraid of and
what we most deny within ourselves. That's why we *must* learn
to love what first seems like our "enemy"; we absolutely must
or we will never know how to love our own soul or the soul of
anything. Please think about that until it makes sense to you. It
eventually will, by the grace of God.

One of the most transformative experiences is entering into
some form of lifestyle solidarity with the powerless, by moving
outside of your own success system, whatever it is. Move around
in the world of others who are not enamored with your world.

This is a good way to feel powerless. *We don't think ourselves into a new way of living; we live ourselves into a new way of thinking.* Lifestyle choices and changes finally convert people. I am not aware that merely believing a doctrine or dogma has ever converted anybody. That should be obvious by now.

Someone once pointed out to me that most of the great founders of religious communities, people like St. Benedict, Francis and Clare of Assisi, Mother Katherine Drexel, Vincent de Paul, Elizabeth of Hungary, Ignatius Loyola, John Baptist de la Salle, and Mother Seton, all started out as what we would now call middle class or even upper class. They first had enough comfort, security, and leisure to move beyond their need for more of it; they saw it did not satisfy. Each in their own way willingly changed sides and worked in solidarity with those who did not have their advantages.   —GCCA

SEEKING GOD'S WILL

Richard so firmly believed in the bias from the bottom and the importance of working with the poor that in 1994 he planned to leave the CAC in New Mexico and move to Africa.

He explains: "In the mid 1990s, the head of the Franciscan Order in Rome said that he wanted each province in the world to send someone to Africa.

"I spoke with my spiritual director about it. We agreed that I was probably experiencing 'success guilt,' feeling that everything had come far too easily to me. I think I still live with this. I really didn't seek or search for such success, but now I am used to it. I am used to having power and used to being listened to and being kowtowed to. It's dangerous when you are always the person that others are listening to. I guess I was afraid I was becoming too well-known. So when this invitation came from Rome, I said, 'I think I should go to Africa.'

"I left CAC for a thirty-day discernment retreat with Mary-knoll. My goal was to discover God's will for my life, but I was fully expecting to go to Africa afterward.

"Near the end of the retreat we each sat down privately with the leadership team of four or five wise people, primarily nuns. They told us what they saw and heard and thought, so we didn't have to take the decision on by ourselves. Nor did we have to follow their recommendations. We could go back to our own superiors and make the final decision.

"Well, the leadership team told me, 'We are convinced that you have a gift for America—to preach the Gospel to a first world country. There's not much point in you talking about the poor in Kenya; you need to talk about it in North America.' It was the consensus of the whole group. They said, 'It's your decision, but we strongly recommend that you stay here and keep doing what you are doing. If you are worried about your success guilt, well, you can worry about it!'

"I remember driving back from San Antonio, Texas, all the way through the Guadalupe Mountains, and everything was beautiful! I felt so happy and so relieved and recommitted to working with the Center for Action and Contemplation."

Learning How to Love

St. Francis of Assisi's emphasis on action, practice, and lifestyle was revolutionary for its time, just as it is now. It is the foundation of Franciscan alternative orthodoxy. For Francis and Clare, Jesus became someone to imitate and not just to collectively worship. Unfortunately, this has hardly ever been the norm or practice of most Christians. We preferred Sunday morning worship services and arguing about how to conduct them or prohibiting each other from attending "heretical" churches.

The Franciscan School found a way to be both very traditional and very revolutionary at the same time by emphasizing practice over theory, or orthopraxy over orthodoxy. In general, the Franciscan tradition taught that love and action are more important than intellect or speculative truth. Love is the highest category for the Franciscan School (the goal), and we believe that authentic love is not possible without true inner freedom (contemplative practice helps with this). Also, love will not be real or tested unless we somehow live close to the disadvantaged (the method), who frankly teach us that we know very little about love.

Orthodoxy teaches us the theoretical importance of love; orthopraxy helps us learn *how to love*. To be honest, even my Franciscan seminary training did not teach me how to love. It taught me how to obey and conform, but not how to love. I'm still trying to learn how to love every day of my life. As we endeavor to put love into action, we come to realize that on our own, we are unable to obey Jesus' command to "Love one another as I have loved you." To love as Jesus loves, we must be connected to the Source of love. Franciscanism found that connection in solitude, silence, and some form of contemplative prayer. Contemplation quiets the monkey mind and teaches us emotional sobriety and psychological freedom from our addictions and attachments. Otherwise, most talk of change is largely an illusion and a pretense.

Early on, Francis found himself so attracted to contemplation, to living out in the caves and in nature, that he was not sure if he should dedicate his life to prayer or to action. So he asked Sister Clare and Brother Sylvester to spend some time in prayer about it and then come back and tell him what they thought he should do. After a few weeks, they both came back. Francis knelt down and put his arms out, prepared to do whatever they told him. Both Clare and Sylvester, in perfect agreement, without having talked to one another, said Francis should not be solely a contemplative; nor should he only be active in ministry. Francis was to go back and forth between the two, much as Jesus did. Francis jumped up with great excitement and immediately went on the road with this new permission and freedom.

Before Francis, the "secular" priests worked with the people in the parishes and were considered "active." Those who belonged to religious orders went off to monasteries and prayed. Francis found a way to do both. Thus, Franciscans were called friars instead of monks. Francis took prayer on the road; in fact, prayer is what enabled him to sustain his life of love and service

to others over the long haul, without becoming cynical or angry.
Francis didn't want a stable form of monastic life. (I wrote my
Bachelor's thesis on this theme in 1966.) Francis wanted us to
mix with the world and to find God amidst its pain, confusion,
and disorder. For me, that is still the greatest art form—to "dance
while standing still"! So you see that in 1987, when I founded
the Center for Action and Contemplation, I was just being a
good Franciscan.   —EL 81, 87, 98; FM disc 1; IFF

The Positive in the Negative

> *We must bear patiently not being good . . . and not being*
> *thought good.*   —St. Francis of Assisi

> *Whoever is willing to serenely bear the trial of being*
> *displeasing to herself, that person is a pleasant place of*
> *shelter for Jesus.*   —St. Therese of Lisieux

In these shocking quotes, Francis and Therese are trying to teach
us to let go of that deep but deceptive human need to "think well
of one's self." That is the ego talking, they would say. Only those
who have surrendered their separateness and their superiority
can do this, of course. Those who have radically "accepted being
accepted," who know that God loves them, already think well of
themselves. Their positive and secure self-image is a divine gift
totally given from the beginning and never self-constructed. It is
quite stable and needs no fanfare.

In a world where imperfection seems to be everywhere, the
humble and the honest have a huge head start in spiritual matters and can readily find God in their most ordinary of lives. "To
the poor in spirit the kingdom of heaven already belongs," Jesus
says in his emphatic opening line of the Sermon on the Mount
(Matthew 5:3).

One thing we all have in common is that we all "sin" (Romans
5:12), transgress, fall into our imperfections, and make mistakes.
There are no exceptions to this. We are also *sinned against* as the

victims of others' failure and our own social milieu. Augustine called this "original sin." But that does not mean we are bad at the core, which is the way it has unfortunately been misinterpreted for much of Christian history.

You must first remember who you are! You must start with the positive and not with a problem, or you never get beyond a kind of negative problem solving. Your core, your deepest DNA, is divine; it is the Spirit of Love implanted within you by your Creator at the first moment of your creation (see Romans 5:5, 8:11, 14–16). We must know that we begin with "original blessing" as Matthew Fox and others have put it. Augustine was just trying to describe the inevitability of sin in an imperfect world (so we would not be surprised). Unfortunately, this poorly named and misunderstood negative notion dominated the next 1,500 years of Christianity. The word "sin" implies culpability, and that was never Augustine's point. In fact, his meaning was quite the opposite: we all carry the wounds of our parents and ancestors, which good therapists all know is true. Your sins are not just your own.

Humble honesty about our positive core, and a compassionate recognition that none of us completely lives out of our full identity, is the most truthful form of spirituality. We all find our lives eventually dragged into opposition, problems, or the negative (sin, failure, betrayal, gossip, fear, hurt, disease, etc.), and especially the ultimate negation: death itself. What I love about healthy Christianity is its utter realism. Both divine election and death in many forms are presented as the school of life. The Divine Life we have been blessed with, which is actually Love itself, is big enough to include all failure and death. The genius of the Christian explanation is that it includes the problem in the solution: the cross of failure becomes the catapult toward transformation. Our sins can even become "happy faults," as we sing on Holy Saturday.

The vulnerable person has every reason to keep growing through everything that happens to them. The overly guarded and self-protected person is scratched and dented by all "the slings and arrows of outrageous fortune," whereas the malleable, bendable, flexible, woundable person is indestructible. Their wounds are their teachers instead of their defeat.

It is crucial that we understand Jesus was never upset with sinners; he was only upset with people who did not think they were sinners! How marvelous that our God-image is a wounded and vulnerable man. This is a most unlikely image for God, unless we are able to comprehend that God is telling us something about the Godself—which is almost incomprehensible: God is also vulnerable.   —EL 101–6, 111–12

Our Holiness Is God's Holiness

There is only one thing you must definitely answer for yourself: "Who am I?" Or, restated, "Where do I abide?" If you can get that right, the rest largely takes care of itself. Paul answers the questions directly: "You are hidden with Christ in God, and God is your life" (Colossians 3:3–4). Every time you start hating yourself, ask, "Who am I?" The answer will come, "I am hidden with Christ in God" in every part of my life. I am bearing both the mystery of suffering humanity and God's glory. Maybe right now I must bear the suffering part to be in solidarity with both humanity and "Christ," which is just another word for everything (see 1 Corinthians 3:21–23, 15:20–28 or Colossians 1:15–20).

God keeps looking at what is good in the human person. What is entirely good in me is called God and, of course, God finds this always and entirely lovable. God fixes God's gaze intently where I refuse to look, on my shared, divine nature as God's daughter or son (1 John 3:2). God looks at me and sees Christ. And one day my gaze matches God's gaze. This is what we mean by prayer. At those times, I will find God entirely lovable and myself fully lovable. Why? Because it is the same set of eyes that is doing the looking (2 Corinthians 3:18), and we henceforth look out at life together and agree on what we see.

All you have to do is receive the gaze and then return what you have received. It is an entire agenda for your whole life. All you really do is complete the circuit, "love returning love" as my father, St. Francis, put it.

We are saved by standing consciously and confidently inside the force field that is Christ, not by getting it right in our private selves. This is too big a truth for the small self to even imagine. We're too tiny, too insecure, too ready to beat ourselves up. We do not need to be correct, but we can always try to remain connected to our Source. The great and, for some, disappointing surprise is that many people who are not correct are the most connected.

All we can do is fall into the Eternal Mercy—into Love— which we can never actually fall out of because "we belong to Christ and Christ belongs to God," as Paul so beautifully stated (1 Corinthians 3:23). Eventually, we know that we are all saved by mercy in spite of ourselves. That must be the final humiliation to the ego.

Our holiness is first of all and really only God's holiness, and that is why it's certain and secure. It is a participation in love, a mutual indwelling, not an achievement or performance on our part. "If anyone wants to boast, let him boast in the Lord," Paul shouts at the end of his long argument (1 Corinthians 1:31). Jeremiah said the same long before Paul (Jeremiah 9:22–23).

—TH 50–51 and GTP disc 5

Everything Is Grace

Mercy is not a virtue that you choose to put on one day. Mercy has to be your way of seeing, a generosity of spirit that draws from your identity, your deepest dignity, which is love. It is basically a worldview of abundance wherein I do not have to withhold, protect, or hoard myself.

I liken this deepest dignity, this True Self at our core, to a diamond buried within us and constantly forming under the intense pressure of our lives. We must search for and uncover this diamond, freeing it from the surrounding debris of guilt and shame. In a sense, our True Self must, like Jesus, be resurrected.

That process is not resuscitation of something old and tired, but a wonderful discovery of something always new—and already perfectly formed.

For the True Self, there is nothing to hate, reject, deny, or judge as unworthy or unnecessary. It has "been forgiven much and so it loves much" (Luke 7:47). Once you live inside the Big Body of Love, compassion and mercy come easily. The detours of the false self were all just delays, bumps in the road, pressure points that created something new in the long run, as pressure does to carbon deep beneath the earth. God uses everything to construct this hard and immortal diamond, our core of love. Diamonds are said to be the hardest substance on this earth. It is this strong diamond of love that will always be stronger than death (Song of Songs 8:6).

Absolutely everything is now made use of in this great economy of grace. "Grace is everywhere," Georges Bernanos said both at the end of his great novel and at the very end of his life.[7] Likewise, nearing her death, Therese of Lisieux said, "Everything is a grace!"[8] Living from your core of love, you can now enjoy unearned love in yourself and allow it in everyone else too. This patient mining process will make you compassionate and forgiving with the unfinished diamonds of others who are on the same journey as you are. This True Self cannot find or know God without bringing everybody else along for the same ride. It is one great big finding and one great big being found all at the same time.

You do not find the Great Love except by finding your True Self along with it, and you cannot find your True Self without falling into the Great Love. As you fall, you will discover that the meaning of the universe, at its deepest and final level, is only mercy.   —TTM and ID 184–85

---

7. Georges Bernanos, *The Diary of a Country Priest* (New York: Carroll & Graf, 2002), 298.

8. Therese of Lisieux, *Story of a Soul: The Autobiography of Saint Therese of Lisieux*, trans. John Clarke (Washington, DC: ICS Publications, 1996), 266.

Cleaning the Lens

True religion is always about love. Love is the ultimate reality. We can probably see this only through prayer. For love can be hidden. We don't see it unless we learn how to see, unless we clean the lens. The Zen masters call it wiping the mirror. In a clear mirror, we can see exactly what's there without distortion. In a perfect mirror I see what's there, not what I'm afraid of, nor what I need to be there. Wiping the mirror is the inner discipline of constantly observing my own patterns, what I pay attention to and what I don't pay attention to, in order to get my own ego out of the way. Lest you think this is only a Buddhist preoccupation, remember St. Teresa of Avila's stark admonition: "For the most part all our trials and disturbances come from our *not* understanding ourselves."[9] This is also the way St. Therese of Lisieux practiced her "science of love." She was always aware of how her own thoughts and feelings could get in the way of her "vocation" of love. We must all learn to observe our own stream of consciousness.

What is my agenda? What is my predisposition? What are my prejudices? What are my angers? I meet people in high levels of church and society who don't appear to have asked these questions or undertaken this discipline. This discernment process is often called the third eye. It refers to the ability to stand away from ourselves and listen and look with some kind of *calm, nonjudgmental objectivity*. Science fiction writer Ray Bradbury coined the term "faith witnessing" to describe this kind of attention. This process can be brutal, but it is absolutely necessary. Otherwise the "I" that I am cannot separate from my identification with my own thoughts and feelings.

So we start with wiping the mirror until we can see what is objectively there. But let's go further than that: wiping the mirror until even the eye that is watching the mirror is not taken too seriously. The watcher can become self-preoccupied, which only

---

9. *Interior Castle*, IV, 1, 9.

distorts things further. So we have to observe, but also *not* let the observer become an accusing tyrant.

If we get past that temptation, we no longer ask questions about whether we're doing it right. We stop pestering our soul with questions like, "Am I pure? Am I holy? Am I good? Is my technique proper?" They all fall away.

When the veil parts and we see *love,* the self-conscious watcher, preoccupied with doing it right, just forgets the self (see Mark 10:18). After worrying that I don't know myself, a lovely question then arises. Who cares? My watching and judging don't change what is, but often become a concern with watching and judging itself. Prayer, however, is not finally self-observation, but rather to "fall into the hands of the living God" (Hebrews 10:31).   —EB 104–5

The Indwelling Presence

Those who have gone to their depths uncover an indwelling Presence. It is a deep and loving "yes" that is inherent within you. In Christian theology, this inner Presence would be described as the Holy Spirit, which is precisely God as immanent, within, and even our deepest and truest self.

Some saints and mystics have described this Presence as "closer to me than I am to myself" or "more me than I am myself." Many of us would describe this, as Thomas Merton did, as the True Self. Yet, it still must be awakened and chosen. The Holy Spirit is given equally to all; but it must be received, too. One who totally receives this Presence and draws life from it is what we call a saint.

That is how "image" becomes "likeness" (Genesis 1:26–27). We all have the indwelling image, but we surrender to the likeness in varying degrees and stages. None of us are morally or psychologically perfect or whole, but a saint or mystic nevertheless dares to believe that he or she is ontologically ("in the inner being") whole, and that it is totally a gift from God. It has nothing to do with "me"!

The Holy Spirit is never created by our actions or behavior, but it is naturally indwelling, our inner being with God. In Catholic theology, we called the Holy Spirit "Uncreated Grace." Culture and even religion often teach us to live out of our false self of reputation, self-image, role, possessions, money, appearance, and so on. It is only as this fails us, and it always eventually does, that the True Self stands revealed and ready to guide us.

The True Self does not teach us compassion as much as it *is* compassion already. And from this more spacious and grounded place, one naturally connects, empathizes, forgives, and loves just about everything. We were made in love, for love, and unto love.

This deep inner "yes" is God in me, already loving God through me. The false self does not really know how to love in a very deep or broad way. It is too opportunistic. It is too small. It is too self-referential to be compassionate.

The True Self—where you and God are one—does not choose to love as much as it is love itself already (see Colossians 3:3–4). Loving from this vast space is experienced as a river within you that flows of its own accord (see John 7:38–39).   —SC 46–48

A Bottomless Well

Love is not really an action that you do. *Love is what and who you are, in your deepest essence.* Love is a place that already exists inside of you, but is also greater than you. That's the paradox. It's within you and yet beyond you. This creates a sense of abundance and more-than-enoughness, which is precisely the satisfaction and deep peace of the True Self. You know you've found a well that will never go dry, as Jesus says (see John 4:13–14). Your True Self, God's Love in you, cannot be exhausted.

Material gifts decrease when you give them away. Spiritual gifts, by contrast, increase the more you use them. Yes! You get more love by letting it flow through you, as modeled by the Trinity. If you love, you will become more loving. If you practice patience, you will become more patient.

Love is not something you can bargain for, nor is it something you can attain or work up to—because love is your very
structural and essential identity—created in the image of the
Trinity. When you are living in conscious connection with this
Loving Inner Presence, you are in your True Self. God is forever
united to this love within you; it is your soul, the part of you
that always says yes to God. God always sees God in you—and
"*cannot* disown God's own self" (2 Timothy 2:13).

—TSFS disc 2

4

2000–Present:
We Love God by Loving Everything

In the end, "God will be all in all."
—1 Corinthians 15:28

Love [people] even in [their] sin, for that is the sem-
blance of Divine Love and is the highest love on earth.
Love all God's creation, the whole and every grain
of sand in it. Love every leaf, every ray of God's light.
Love the animals, love the plants, love everything. If you
love everything, you will perceive the divine mystery in
things. Once you have perceived it, you will begin to
comprehend it better every day. And you will come at
last to love the whole world with an all-embracing love.
—Fyodor Dostoyevsky, *The Brothers Karamazov*

The only way I know how to love God and to teach you
how to love God is to love what God loves. To love God
means to love everything . . . no exceptions.
—Richard Rohr, FM disc 2

GROWTH IN SPIRIT

Richard talks to us about his evolution in love: "I do not know if
I have become more loving as I have grown older, although I do

*hope so. I do think I have grown in Spirit. By growth in Spirit,
I mean that my sensitivities to the flow of love, to the opposite
of love, and to active resistances to love are far more obvious to
me now—both in myself and in others. This is a great burden
to carry. My 'weather vane' is far more developed now, which
makes me mourn the lack of love everywhere, but most especially in myself. This does not make life in this world easier, but
much harder, because you see so many things are counterfeits
of love. It makes you very critical of the culture, the liberals as
much as the conservatives, myself as much as anybody else. It's a
great burden to begin to see where love is and where love isn't."*

Fourth and Walnut

One day at the corner of Fourth and Walnut (now Muham-
mad Ali Blvd.) in Louisville, Kentucky, Thomas Merton had an
epiphany. At this intersection, Merton says, "I was suddenly
overwhelmed with the realization that I loved all these people,
that they were mine and I theirs, that we could not be alien to
one another even though we were total strangers. It was like
waking from a dream of separateness. . . ."[1] This is an experience of universal love, which I would define as recognizing one's
self in the other.

A bit further on, Merton writes, "Then it was as if I suddenly
saw the secret beauty of their hearts, the depths of their hearts
where neither sin nor desire nor self-knowledge can reach, the
core of their reality, the person that each one is in God's eyes."[2]

Merton—as well as anyone deserving of the title mystic—
believes that God is always recognizing Godself in you and
cannot *not* love it. This is God's "steadfast love" (*hesed*) of
humanity. That part of you has always loved God and always
will. You must learn how to consciously abide there. As Meister
Eckhart says, "The eye with which I see God is the same one

---

1. Thomas Merton, *Conjectures of a Guilty Bystander* (Garden City,
NY: Image Books, 1968), 156.
2. Ibid., 158.

with which God sees me. My eye and God's eye is one eye, and one sight, and one knowledge, and one love."[3]

There is a part of you that has always said yes to God, and that is the Anointed One, the Christ, the True Self that you already are. Within prayer you quite simply receive and return God's gaze of love. God is recognizing Godself in you, and you are recognizing yourself in God. Once the mirror begins to reflect in both directions, it will gradually move you toward a universal seeing. Once accepted in yourself, the divine image is then seen everywhere else too—and just as gratuitously.

Merton continues:

> If only they could all see themselves as they really are. If only we could see each other that way all the time. There would be no more war, no more hatred, no more cruelty, no more greed. . . . I suppose the big problem would be that we would fall down and worship each other. But this cannot be seen, only believed and "understood" by a peculiar gift.[4]
>
> —TSFS disc 2

Five Points, Sunset, and Bridge

The Center for Action and Contemplation is on a street called Five Points in Albuquerque. Where the street ends at the intersection with Bridge Boulevard and Sunset, five roads come together. Every weekday I go through this intersection on my way to the post office, taking and picking up mail for my little hermitage, for the Franciscans at Holy Family Parish, and for the CAC. I just feel so useful and helpful bringing mail back and forth. It's an obsession! Everyone at the post office knows me. They show me the back rooms and the leftover mail. It's great stuff!

The stop light at the five-way intersection seems interminably long. One day, in my usual type-A personality, wanting to

3. Johannes Eckhart, *Meister Eckhart's Sermons*, Sermon IV, "True Hearing," http://www.ccel.org/ccel/eckhart/sermons.vii.html, 32–33.
4. Merton, *Conjectures of a Guilty Bystander*, 158.

get across Bridge Blvd. to the post office, it seemed even longer than usual. And I felt God saying to me (as clear as you
can hear something without an actual audible voice speaking),
"Richard, are you really going to be any happier on the other
side of Bridge?"

For me the message was clear. If I'm not happy on this side of
Bridge, I'm not going to be happy on that side of the street. So
why not just be happy now? It's that simple . . . and that hard.
The stoplight has become a little daily meditation place. Okay,
here I get to practice it again. Everything is right here, right now.
If I can't experience God and love myself and everything else on
this side of Bridge Blvd., I probably won't be able to do it on the
other side either.

I cannot think of any spiritual practice I could recommend
which will transform your life into love and into God better
than simply living in the naked now, in the sacrament of the
present moment. There is nothing you can figure out about this,
so don't over-think it. All you can really be is an alert presence.
There's no separation between the secular and the sacred.

(The CAC staff tease me and say they're going to put up a
plaque at the corner of Five Points, Sunset, and Bridge after I die.
"This is where he was finally converted," it will say.)   —LEN

God Comes Disguised as Our Life

The genius of the biblical revelation is that we will come to God
through "the actual," the here and now, or quite simply *what is*.
As Paula D'Arcy says, "God comes to us disguised as our life."
But for most "religious" people this is actually a disappointment!
They seemingly would rather have church services than ordinary
life. The Bible moves us from sacred *place* (why the temple had
to go) or sacred *action* (why the law had to be relativized) or
mental belief systems (why Jesus had no prerequisites in this
regard) to time itself as sacred *time*. "I am with you always, yes,
to the very end of time" is the last verse of Matthew's Gospel
(28:20). And space itself is sacred *space*, "the whole world is
filled with his glory" (Psalm 72:19).

Life is not about becoming spiritual beings nearly as much as about becoming human beings, following the lead of Jesus in his incarnation. We already are spiritual beings, inherently so; but as is evident from the daily newspaper, we have a very hard time being basically human. We just don't know, honor, or recognize that we are from the beginning "hidden with Christ in God" (Colossians 3:3). The Bible tries to let you in on the secret, by slowly *revealing God in the most ordinary*. That's why so much of the text seems mundane, practical, specific and, frankly, unspiritual! Don't you get tired of the wars, adulteries, rapes, murders, and the machinations of kings in the Bible? Yet this very pull-back can create the thrust toward a positive answer as you search for resolution and presence.

Speaking of mundane or ordinary, let me give you what might seem like a silly example from my own life. Several years ago, I was standing in the cleaning supplies aisle at a local supermarket, staring at boxes of laundry detergent. Something came over me and all of a sudden everything was wonderful. For a moment, the veil parted and I knew, "This is it! It doesn't get any better than this." I must have stood there for five minutes, smiling at the Tide boxes. Fortunately, no one else was in that aisle. Who of us would think a sacred experience like this could happen in a supermarket? But it can. The division between secular and sacred breaks down when you learn how to see. It's all good. It's all okay. And love oozes and shines through everything. For just a moment, I tasted the Real. In a box of Tide!

—TH 15–17 and TSFS disc 4

MASCULINE SPIRITUALITY

For several years, Richard read all the books he could find on male initiation. Drawing from indigenous and elders' wisdom around the world, he developed Men's Rites of Passage, which many men found to be a powerful transformative experience. He sums up the heart of his work with masculine spirituality in this way:

"The underlying assumption of all men's work across cultures is that men who have not made journeys of powerlessness cannot be trusted with power. They will always abuse it. That's why the male had to be sent on journeys of powerlessness before he could be released into society. It's interesting that the recognition of one's powerlessness is also the First Step of the Twelve-Step program. It also relates to the vulnerability of the Trinity. Vulnerability is essential to the free flow of love, and the male has major resistance to vulnerability.

"The young male needed initiation because he was considered the loose cannon in the family unit. The uninitiated male tended to seek his own privilege, advantage, comfort, and promotion. That doesn't need much proof. Just look at history. Unbridled ambition takes the form of power, violence, and war when it isn't balanced by the feminine and vulnerability."

Passing from Death to Life Now

How do we explain the larger-than-life, spiritually powerful individuals who seem to move events and history forward? One explanation is that they have somehow been "initiated"—initiated into their True Self, the flow of reality, the great pattern, or into the life of God. Initiation experiences took specific ritual forms in every age and every continent for most of human history. They were considered central to the survival of most cultures and to the spiritual survival of males in particular.

Many cultures and religions saw the male, left to himself, as a dangerous and even destructive element in society. Rather than naturally supporting the common good, the male often sought his own security and advancement. The same could probably be said of many modern Western women, but historically, women were "initiated" by their subjugated position in patriarchal societies, by the "humiliations of blood" (menstruation and labor), by the ego-decentralizing role of child-rearing, and by their greater investment in relationships.

For many years I have been studying, creating, and promoting men's rites of passage focusing mainly on destabilizing the ego.

As I am a man and have not studied women's journeys in particular, most of my comments will be focused on male initiation. Female readers, please use your best discretion to apply (or not) these principles to your own experience. I also want to emphasize that before you can let go of your ego, you first have to have one! The ego has an important place and role; it is simply not the whole story of who you are.

In the larger-than-life people I have met, I always find one common denominator: in some sense, *they have all died before they died*—and thus they are larger than death too! Please think about that. At some point, they were led to the edge of their private resources, and that breakdown, which surely felt like dying, led them into a larger life. They went through a death of their various false selves and came out on the other side knowing that death could no longer hurt them. *They fell into the Big Love and the Big Freedom—which many call God.*

Throughout most of history, the journey through death into life was taught in sacred space and ritual form, which clarified, distilled, and shortened the process. In sacred space, you can do things that would never work in secular space (male circumcision being the most common example). Since rites of passage have fallen out of favor in our consumer cultures, many people don't learn how to move past their fear of diminishment, even when it stares them down or gently invites them. This lack of preparation for the "passover," the absence of training in grief work and letting go, and our failure to entrust ourselves to a bigger life, have contributed to our culture's spiritual crisis.

All great spirituality is about letting go. Instead we have made it to be about taking in, attaining, performing, winning, and succeeding. True spirituality echoes the paradox of life itself. It trains us in both detachment and attachment: detachment from the passing so we can attach to the substantial. But if we do not acquire good training in detachment, we may attach to the wrong things, especially our own self-image and its desire for security. Initiation is one's initial training in an essential letting go in order to allow oneself to be reconstructed on a new foundation.

Reality is God's greatest ally; full Reality always relativizes us in a most essential way. Such an initiation into death, and therefore into life, rightly "saves" a person. Catholics call it the paschal mystery or the passion of the Christ. The word passion (*patior*) means to "allow" or "suffer reality." It is not a doing, but *a being done unto*.

Union with God, union with *what is*—that is to say, union with everything—has always been the final goal of any initiatory experience. One taste of the Real had to be given early in life to keep the initiate hungry, harmonious, and holy—so he could never be satisfied with anything less than what he once knew for sure!   —AR 1–5, 7–9, 29–30; BSMG; and BSHM

BEING IN LOVE VS. LOVING

Richard shared insights with us that came to him after a time of prayer, further distilled as he journaled about the difference between being in love and loving:

"*For me, being in love is whenever an event, a person, an animal evokes your soul, receives your soul, and then reflects your own soul back to you. You feel like you're receiving your own self by their love for you and by them allowing you to love them. It's a mutual, Trinitarian flow of relationship. When you have such a wonderful experience of falling in love, you know this is what life is all about.*

"*But there are people, events, and animals which don't reciprocate and don't know how to receive your soul and bounce it back to you. If, by the grace of God, you make the choice to love anyway and send your love to that person who is not beautiful in your eyes, who will not receive any love you give them, much less be able to bounce it back, that is the decision to love. It's a unilateral sending of love and letting go of any concern about whether it's received or not.*

"The second kind of love is less common I think, certainly in my experience. It demands such depth, such deliberate choice, such spaciousness to realize that mutuality isn't being evoked, and your love may not be received or reciprocated; but you're going to love anyway.

"Love is a choice, a decision. If love is dependent on feelings, there are times when we won't be loving. Even married people don't always feel intense love for their partners. But we can choose to give ourselves anyway."

Divine Love

Divine love is a capacity for self-giving for its own sake. The outpouring is not seeking any particular goal, nor does it seek any preference of object. The love we're talking about is not "I will outpour to this good-looking person, but I won't outpour to this not-so-good-looking person." If it's divine love, it's not determined by the object but by the subject, the one who's doing the loving.

Psychiatrist and author Scott Peck suggested that outpouring love seeks the spiritual good of the other. This is a helpful clarification. If you're not seeking another's good, then your "love" is self-referential. You're doing something for someone because you have a goal in mind or so that you can appear loving.

Now I know it takes an entire life of fits and starts, doing it wrong a thousand times, before you get it. And God must understand this is the human path. It may even necessitate that we do love wrong at first, in a way that is self-referential and not outpouring. You almost need to do it wrong to know what right is. That's the human way of learning. The path to perfection is necessarily imperfect.

Our human minds can't even imagine infinite mercy and love. That's where faith comes in. We trust it—because of Scripture and our Tradition. And some of our experience is beginning to tell us it's true: this love is infinitely available and is not

determined by the worthiness of the object. Letting go of our
human frame of reference is foundational to conversion.

—IDA disc 5

Intimacy

In the Hebrew Scriptures, there are many passages that have
YHWH speaking of Godself as a jealous lover. God desires our
response. That is the opening for mutuality: that God could
somehow need and want me. Is that possible? Is that con-
ceivable? Process theologians today suggest that if the Formless One—the Great Spirit, God, whom we Christians call the
Father—needed to take form as Jesus the Son, there is a sense in
which God needs form to know Godself. They say that God is
growing with us and through us and interfaces with us by taking
on and living in solidarity with our pain and our joy. Now this
might sound like blasphemy to some, but it has a beautiful level
of meaning for me.

Some people like God being unchangeable, eternal, and
self-sufficient, not contingent on anything else. But I think the
Scriptures show God at a mystical level needing and desiring
our response. Mystics in the Catholic and Sufi tradition talk
as if they matter to God. This is what a love relationship does
for you. You feel that your presence or absence matters to the
other person. You feel wanted. You feel "at home" when you are
together.

YHWH pursues a relationship with Moses, and Moses calls
himself a friend of God. There is mutual self-revelation, self-disclosure. This leads to the next stage of intimacy which we might
call inter-being or mutual indwelling—where you actually experience some of yourself over there in that other person and some
of the other person in you. That is what every mystic knows.
It is not just poetry. It is very real. Language eventually breaks
down and cannot do justice to intimacy, whether human-to-hu-
man or human-to-divine. But still we try to express the wonder
and ecstasy of union.

Inter-being, coinherence, is the true shape of reality. That is consciousness. The Latin *conscire* means knowing with or knowing together. My knowing is not just my knowing. The very word that is frequently used for "knowing" in the Hebrew Bible, *yada*, is the same word as sexual intercourse. It implies an overlapping between nakedness, self-disclosure, and true knowledge. People who have been married for years and who love one another deeply know what the other is feeling and thinking. And that is beautiful. That's consciousness. It's beyond your own knowing; it's a shared knowing that comes about through love.

—IDA disc 4

Thisness

The Franciscan School says loving is the highest level of knowing. It is true knowing. If you do not love something, you cannot know it because you'll approach it with a critical, analytical, judgmental, negative mind. That is why it becomes important to love all things. You cannot really know reality without loving it; and that in a word is contemplation. The contemplative mind is different than the rational mind. The rational mind tries to know by analysis alone; the contemplative mind tries to know things by living in intimacy with them. And that applies not only to people, but to animals, trees, and anything you honor. I had an aunt who was a Sister of the Precious Blood in Wichita, Kansas, and she just loved beetles. She was a biology teacher and her walls of beetles brought her to ecstasy and excitement.

That's the principle of particularity or *thisness*. We call it *haecceity* in the Franciscan School. You cannot love universals. You start with particulars: this woman, this man, this beetle, this moment. That is where the heart opens and intimacy is learned. You cannot love concepts, forces, or ideas—which is ideology, a kind of idolatry. Ideological love is not love at all; it is not incarnational or intimate. Rather, it is the ego wrapping itself around opinions.

Inter-being, mutuality, and reciprocity are normally learned and deepened through the contemplation and encounter of specific, concrete things. Love must be tested with a particular person or creature. Intimacy is the mutual humble desire of two beings coming together from their different ground. You don't need to give up your ground, your selfhood; but you're able to detach from it so that you can honor the other.   —IDA disc 4

Loving the "Other"

Plenty of people in Richard's life have challenged his ability to love. He gets a fair amount of hate mail and has been called a heretic by some. But he tries to understand where they are coming from. Often, he can say, "I was there once myself. And God still loved me." He can understand conservatives because he came from conservative beginnings and can see the good that they are trying to protect. He realizes that we all understand things from our own viewpoint and that "every viewpoint is a view from a point." He tries to find the sliver of truth hiding in what a person is saying. That allows him to start with a "yes" instead of a "no." Beginning with "yes" opens our hearts and minds to learn; starting with "no" closes us off to possibility. Richard believes that meeting those who are different from him with an open mind holds opportunity for growth and transformation.

Richard's quote on the back of a CAC T-shirt says something similar: "You cannot build on death. You can only build on life. We must be sustained by a sense of what we are for *and not just what we are* against."

In his everyday speech, Richard tries to pass his words through three gates: Is it true? Is it loving? Is it necessary? He sees the need to speak truth, especially to power, but to do so in a way that would build people up rather than tear them down. Richard observes that a great deal of chatter flows from nervousness and fear of silence, filling up a scary emptiness. Even in his muchness of speaking, Richard focuses on saying only what he feels is essential and valuable. He invites his listeners and readers to hold space for contemplative stillness.

Yes Must Precede No

Faith in God is not just faith to believe in spiritual ideas. It's to have confidence in Love itself. It's to have confidence in reality itself, that at its core, it's okay, that God is in it, that God is revealed in everything. Faith is about learning to say yes to the moment right in front of you. Only after you say your *yes* do you recognize that Christ is here, in this person, in this event. You say *yes* and then you recognize it is the Lord. God is in all things; this universal Presence is available everywhere.

Most of us learned to say *no* without the deeper joy of *yes*. We were trained to put up with all the "dying" and just take it on the chin. (When I entered the novitiate, we still had whips for self-flagellation in our cells.) Saying no to the false self does not necessarily please God or please anybody, and surely not you. There is too much resentment and self-pity involved in this kind of false dying. *There is a good dying and there is a bad dying.* Good dying is unto something bigger and better; bad dying is just stupid dying that profits nobody. It is too much *no* and not enough *yes*. You must hold out for *yes*! Don't be against anything unless you are much more for something else that is better. "I want you to be you, all of you, your best you!" is what true lovers say to one another, not just, "I do not like this about you," or, "Why don't you change that?"

God tries to first create a joyous *yes* inside you, far more than any kind of *no*. Then you have become God's full work of art, and for you, love is now stronger than death, and Christ is surely risen in you. Love and life have become the same thing. Just saying *no* is resentful dieting, whereas finding your deepest *yes*, and eating from that table, is a spiritual banquet. You see, death and *no* are the same thing. Love and *yes* are even more the same thing.

The True Self does what it really loves and therefore loves whatever it does. I am sure that is what Joseph Campbell meant by his oft misunderstood line, "Follow your bliss."

—H April 10, 2016 and ID 182–83

How You Love Anything Is How You Love Everything

Authentic love is of one piece. How you love anything is how you love everything. Jesus commands us to "Love our neighbors as we love ourselves," and he connects the two great commandments of love of God and love of neighbor, saying they are "like" one another (Matthew 22:40). So often, we think this means to love our neighbor with the same amount of love—*as much as* we love ourselves—when it really means that it is the same Source and the same Love that allows me to love myself, others, and God at the same time! That is unfortunately not the way most people understand love, compassion, and forgiveness; but it is the only way they ever work. *How you love is how you have accessed Love.*

You cannot sincerely love another or forgive another's offenses inside of dualistic consciousness. Try it, and you'll see it can't be done. We have done the people of God a great disservice by preaching the Gospel to them but not giving them the tools whereby they can obey that Gospel. As Jesus put it, "cut off from the vine, you can do nothing" (John 15:5). The "vine and the branches" are one of the greatest Christian mystical images of the non-duality between God and the soul. In and with God, I can love everything and everyone—even my enemies. Alone and by myself, willpower and intellect will seldom be able to love in difficult situations over time. Many sophisticated folks try to love by themselves. They try to obey the second commandment without the first. It usually does not work long-term, and there is no one more cynical than a disillusioned idealist. (This was my own youthful generation of the 1960s.)

Finally, of course, there is a straight line between love and suffering. If you love greatly, it is fairly certain you will soon suffer, because you have somehow given up control to another. Undoubtedly, this is why we are told to be faithful in our loves, because such long-term loyalty will always lead us to the necessary pruning (John 15:2) of the narcissistic self.

Until we love and until we suffer, we all try to figure out life and death with our minds; but afterward a Larger Source opens up within us and we "think" and feel quite differently: "Until knowing the Love, which is beyond all knowledge" (Ephesians 3:19). Thus, Jesus would naturally say something like, "This is my commandment, you *must* love one another!" (John 13:34). Love initially and safely opens the door of awareness and aliveness, and then *suffering for that love* keeps that door open and available for ever greater growth.   —NN 128

FREEDOM ON THE EDGE OF THE INSIDE

Richard credits the Franciscan Order and his open-minded superiors with providing him the structural freedom to teach an "alternative orthodoxy." There is a long heritage in the Catholic Church of welcoming diverse views and debate on theology. Richard says that if you're on the outside, all you can do is throw rocks; if you're too deeply embedded on the inside, you have to speak the party line. "On the edge of the inside," Richard is able to serve his Tradition as a prophet, offering constructive criticism with love and respect.

"Did I tell you that I was once investigated by the Vatican?" Richard asks. "I got this letter from a cardinal saying that my orthodoxy was being questioned and they wanted me to answer some questions. I answered six or eight questions with about two paragraphs each. I tried to get right to the point of why I felt what I was teaching was good theology, or the Perennial Tradition of the Catholic faith. For four months I waited, expecting to be called to Rome for further questioning. Instead, I got a letter back from the same cardinal saying, 'You have answered all of our questions to this office's satisfaction. God bless you in your ministry.' So I dodged that bullet.

"Many times, my former archbishop went to the Franciscan provincial (the head of the province), saying, 'We're concerned about something that Richard is teaching.' Every time

my provincial would say, 'We do not have a problem with this teaching. He might say things with a different twist, but he is, in fact, quite orthodox and is concerned about being orthodox. That is where his authority comes from. He's preaching the Gospel with our blessing. . . ' or something to that effect. It always worked. They are not about to take on the whole Franciscan Order, which has been here in New Mexico much longer than the bishops!

"That's why I can write and preach the way I do, quoting scriptural and theological sources, the Councils of the Church, and the saints and mystics to back me up. I admit that some of the things I say—like 'cosmic Christ'—sound different and unfamiliar. But Franciscans have always paid attention to different things than the mainline church. The cosmic Christ, for example, is plainly taught in John 1, Colossians 1, and Ephesians 1, but most Christians were paying attention to different things, to the historical Jesus. My Franciscan education has given me enough confidence and access to the Tradition so that I can defend myself. Belonging to a community protects me as well. The typical diocesan priest does not have that kind of theological and structural cover, which is why both reformers and heretics often come from religious orders."

Where You Can't Be Bought Off

When Francis said, after kissing the leper, "I left the world," he was saying that he was giving up on the usual payoffs, constraints, and rewards of business-as-usual and was choosing to live in the largest Kingdom of all. To pray and actually mean "thy Kingdom come," we must also be able to say "my kingdoms go." At best, most Christians split their loyalties between God and Caesar, but Francis and Clare did not. Their first citizenship was always, and in every case, elsewhere, which paradoxically allowed them to live in this world with joy, detachment, and freedom (see Philippians 3:20).

When you agree to live simply, you put yourself outside of others' ability to buy you off, reward you falsely, or control you by money, status, salary, punishment, and loss or gain. This is the most radical level of freedom, but, of course, it is not easy to come by. Francis and Clare had little to lose, no desire for gain, no loans or debts to pay off, and no luxuries that they needed or wanted. Most of us can only envy them.

When you agree to live simply, you do not consider the immigrant, the refugee, the homeless person, or the foreigner as a threat to you or as competition with you. You have chosen their marginal state for yourself—freely and consciously becoming "visitors and pilgrims" in this world (1 Peter 2:11). A simple lifestyle is quite simply an act of solidarity with the way most people have lived since the beginnings of humanity. It is thus restorative justice instead of the very limited notion of retributive justice.

When you voluntarily agree to live simply, you do not need to get into the frenzy of work for the sake of salary or for the ability to buy nonessentials or to raise your social standing. You enjoy the freedom of not climbing. You might climb for others, but not only for yourself.

When you agree to live simply, you have time for spiritual and corporal works of mercy because you have renegotiated in your mind and heart your very understanding of time and its purposes. Time is *not* money, despite the common aphorism. Time is life itself!

When you agree to live simply, people cease to be possessions and objects for your consumption or use. Your lust for relationships or for others to serve you, your need for admiration, your desire to use people or things as commodities for your personal pleasure, or any need to control and manipulate others, slowly— yes, very slowly—falls away. Only then are you free to love.

—EL 36–40

A NEW REFORMATION

Some time ago, Richard was called before the archbishop because it had been reported that Richard used tortillas during the Eucharist at a wedding in northern New Mexico. "We often used tortillas as communion wafers. In fact, they are almost identical to what Jesus would have actually used!" Richard further explains. "Tortillas are the bread of the people here; and these particular tortillas were made by the bride's mother. But the archbishop was concerned about what ingredients were used in the tortillas. I ended up telling him I would not use tortillas any more if that's what he preferred. Perhaps they had salt or baking soda in them, and apparently Jesus does not like such things (I did not say that!)."

Judy, one of the editors of this book, first heard this story from Richard at a Center for Action and Contemplation board meeting. The board had just read Richard's suggested vision statement, which began with: "The CAC supports a new reformation—from the inside. . . ."

"Richard," Judy asked, "if the archbishop is upset about a tortilla, don't you think 'a new reformation' might raise a few red flags?"

Without missing a beat, Richard responded, "I'm willing to go down for a reformation; but I won't go down for a tortilla!"

Richard has had to do soul searching about other important issues, such as the time he attended and spoke at his lesbian friends' wedding in the backyard of the CAC's then guesthouse. He did not preside at the wedding and dressed in "civilian" clothes so it would be clear that he was there not as a priest, but as a friend. Again, Richard was brought before the archbishop. Why did he decide to talk at the wedding? This was part of his answer:

"The Book of Wisdom says, 'Yes, you love all that exists, you hold nothing of what you have made in abhorrence, for had you hated anything, you would not have formed it. And how, had you not willed it, could a thing persist, how be conserved if not called forth by you? You spare all things because all things are yours, Lord, lover of life, you whose imperishable spirit is in all' (11:25–26). I know that God loves LGBTQ people just as much as God loves everyone else. How dare we tell God who

God can and cannot love? It is obvious to me that God loves all that God has created! I also know that committed love always pleases God. So it felt like the right thing to attend my friends' wedding ceremony."

The Greatest Commandments

> *Beloved, let us love one another, because love is of God; everyone who loves is begotten by God and knows God. Whoever is without love does not know God, for God is love. In this way the love of God was revealed to us: God sent God's only Son into the world so that we might have life through him. In this is love: not that we loved God, but that God loved us and sent God's Son as expiation for our sins. Beloved, if God so loved us, we also must love one another. No one has ever seen God. Yet, if we love one another, God remains in us, and God's love is brought to perfection in us.* —1 John 4:7–12, NAB

"Whoever *loves* is born of God and knows God." Unfortunately, many Christians think, "If I read the Bible, I'm born of God; or if I go to church, I know God; or if I obey the commandments, I know God." Yet John says it's simply about loving. Note that the inverse is true also. "Whoever is without love does not know God, for God is love."

> *As the Father loves me, so I also love you. Remain in my love. If you keep my commandments, you will remain in my love, just as I have kept my Father's commandments and remain in his love. I have told you this so that my joy may be in you and your joy may be complete. This is my commandment: love one another as I love you. No one has greater love than this, to lay down one's life for one's friends. You are my friends if you do what I command you. . . . This I command you: love one another.* —John 15:9–14, 17, NAB

We might expect Jesus to say, "There is no greater love than to love God." But he says, "There is no greater love than to lay down your life for your friends."

Both of these Scriptures emphasize the centrality and the importance of love. The beginning and end of everything is love. Only inside of the mystery of love—mutual self-emptying and infilling—can we know God. If we stay outside of that mystery, we cannot know God.

When most of us hear the word "commandment," we likely think of the Ten Commandments. But Jesus speaks of a "new" commandment surpassing and summing up the "ten" of the Hebrew Bible (Exodus 20:1–17; Deuteronomy 5:6–21): "This is *my* commandment: Love one another." He also says: "The entire law and the prophets is summed up in the two great commandments: to love God and to love one another" (see Matthew 22:36–40).

Perhaps we don't want to hear this commandment because we can never live up to it through our own efforts. We'd like to whittle it down to a little commandment, like "Come to church on Sunday." But who of us can say we have really loved yet? We're all beginners. We're all starting anew every day, and we're failing every day. Loving as imperfect, egoic human beings keeps us in utter reliance upon the mercy, compassion, and grace of God. We can never fully succeed by ourselves.

It seems God gave us a commandment that we could not obey. Perhaps this is so we would have to depend upon the Holy Spirit. This is the greatness, the goodness, the wonder, the impossibility of the Gospel, that it asks of all of us something we—alone, apart, separate—cannot do! Only by living in love, in communion—God in us and we in God (see John 17:20–26)—do we find, every once in a while, a love flowing through us and toward us and from us that is bigger than our own. And we surely know it's not "we" who are doing it!

—H May 13, 2012

Seeing Truly

The movement to full wisdom has much to do with necessary shadow work and the emergence of healthy self-critical thinking, which alone allows you to see beyond your own shadow and disguise and to find who you are "chosen in Christ from the beginning of the world" (see Ephesians 1:4+). The Zen masters are saying the same thing when they speak of "the face you had before you were born." This metaphysical self cannot die and always lives in God; it is your True Self, and is probably what we mean by the soul.

Jesus said, "The lamp of the body is the eye" (Luke 11:34). Spiritual maturity is largely a growth in seeing. Full seeing seems to take most of our lifetime. There is a cumulative and exponential growth in perception for those who do their inner work. There is also a cumulative closing down in people who have denied all shadow work and humiliating self-knowledge. This is the classic closed mind and heart that we see in some older people. The Nuremburg trials, where many Nazis remained in total denial and maintenance of their positive self-image, are a stark example of this. The longer you persist in not asking for forgiveness, the harder it becomes because you have more and more years of illusion to justify. Allow conversion when you are young, if possible!

All physical shadows are created by a mixture of darkness and light, and this is the only spectrum of human vision. *We cannot see inside of total light or total darkness.* Think about that. As the shadows of things gradually show themselves as understandable and real, you lose interest in idealizing or idolizing persons or events, especially yourself. As Jesus says to the rich young man, "Only God is good" (Mark 10:18). All created things are a mixture of good and not so good.

This does not mean you *stop* loving other people; in fact, it means you actually *begin* to truly love people and creatures! It does not mean self-hatred or self-doubt, but finally accepting both your gifts and your weaknesses as fully your own; they no longer cancel one another out. You can eventually do the same for others too, and you do not let one or the other fault in a person destroy your larger relationship with them. Now you understand the importance of contemplative (non-dualistic) thinking as absolutely necessary for human flourishing. It is the change that changes everything else. It makes love, forgiveness, and patience possible. Without it, we are trapped inside of our judgments.   —FU 130, 134

BIRTH OF THE LIVING SCHOOL

In the early 2000s, Father Thomas Keating invited Richard and many other Christian leaders, both Catholic and Protestant, to a meeting in Snowmass, Colorado. Richard says, "From there, we were all sent out to see if we could get a seminary in the United States to put the teaching of the contemplative mind front and center in their curriculum. As of now, not a single denominational seminary has been able to do it. Most seminaries just train students in their academic and denominational theology. Contemplative epistemology and theology are seen as superficial add-ons rather than the core of the matter. Since no one else was going teach in this way, we decided to try it ourselves. And this became our own Living School."

The Living School for Action and Contemplation, which launched in 2013, grew out of Richard's long-time dream. Each fall the school accepts almost two hundred students who engage in onsite and online learning over the course of two years. Richard serves as Academic Dean, teaching alongside core faculty members James Finley and Cynthia Bourgeault. It is an ecumenical school with religious priests, ministers, sisters, brothers, and lay people of all genders in each program. While seminaries are closing at an increased rate, the school has to turn away many qualified applicants for lack of space. Richard muses, "What does this say about the state of Christianity in the United States and in the West?"

The Living School seeks to deepen students' engagement with their True Selves and with the world, growing their capacity to embody their unique calling. The program grounds "multipliers" in the Christian contemplative tradition so that they can spread wisdom and compassion in their own communities and professional fields. Richard hopes Living School alumni are models of love, preaching more through their lived example—mirroring union with God—than through the words they use.

Universal Union

> *The place which God takes in our soul he will never vacate, for in us is his home of homes, and it is the greatest delight for him to dwell there. . . . The soul who contemplates this is made like the one who is contemplated.*
> —Lady Julian of Norwich, *Showings*

> *On that day, you will know that you are in me and I am in you.* —John 14:20

"That day" that John refers to has been a long time in coming, yet it has been the enduring message of every great religion in history. It *is* the Perennial Tradition. Yet union with God is still considered esoteric, mystical, a largely moral matter, and possible for a very few, as if God were playing hard to get. Nevertheless, divine and thus universal union is still the core message and promise, the goal of all religion.

Place does not exist except in God. There is no time outside God. God is the beauty in all beauty. Those who allow divine friendship enjoy divine friendship, and it is almost that simple. You are that which you are looking for, and that is why you are looking for it. God's life and love flow through you as soon as *you* are ready to allow it. That is the core meaning of faith— to dare to trust that God could and does have an eternal compassion toward you. Everyone who asked Jesus to heal them or help them had somehow made that simple act of trust that he cared—and so the flow happened and they were healed. No other preconditions were ever required.

If you are seeking the divine, you have already made contact with the divine in yourself. If you have not made contact with the divine in yourself, you will likely be bored with any notion of spiritual search. If you have, you will seek and find it everywhere. The modern divine–human divorce seems to be on the grounds of both "incompatibility" and "irreconcilable" differences. Religion itself must bear most of the responsibility for causing this divorce by, in effect, increasing the distance between God and humanity instead of proudly announcing that the problem is already solved and the perceived gap has been overcome from the very beginning: "Before the world was made, he chose us" (Ephesians 1:4).

Jesus fully accepted and enjoyed his divine/human status. "I and the Father are one," he said (John 10:30), which was shocking to his Jewish contemporaries, for he looked just like one of them, and apparently they did not like themselves. No wonder they called it blasphemy and picked up stones to kill him (John 10:33). It is formally incorrect for Christians to simply say, "Jesus is God." It misses the major point and goal of the whole incarnation. Jesus does not equal God per se, which is for us the Trinity. Jesus, much better and more correctly, is *the union between God and the human.* That is a third something—in which we are invited to share. Once we made Jesus *only* divine, we ended up being *only* human, and the whole process ground to a halt. That is the way the dualistic mind works, I am very sad to say.

When we tried to understand Jesus outside the dynamism of the Trinity, we did not do him or ourselves any favor. Jesus never knew himself or operated as an independent "I" but only as a "Thou" in relationship to his Father and the Holy Spirit, which he says in a hundred different ways. The "Father" and the "Holy Spirit" are a relationship to Jesus. *God* is a verb more than a noun. God is love, which means relationship itself (see 1 John 4:7–8).

Christianity lost its natural movement and momentum—out from that relationship and back into that relationship—when it pulled Jesus out of the Trinity. It killed the exciting inner experience and marginalized the mystics who really should be center stage. Jesus is the model and metaphor for all of creation that is being drawn into this flow of love, and thus he always says, "Follow me!" and, "I shall return to take you with me, so that where I am, you may be also" (John 14:3). The concrete, historical body of Jesus represents the universal Body of Christ that "God has loved before the foundation of the world" (John 17:24). He is the stand-in for all of us. The Jesus story is the universe story. Jesus hands on his union with God (which he never doubts) to us—to never doubt. Quite simply, this is what it means to "believe" in Jesus.

The spiritual wisdom of divine union is first beautifully expressed in writing in the Vedas (the oldest source of Hinduism, around three thousand years old), and it is one of its "grand pronouncements." The phrase in Sanskrit is *Tat Tvam Asi,* which is a thought so condensed that I am going to list all likely translations, and know that however you hear it, it is still true and is the Perennial Tradition of religion:

YOU are That!
You ARE what you seek!
THOU art That!
THAT you are!
You are IT!

The meaning of this saying is that the True Self, in its original, pure, primordial state, is wholly or partially identifiable or even identical with God, the Ultimate Reality that is the ground and origin of all phenomena. That which you long for, you also are. In fact, that is where the longing comes from.

Longing for God and longing for our True Self are the same longing. And the mystics would say that it is God who is even doing the longing in us and through us (that is, through the divine indwelling, or the Holy Spirit). God implanted a natural

affinity and allurement between Godself and all of God's creatures. The limited and the limitless would otherwise be incapa-
ble of union; the finite and the infinite could never be reconciled
into one.

Religion has only one job description: to make one out of
two. For Christians, that is "the Christ Mystery," whereby we
believe God overcame the gap from God's side. God does all the
work, the heavy lifting, and always initiates the longing. Some
call it "prevenient grace," which makes the point quite well. The
deepest human need and longing is to overcome the separateness, the distance from what always seems "over there" and
"beyond me," like a perfect lover, a moment of perfection in art,
music, or dance, and surely a transcendent God.

God is saying in all incarnations that "I am not totally Other.
I have planted some of me in all things that long for reunion."
It is mimicked and mirrored in erotic desire and the sexual pair-
ing of animals, which is why the Song of Songs, Rumi, Hafiz,
Kabir, and John of the Cross could use only highly erotic images
to communicate their mysticism. Absolute otherness will create only absolute alienation. (Add to that any notion of God
as petty, angry, or torturing, and the mystical journey is over.)
So God created human similarity and compassion in Jesus to
overcome this tragic gap. God-in-you seeks and loves God, like
a homing device that never turns off.   —ID 95–100

The Principle of Likeness

> Deep calls unto Deep.   —Psalm 42:7

> Be the change you want to see in the world.
> > —Mohandas Gandhi

To have a spiritual life is to recognize that there is always a similarity and coherence between the seer and the seen, the seeker
and what they are capable of finding. You will seek only what
you have partially already discovered and seen within yourself
as desirable. Spiritual cognition is invariably re-cognition.

Call it the "Principle of Likeness," if you will. The enormous breakthrough is that when you honor and accept the divine image within yourself, you cannot help but see it in everybody else, too, and you know it is just as undeserved and unmerited as it is in you. That is why you stop judging, and that is how you start loving unconditionally and without asking whether someone is worthy or not. The breakthrough occurs at once, although the realization deepens and takes on greater conviction over time.

Non-dual people will see things in their wholeness and call forth the same unity in others, simply by being who they are. Wholeness (head, heart, and body, all present and positive) can see and call forth wholeness in others. This is why it is so pleasant to be around whole and holy people.

Dualistic or divided people, however, live in a split and fragmented world. They cannot accept or forgive certain parts of themselves. They cannot accept that God objectively dwells within them (1 Corinthians 3:16–17). This lack of forgiveness takes the forms of a tortured mind, a closed heart, or an inability to live calmly and comfortably inside their own body. The fragmented mind sees parts, not wholes, in itself and others. It invariably creates antagonism, reaction, fear, and resistance—"push-back"—from other people.

What you see is what you get. What you seek is also what you get.

We mend and renew the world by strengthening inside ourselves what we seek outside ourselves, not by demanding it of others or trying to force it on others.

This truth may sound like the Law of Attraction that has been so widely discussed, and often called the "Secret," but there is one major difference. Perhaps, like many people, you use the Law of Attraction to draw to yourself the good things you want in life—love, a successful relationship, stability. This is fine as far as it goes. The true contemplative mind, however, does not deny the utter "facticity" of the outer world. In fact, much of its suffering comes from seeing and accepting things exactly as they are. The Secret seems to be saying that your mind creates the outer world. I am saying that *you do create your response to it, and that response, for all practical purposes, is your reality.*

- If you want others to be more loving, choose to love first.
- If you want a reconciled outer world, reconcile your own inner world.
- If you are working for peace out there, create it inside as well.
- If you notice other people's irritability, let go of your own.
- If you wish to find some outer stillness, find it within yourself.
- If you are working for justice, treat yourself justly, too.
- If you find yourself resenting the faults of others, stop resenting your own.
- If the world seems desperate, let go of your own despair.
- If you want a just world, start being just in small ways yourself.
- If your situation feels hopeless, honor the one spot of hope inside you.
- If you want to find God, then honor God within you, and you will always see God beyond you. For it is only God in you who knows where and how to look for God.

Some Eastern religions have called this *karma*, the correspondence between who you are and what you can make happen. But this truth is not found only in the East. Jesus said the same, almost exactly (Luke 6:36–38):

> Do not judge and you will not be judged,
> Do not condemn and you will not be condemned,
> Grant pardon, and you will be pardoned,
> Give, and there will be gifts for you. . . .
> The amount you measure out is the amount you will be
>   given back.

Now you can finally understand the words of Matthew 7:8: "Seek and you will find, knock and the door will be opened for you." Your desire to seek reflects a part of who you already are. *You desire only what you have already partially found.*

—NN 159–62

A BIGGER OCEAN

The idea of "chains flying" and being freed to live in bigger and bigger fields seems to be a recurring pattern in Richard's life. "That keeps happening," he says. "There's no doubt that the 'chains' keep breaking. The big reason is not just my theology, but the opportunities I've had for traveling around the world and meeting different cultures, religions, and people who weren't in my little pond. That forced me to begin to live in a very big ocean. This was supposed to be the meaning of 'catholic' in the first place. I just had the freedom to go there experientially, whereas a lot of people have never had that exposure. Your own little boundaries mean less and less when you are in the bigger world."

Traveling also helped Richard see that there are many ways of loving. In each culture, love looks different. The people he's met all around the world have taught him that love has "ten thousand varieties."

If It Is True, It Is True Everywhere

There is one Body, one Spirit, "one and the same hope," there is one Lord, one faith, one initiation, and one God who is Father of all, over all, through all, and within all.
—Ephesians 4:4–6

Christ likes us to prefer truth to himself, because before being Christ, he is truth. If one turns aside from him to go toward the truth, one will not go far before falling into his arms. —Simone Weil, *Waiting for God*

Jews or Christians, or those of any other religion, should not feel that they were the first people who could know God's eternal patterns and presence. After all, those patterns are "perfectly plain since God has made it plain. Ever since God created the world, God's everlasting power and deity—however invisible— have been there for the mind to see in the things that God has made" (Romans 1:19–20). How could any God worthy of the name be limited, stingy, entirely invisible, or need to squeeze that which is Being itself into any specific time frame, culture, or vocabulary? If it is true, then all people of goodwill will be able to see it. That is what we mean by the "Perennial Tradition" that keeps recurring in new formulations.

As St. Bonaventure put it, "[God] is an intelligible space whose center is everywhere and whose circumference is nowhere. . . . [God] is within all things, but not enclosed, outside all things but not excluded, above all things, but not aloof, below all things but not debased. . . . [God] is supremely one and all-inclusive, [God] is therefore 'all in all'" (1 Corinthians 15:28).[5] You can either accuse St. Paul and St. Bonaventure, who is proclaimed a "Doctor of the Church," of pantheism, or admit that *we* are the ones who do not get it yet.

God is very clearly not a mere tribal God, and one would think the three monotheistic religions would have understood that message first and best. No group will ever confine or control God (see John 3:6–8, 4:23–24) to any little tent or temple, which has been the temptation since Exodus, yet every religion falls into it. How could anyone imagine God being small and still call this phenomenon God? History, the shrinking globe, and Jesus' proclamation of the Kingdom of God are demanding of us a very big tent and a universal temple. It is God's one world, and if the supposed God-lovers cannot see this, one wonders if there is any hope for this planet.   —ID 127–30

5. Bonaventure, "The Soul's Journey to God," in *Classics of Western Spirituality* (Paulist Press, 1978), V:8.

Oneing

Lady Julian of Norwich, one of my favorite mystics, uses the idea of "oneing" to describe divine union. In Chapter 53 of *Revelations of Divine Love*, she writes, "The soul is preciously knitted to [God] in its making by a knot so subtle and so mighty that it is oned into God. In this oneing, it is made endlessly holy. Furthermore, [God] wants us to know that all the souls which are one day to be saved in heaven without end are knit in this same knot and united in this same union, and made holy in this one identical holiness."

In *Showings* Julian says, "By myself I am nothing at all, but in general, I AM the oneing of love. For it is in this oneing that the life of all people exists" (Chapter 9). She continues: "The love of God creates in us such a oneing that when it is truly seen, no person can separate themselves from another person" (Chapter 65), and "In the sight of God all humans are oned, and one person is all people and all people are in one person" (Chapter 51).

This is not some 21st century leap of logic or mere "New Age" optimism. This is the whole point. It was, indeed, supposed to usher in a new age—and it still can and will. Radical union is the recurring experience of the saints and mystics of all religions. Our job is not to first discover it, but only to retrieve what has been re-discovered—and enjoyed, again and again—by those who desire and seek God and love. When you have "discovered" it, you will be just like Jacob "when he awoke from his sleep" and shouted "You were here all the time, and I never knew it!" (Genesis 28:16).

As John said in his first letter, "I do not write to you because you do *not* know the truth, I am writing to you here because *you know it already*"! (1 John 2:21). I can only convince you of spiritual things because your soul already knows what is true, and that is why I believe and trust Julian's showings too. For the mystics, there is only one Knower, and we just participate in the knowing through relationship.

—ID 95; IDA disc 7; TH 45–46; O 1, no. 1: 14

Seeing with God's Eyes

God refuses to be known in the way we know all other objects; God can only be known by loving God. Yet much of religion has tried to know God theologically, by words, theories, doctrines, and dogmas. Belief systems have their place; they provide a necessary and structured beginning point, just as the dualistic mind is good as far as it goes. But then you need the non-dual or mystical mind to love and fully experience limited ordinary things and to peek through the cloud to glimpse infinite and seemingly invisible things. This is the contemplative mind that can "know spiritual things in a spiritual way," as Paul says (1 Corinthians 2:13).

What does it mean when Jesus says you should love God with your whole heart, with your whole soul, with your whole mind (not just your dualistic mind), with your whole strength? What does it mean, as the first commandment instructs us, to love God more than anything else? To love God is *to love what God loves*. To love God means to love everything . . . no exceptions.

Of course, that can only be done with divine love flowing through us. In this way, we can love things and people, as John Duns Scotus says, in themselves, for themselves—not for what they do for us. That's when we begin to love our spouse and neighbors apart from what they can do for us or how they make us look. We love them as living images of God.

Now that takes work: constant detachment from ourselves—our conditioning, preferences, and knee-jerk reactions. We can only allow divine love to flow by way of contemplative, non-dualistic consciousness, where we stop eliminating and choosing. This is the transformed mind (Romans 12:2) that allows us to see God in everything, and empowers our behavior to almost naturally change.

Religion, from the root *religio*, means to reconnect, to bind back together. I would describe mystical moments as those attention-grabbing experiences that overcome the gap between you and other people, events, or objects, and even God, where the illusion of separation disappears. The work of spirituality is to look with a different pair of eyes (non-dual eyes) beyond what Merton calls "the shadow and the disguise" of things until you can see them in their connectedness and wholeness. In a very real sense, the word "God" is just a synonym for everything. So if you do not want to get involved with everything, stay away from God.   —EENN disc 2 and FM disc 2

Everything Belongs

Like Jesus, St. Francis did not go down the self-protective and exclusionary track. They both knew what they were for—and *who* they were—not just what they were against. That is the heart of the matter. Jesus and Francis had a genius for not eliminating or punishing the so-called negative side of the world, but incorporating it and using it. Francis, merely imitating Jesus, goes to the edge of town and to the bottom of society; he kisses the leper, loves the poor, and wears patches on the outside of his habit so everyone will know that this is what he's like on the inside. Francis doesn't hide from his shadow side, but weeps over it and welcomes it as his teacher.

The history of almost every religion begins with one massive misperception; it begins by making a fatal distinction between the sacred and the profane. Low-level religions put all their emphasis on creating sacred places, sacred time, and sacred actions. While I fully appreciate the need for this, it unfortunately leaves the majority of life "un-sacred."

In authentic mystical moments, any clear distinction between sacred and profane quickly falls apart. One henceforth knows that all of the world is sacred because most of the time such moments happen in secular settings. For examples, look at the lives of Abraham and Sarah, Moses, Elijah, Mary, and Jesus. Our Franciscan official motto is *Deus Meus et Omnia*, "My God and all things." Once you recognize the Christ as the universal truth of matter and spirit working together as one, then everything is holy. Once you surrender to this Christ mystery in your oh-so-ordinary self and body, you begin to see it in every other ordinary place too.

You don't have to go to sacred places to pray or wait for holy days for good things to happen. You can pray always, and everything that happens is potentially sacred if you allow it to be. Once we can accept that God is in all circumstances, and that God can and will use even bad situations for good, then everything becomes an occasion for good and an occasion for God. "*This* is the day God has made memorable, let us rejoice and be glad in it!" (Psalm 118:24).

Your task is to find the good, the true, and the beautiful in everything, even and most especially in the problematic. The bad is never strong enough to counteract the good. You can most easily learn this through some form of contemplative practice. Within contemplation you must learn to trust your Vital Center over all the passing jerks and snags of emotions and obsessive thinking. Once you know you have such a strong and loving soul, which is also the Indwelling Spirit, you are no longer pulled to and fro with every passing feeling. You have achieved a peace that nothing else can give you, and that no one can take from you (John 14:27).

Divine Incarnation took the form of an Indwelling Presence in every human soul and surely all creatures in some rudimentary way. Ironically, our human freedom gives us the ability to stop such a train and refuse to jump on board our own life. Angels, animals, trees, water, and yes, bread and wine seem to fully accept and enjoy their wondrous fate. Only humans resist and deny their core identities. And so we people can cause great havoc and thus must be somehow boundaried and contained. But the only way we ourselves can refuse to jump onto the train of life is by any negative game of exclusion or unlove—even of ourselves. If you read the Gospel texts carefully, you will see that the only people Jesus seems to "exclude" are those who are excluding others. Exclusion might be described as the core sin. Don't waste any time rejecting, excluding, eliminating, or punishing anyone or anything else. Everything belongs, including you.   —FM disc 1; EL 10; FMU

Love Is Stronger than Death

I believe the meaning of the Resurrection of Jesus is summed up in the climactic line from the Song of Songs, "love is stronger than death" (8:6). If the blank white banner that the Risen Christ usually holds in Christian art should say anything, it should say: "Love will win!" Love is all that remains. Love and life are finally the same thing, and you know that for yourself once you have walked through death.

Love has you. Love *is* you. Love alone, and your deep need for love, recognizes love everywhere else. Remember that you already are what you are seeking. Any fear "that your lack of fidelity could cancel God's fidelity, is absurd" (Romans 3:3), says Paul. Love has finally overcome fear, and your house is being rebuilt on a new and solid foundation. This foundation was always there, but it took you a long time to find. "It is love alone that lasts" (1 Corinthians 13:13). All you have loved in your life and been loved by are eternal and true.

Two of the primary metaphors of final salvation are Noah's ark (Genesis 6:19) and "the Peaceable Kingdom" (Isaiah 11:6–9). Interestingly enough, both are filled with images of animals—as worth saving and as representative of paradise regained.

My fellow Franciscan friar, Father Jack Wintz, has written a theologically solid book on why we can consider all things loved, loving, and lovable as participating in eternity, including animals.[6] What made us think humans were the only ones who love and are lovable? If unconditional love, loyalty, and obedience are the tickets to an eternal life, then my black Labrador, Venus, will surely be there long before me, along with all

---

6. Jack Wintz, O.F.M., *Will I See My Dog in Heaven?* (Orleans, MA: Paraclete Press, 2009).

the dear wild animals who care for their young at great cost to themselves and accept their fate far better than most humans.

—ID 178–79

VENUS

During one of our last interviews, we first inquired about Richard's dog, Venus, whose absence was notable. Richard said she just didn't want to come with him to the office, and it was clear she was not feeling well. Richard acknowledged that it has been God's special grace to allow Venus to be with him for fifteen wonderful years.

Several years ago, Richard reflected on how much Venus means to him.

Which Venus?

I so love and enjoy my eleven-year-old Labrador named Venus, and I dread the thought of her passing. I would so miss her unconditional love. I would sooner go first, but that would only leave her feeling confused and abandoned.

I also look most nights at the lovely New Mexico sky and see the planet Venus in the heavens. There she shines and sparkles for all to see who are willing to look and enjoy. Which is the better Venus? As always, I will choose earth over sky, my dog over distant planets. But the planet keeps me connected to all of you and to the universe; my dear black Lab keeps me connected to myself and to life itself. Both connect me to God.

—B April 9, 2012

SOMEONE TO LOVE

We asked Richard how the dogs throughout his life—including Peanut Butter, his toy poodle at New Jerusalem—may have helped with some of the loneliness inherent in the celibate experience.

He replied, "I really think human beings need someone to love, someone to begin that flow and to keep it going. I think a lot of us (and not just celibates) don't keep that flow going. The goal of the celibate relationship—God—is not always obvious. The essential question is how do you love God?

"I often wonder if there doesn't have to be an object (which really becomes a subject) whose beauty draws you out of yourself. It can be an animal to whom you give yourself and through whom you feel yourself given back to. This is why my dogs have been important in my life.

"I do think there's a wonderful structural meaning to celibacy. I know I could never have lived the life I've lived in terms of the years being on the road, the time to write books and go on extended hermitage retreats—I never could have done it if I had been married and had children. So structurally, it was a good thing.

"But it was also a dangerous thing, because it allowed me to live periods of my life self-absorbed. There wasn't an 'other' present to demand the flow and require me to keep the conduit open the way a partner or children can. There's a danger of being too much in control of what you allow to affect you."

Well, Richard has clearly allowed Venus to affect him. Here he shares a familiar daily encounter.

Pure Consciousness

Venus has the most amazing ability to make eye contact with me. She did it this morning. She comes to my bed at 5:30 and she puts her head on the side of my bed and looks at me. And I roll over and try to get my eyes open and look back at her. She can sustain this gaze. She just keeps looking at me. It is said that the eyes are the windows to the soul. Human beings can't sustain eye contact for long. We get nervous and afraid, maybe because we're afraid people will see there's nothing in here or they won't like us. But Venus just keeps looking at me and I wonder: What does she see? What is she thinking? What is it that she sees and likes in me? I'm convinced these beings that we thought lived at a rudimentary level of consciousness can see the one thing necessary. They don't get lost in labeling and categorizing.

Almost all of nature just does its thing and does it without that *self*-consciousness that we humans call a gift. And it is a gift. It brings us freedom and enjoyment. But it also brings us judgment, categorization, pigeonholing, and deciding who's in and who's out, who's up and who's down, who's right and who's wrong, who's saved and who's lost. At that moment of labeling, love fails. The flow cannot happen. You will not see the divine image in the other because at that point you're not drawing upon the divine image in yourself.

When you can draw upon the divine image in yourself, when you can see with the third eye—the eye of God—love will come from that place within you that knows you already participate in Love. It doesn't need to categorize or moralize. It doesn't need to decide who's right and who's wrong. It just is.

That's naked being. I think that's the way my dog looks at me, and I really wish I could look at reality the way Venus looks at reality—instead of having all this education and awareness that's not awareness at all. It's not pure consciousness, just letting it be and letting the being of this thing touch my naked being. That's probably the simplest definition of contemplation I can give you. But it doesn't happen naturally. It has to be practiced. And it demands a lot of letting go.

But if we can practice that contemplative mind, I have no doubt we will experience foundational participation. We will rebuild the Great Chain of Being, and out of that plenitude—out of that sense of satisfaction, enoughness, and abundance—you simply find it much easier to live simply. It's not that you have to be taught to live simply. You simply don't need all this stuff because you've found your satisfaction at an inner, deeper level. Once you've got it in here, you don't need it out there. And that's the connection between spirituality and our attempt to live a simpler and more responsible life in this world.   —GCB

THE DIVINE GAZE

Richard shares how it seems Venus intuitively understands him: "I've had times at the house where I just got an angry email or letter, where I am sitting there emotionally disrupted. I will look over at her and she's staring up at me. Does she know that I am upset and she's trying to comfort me? And she will just hold the stare. Oh my God, it feels like the divine gaze. It really does!"

As we write this, our hearts are hurting and our prayers are constant for Richard and Venus. Here is the email Richard sent yesterday, on March 29, 2017, to the CAC staff:

Dearest,

Now I have to live what I teach too easily.

It seems my dear Venus is suffering from a fast-growing tumor on her liver, now the size of a grapefruit. Last Wednesday I spent the whole horrible night on the floor with her, as she groaned and panted in pain. Since then she has been on pain medicine and seems to be more lively than the last six months, making me think this has been hurting her for some time. But she is stoic and loyal and never lets me know when she is hurting.

At her age of fifteen, the vet recommends that her life has come to its end, and it would be wise for me to put her to sleep. So that will happen this week, and I will bury her here in my front yard. I must let her go.

St. John Chrysostom said, "Weep then at the death of a dear one as if you were bidding farewell to one setting out on a journey." That is the only way I can get through this. I cannot think that I am putting her to death.

Pray for me. She has been my loyal friend and it is so very, very, very hard to let her go! I know many of you fully understand. There is no easy consolation in this, but it is teaching me immense sympathy for parents who lose a child or individuals who lose a lifetime lover.

Thank you so much,

Richard

Living before You Die

All the world can give us is small mind. But small mind, without the unitive experience of big mind, makes us feel unbearably alone. We feel lost, existentially guilty, and often fragile and powerless. A lot of guilt is not about this or that particular sin; it's really a guilt *about not having lived yet.* We call that existential or primal guilt. It's deeper than guilt for an offense we can name. It feels like shame, not about anything in particular, but about who we are and who we aren't. Many of us suffer from this shame.

There is a certain fear of death that comes from not having lived yet. I've had to face death myself when I've had cancer. I don't think I was afraid of death, but I also knew *I had already lived.* Once you know you have touched upon this mystery of life, you are not afraid of death. But there's an existential terror about losing what you've never found. Something in me says, "I haven't done 'it' yet." I haven't experienced the stream of life yet. I haven't touched the real, the good, the true, and the beautiful—which is, of course, what we were created for.

When we know we have experienced the stream of life, we will be able to lie on our deathbed like Francis and say, "Welcome, Sister Death." I'm not afraid to let go of life, because *I have life.* I am life. I know life is somehow eternal, and another form is waiting for me. It is the last threshold, but I've been over this threshold before. I think this is what Paul means when he speaks of "reproducing the pattern of Jesus' death and knowing the power of his resurrection" (Philippians 3:10). It is an actual pattern that we must live through at least once—and then we understand something forever.

But if we've never lived, we will be terrified of death. We will have no assurance that this isn't the end. Jesus said, "I am life." He came to promise us that this mystery called life and love is eternal, but that we have to enter into it *now*. Not later, but now.

—EB 164–65

THERESE OF LISIEUX AND THE BUTTERFLY

A few years ago, Bob Colaresi, a Carmelite priest from Chicago, invited Richard on a pilgrimage to the community of Therese of Lisieux in France. "Of course, I was thrilled! Therese is one of my favorite mystics." Richard shared the following story with us.

"Our small group of five visited the infirmary where Therese of Lisieux died. I stood nearest the window. I could see the black hole in the bushes that Therese likened to her own soul when she was in pain, dying of tuberculosis, and trying to believe that Jesus still loved her. The sister guiding our tour was telling us the story of Therese's death when she suddenly paused and said, 'We have a visitor!' The way she said it, we all just got goose bumps!

"We followed the sister's gaze and saw by the window a beautiful orange and yellow butterfly. It was only April 3, way too early for butterflies to even be in northern France. She said, 'Let it out, let it out!' Since I was closest to the window, I tried to open the latch; but I didn't understand how it worked and just kept struggling with it. All of a sudden, I felt as though I were levitating. I had to look down at my feet to make sure I was still on the ground. I was definitely standing on the ground, but I felt such ecstatic feelings of presence, joy, love, and power. All the blood seemed to flow out of my head.

"The sister could only see me from behind. She asked, 'What's wrong? Open the window. The butterfly wants out! The butterfly wants out!' I finally got the window open and the butterfly flew away. I turned around and the others told me my face was white. 'What just happened?' I asked. But I knew I had just been visited. I don't know how else to say it: Therese was there.

"*The sister came running over to me and came close, her veil a shield between our faces and the others, just like when I was little and my teacher didn't want the other children to hear what she was saying. The sister told me, 'I don't know who you are, but you're supposed to have this. I knew I was supposed to bring it this morning.' She pulled something out of her pocket and gave it to me. She said, 'Put it in your pocket. Don't open it until you're alone.' She spoke with such authority, the way nuns often do.*

"*Well, I was still in ecstasy! I felt like I floated through the rest of the tour. We got to see Therese's house and the stairs she was climbing when she had her great moment of conversion. We stood in the places where photos of her had been taken. It just made her seem so real.*

"*After lunch, I finally got to my room and opened the small package. Inside was a first-class relic, certified to be a part of Therese's bone. The nun was the archivist and said that she just knew she was supposed to bring that relic on this particular day.*

"*The sister wrote to Bob afterward and said, 'I think that priest, whoever he is, is supposed to get out and communicate the Little Way of Therese. The release of the butterfly may have symbolized the release of her message after her dying.'*

"*That really has been a lot of my message. The Little Way is the spirituality of imperfection; that we come to God not by doing it right, but by doing it wrong. Unlike the Church of Therese's time and my own pre–Vatican II Church taught, we don't come to God by being perfect and doing great big, heroic things. Now, I don't say it with the love and beauty that she did. But it just became a tremendous confirmation for me that what I am teaching is what I am supposed to be teaching.*

[It's interesting to note that the original Greek word for soul was psyche, *which means "butterfly." Soul and True Self have always been hard to pin down; they are elusive and subtle like butterflies.—ID 15]*

"*In her autobiography, Therese promised to spend her heaven doing good on earth. Even Sister Ilia Delio, who's a scientist and doesn't talk the way many of us sentimental Catholics do, says that Therese has a record of quantum entanglement like no other saint she knows. Everybody who loves Therese has such stories. She gets involved in your life.*

"*I don't doubt that myself. I do believe Therese is somehow present in my life; and I think she is present in millions of lives. There is something beautiful happening through this woman who said she wanted to perfect 'the science of love.'*

"*In her autobiography, Therese tells how she struggled to be loving in the little everyday moments of life in community. They are things we can all relate to. Just to give you one example: In any community, there are some people to whom you are not naturally attracted or who even tick you off. There was a can-tankerous older sister in Therese's community, Sister St. Pierre, whom nobody liked. Therese volunteered to be her helper. Sis-ter St. Pierre had to have her sleeves rolled back correctly and her food cut a certain way. She had to be helped up just so and supported as she walked. And all the time she was complaining, 'You are not holding me right. I am going to fall!'*

"*No sister wanted that job because there was no pleasing Sister St. Pierre. She was just so cranky and bothersome. But Therese, despite her struggles with her own inner feelings and thoughts, managed to perfect the science of love so well that the other sisters thought St. Pierre was Therese's best friend. Even St. Pierre is supposed to have said at the deposition for Therese's canonization, 'I always thought I was Therese's favorite!'*

"*St. Teresa of Calcutta took Therese's name because of that line in Therese's autobiography: 'I want to do little things with great love.' It's not a matter of doing great things. If you are just picking up a book with conscious love, this is the Little Way. And I think whatever you do in conscious union and love is prayer. Therese and Francis are for me the best teachers of the Little Way. So many of our Catholic saints are not. They are more examples of heroic martyrdom and the message they give is 'If I am perfect, God will love me.' Because I'm a One on the Enneagram and so programmed to think that way anyway, I really needed to be released from that pursuit of perfection. And both Francis and Therese did that for me."*

Seeing the Divine Image

You cannot earn God. You cannot prove yourself worthy of God. Knowing God's presence is simply a matter of awareness, of enjoying the now, of deepening one's own presence. There are moments when it happens. Then life makes sense. I am able to see the divine image in myself, in you, and eventually in all things. Finally, the seeing is one. How you see anything is how you will see everything.

Jesus pushes seeing to the social edge. Can you see the image of Christ in the *least* of your brothers and sisters? He uses that as his only description of the final judgment (Matthew 25). Nothing about commandments, nothing about church attendance—simply a matter of our ability to see. Can we see Christ in the "nobodies" who can't play our game of success? In those who cannot reward us in return? When we can see the image of God where we are not accustomed to seeing the image of God, then we see with eyes not our own.

Finally, Jesus says we have to love and recognize the divine image even in our enemies. He teaches what many thought a leader could never demand of his followers: *love of the enemy.* Logically that makes no sense. But soulfully it makes absolute sense, because in terms of the soul, it really is all or nothing. *Either we see the divine image in all created things, or we don't see it at all.* We see it once, and the circle keeps moving outward, widening its embrace.

The Christian vision is that the world is a temple. If that is true, then our enemies are sacred, too. Who else created them but God? The ability to respect the outsider is probably the litmus test of true seeing. And it doesn't stop with human beings and enemies and the least of the brothers and sisters. It moves to frogs and pansies and weeds. *Everything* becomes enchanting with true sight. One God, one world, one truth, one suffering, and one love. All we can do is participate.   —EB 55, 57–59

Love God in What Is Right in Front of You

The God Jesus incarnates and embodies is not a distant God that must be placated. Jesus' God is not sitting on some throne demanding worship and throwing down thunderbolts like Zeus. Jesus never said, "Worship me"; he said, "Follow me." He asks us to imitate him in his own journey of full incarnation. To do so, he gives us the two great commandments: 1) Love God with your whole heart, soul, mind, and strength, and 2) Love your neighbor as yourself (Mark 12:28–31; Luke 10:25–28). In the parable of the Good Samaritan, Jesus shows us that our "neighbor" even includes our "enemy" (Luke 10:29–37).

So how do we love God? Most of us seem to have concluded we love God by attending church services. For some reason, we thought that made God happy. I'm not sure why. That idea probably has more to do with clergy job security! Jesus never talked about attending services; although church can be a good container to start with, and we do tend to become like the folks we hang out with. The prophets often portray God's disdain for self-serving church services. "The sanctuary, the sanctuary, the sanctuary" is all we care about, Jeremiah shouts (7:4). "I hold my nose at your incense. What I want you to do is love the widow and the orphan," say both Isaiah and Amos (Isaiah 1:11–17; Amos 5:21–24), as do Jeremiah, Hosea, Joel, Micah, and Zechariah in different ways. The prophetic message is absolutely clear, yet we went right back to loving church services instead of Reality. I believe our inability to recognize and love God in what is right in front of us has made us separate religion from our actual lives. There is Sunday morning, and then there is real life.

The only way I know how to teach anyone to love God, and how I myself can love God, is to love what God loves, which is everything and everyone, including you and including me! "We love because God first loved us" (1 John 4:19). "If we love one another, God remains in us, and [God's] love is brought to perfection in us" (1 John 4:12). Then we love with an infinite love. Only the contemplative and trustful mind can do that.

As our freedom from our ego expands—as we get ourselves out of the way—there is a slow but real expansion of consciousness so that we are not the central reference point anymore. We are able to love in greater and greater circles until we can finally do what Jesus did: love and forgive even our enemies. Most of us were given the impression that we had to be totally selfless, and when we couldn't achieve that, many of us gave up altogether. We should seek "a harmony of goodness," says John Duns Scotus, which means harmonizing and balancing necessary self-care with the constant expansion beyond ourselves to loving others in themselves and for themselves. Imagining and working toward this harmony keeps us from giving up on impossible and heroic ideals. Now the possibility of love is always right in front of us and always concrete; it is no longer a theory, a heroic ideal, or a distant goal.   —FM disc 2

INCREASING LOVE IN THE WORLD

We asked Richard what he thinks is the most effective way to increase love in the world. His response: "To not separate ourselves from the suffering of the world. When we're close to those who are in pain, their need evokes love in us. Very few of us have the largess, the magnanimity to just decide to be loving. Someone has to ask it of us, as our marriage partners and children do. We have to place ourselves in situations with people who are not like us, outside our systems of success and security, so we can read life from another perspective. The needs we witness will pull us toward love, toward generosity and compassion.

"I think that's what the icon of the cross is meant to do on a spiritual level. The bleeding body pulls us into itself and into bleeding humanity, too. I experience this pull watching the news, witnessing the suffering of people all over the world. As many have observed, we should live life with the Bible in one hand

and the newspaper in the other. I realize cable news is pretty
superficial, but it takes me out of my little hermitage where I
can live far too peacefully and comfortably. It makes me aware
that right now there is a woman in Syria holding her baby in
her arms while running for her life. I must take that in and be
in solidarity with her in whatever ways I can, witnessing what
she is going through: the anxiety, the pain, the fear. That's what
teaches us how to love."

What then do you do with that pain?

"Many are called to activism, which is necessary and good.
My primary work is to send prayer and love toward those who
are hurting. I do believe consciousness is the deepest level of
reality. I also use my voice, through my teaching and writing,
to awaken others to the reality of suffering in the world and
to encourage them to allow God's love to flow through them,
transforming and healing pain. I hope that our Living School is
helping to train and equip transformed people to meet the suffering in the world."

The Third Way

As I explore transformation as a process of letting go of the ego's
needs and accomplishments, you may think I'm overemphasiz-
ing detachment. But when you look at Jesus on the cross, you
see that Christianity also fosters *attachment*. Jesus tells us to
love and to pay the price for loving. The heart and the soul are
the first to attach to things and fall in love. Look at the image of
the Sacred Heart of Jesus. His heart is out in front of his chest. It
may not be great art, but it is great theology. The heart is given,
and the price is paid. When we attach, when we fall in love, we
risk pain and we will always suffer for it. The cross is not the
price that Jesus had to pay to convince God to love us. It is simply where love will lead us.

Jesus names the agenda: If we love, if we give ourselves to feel
the pain of the world, it will crucify us. (This understanding of
the crucifixion is much better than thinking of Jesus as paying
some debt to an alienated God who needs to be appeased into

loving us.) We may prefer to remain aloof and detached, but that's not the Christian way. *The Christian way is to risk the attachments of love—and then keep growing in what it actually means to love.*

As we start trying to love, we begin to realize that we're actually not loving very well. We are mostly meeting our own needs. The word for this is "codependency." This kind of love is still impure and self-seeking and thus is not really love at all. So we have to pull back and learn the great art of detachment, which is not aloofness, but the purifying of attachment. Our religion is neither solely detachment nor solely attachment; it's a dance between the two. It's neither entirely isolation, as symbolized by the desert, nor is it complete engagement, as symbolized by the city. Jesus moves back and forth between desert and city. In the city, he feels himself losing perspective, love, and center; so Jesus goes out to the desert to discover the real again. And when Jesus is in the desert, his passionate union with the Father drives him back to the pain of the city.

The transformative dance between attachment and detachment is sometimes called the Third Way. It is the middle way between fight and flight, as Walter Wink describes it.[7] Some prefer to take on the world: to fight it, to change it, fix it, and rearrange it. Others deny there is a problem at all; it suits their needs as it is. "Everything is beautiful," they say and look the other way. Both instincts avoid holding the tension, the pain, and the essentially tragic nature of human existence.

The contemplative stance is the Third Way. We stand in the middle, neither taking the world on from another power position nor denying it for fear of the pain it will bring. We hold the dark side of reality and the pain of the world *until it transforms us,* knowing that we are both complicit in the evil and can participate in wholeness and holiness. Once we can stand

---

7. See Walter Wink, *Jesus and Nonviolence: A Third Way* (Minneappolis: Fortress Press, 2003).

in that third spacious way, neither directly fighting nor denying and fleeing, we are in the place of grace out of which genuine newness can come. This is where creativity and new forms of life and healing emerge.   —EB 169–71

Transforming Our Pain

Spirituality is always eventually about what you do with your pain. It seems our culture has lost its own spiritual foundation and center, and as a result we no longer know what to do with universal pain. If we do not transform our pain, we will always pass it on—to our partner, our spouse, our children, our friends, our coworkers, our "enemies." Usually we project it outward and blame someone else for causing our pain. Of course, this is the opposite of loving.

In terms of the soul, no one else is your problem. *You* are invariably the primary problem. *You* are always the locus of conversion and transformation. I believe the message of the crucified Jesus is a statement about what to do with your pain. It's primarily a message of transformation, and not a transaction to "open the gates of heaven" unless you are talking about being drawn into heaven *right now*. For some unfortunate reason, Christians have usually "used" Jesus as a mere problem solver, one who would keep us personally from pain later. That kept us in a very small, self-centered world. The big loss was that we missed Jesus' message of how to let God transform us and our world here and now.

The book of Revelation presents the paradoxical image of a Lamb who is simultaneously slaughtered and standing, victim and victorious (see Revelation 5:6 and throughout). This is the transformative mystery in iconic form. We must put together these two seeming opposites in our own life. We, too, can be both. Only the Spirit can teach us the paradox of Jesus' death and resurrection, the pattern of all growth, change, and transformation. It is equally hard to trust both sides—the dying itself and the promised new state.

Was God trying to solve a problem through what looked like the necessary death of Jesus? Or was God trying to reveal something central about the nature of God? Christians have historically taught that God was saving us *from* our sins. Maybe an even better way to say it is that Jesus was saving us *through* our sins. As Paul says with great subtlety, Jesus "became sin that we might become the very goodness of God" (2 Corinthians 5:21). In other words, Jesus becomes the problem to show us how to resolve the problem. The actual impact of this has yet to hit most Christians.

We are generally inclined to either create victims of others or play the victim ourselves, both of which are no solution but only perpetuate the problem. Jesus instead holds the pain— even becomes the pain—until it transforms him into a higher state, which we call the risen life. The subsequent New Testament texts do not reveal any self-pity, resentment, or anger in Jesus. He never asks his followers to avenge his murder. Compare this to almost all historical stories of the death of a leader. An utterly new attitude has been released in history; it's a Spirit of love, compassion, and forgiveness. As Jesus prayed on the cross, "Father, forgive them, they know not what they do" (Luke 23:34).   —OT disc 1 and HAD 19, 22–23

Grace Is Key

The following three paragraphs came to me clearly in a very short time while I was walking along the Pacific Ocean during my Lenten hermitage in 2012. I think they sum up why, for me, grace is the key to accepting all deaths—and experiencing all resurrections.

1. *The goodness of God fills all the gaps of the universe, without discrimination or preference.* God is the gratuity of absolutely everything. The space in between everything is not space at all but Spirit. God is the "Goodness Glue," the love that holds the dark and light of things together, the free energy that carries all death across the Great Divide

and transmutes it into Life. When we say that Christ "paid the debt once and for all," it simply means that God's job is to make up for all deficiencies in the universe. What else would God do? What else would Love do? Basically, grace is God's first name, and probably last too. *Grace is what God does to keep all things God has made in love and alive—forever.* Grace is God's official job description. Grace is not something God gives; grace is who God *is.* If we are to believe the primary witnesses, an unexplainable goodness is at work in the universe. (Some of us call this phenomenon God, but the word is not necessary. In fact, sometimes it gets in the way of the experience, because too many have named God something other than grace.)

2. *Death is not just our one physical dying, but it is going to the full depth, hitting the bottom, going the distance, beyond where I am in control, and always beyond where I am now.* No wonder it is scary. Such death is called "the descent into hell" in the early Apostles' Creed, while in other sources, "the pit," "the dark night," "Sheol," or "Hades." We all die eventually; we have no choice in the matter. But there are degrees of death before the final physical one. If we are honest, we acknowledge that we are dying throughout our life, and this is what we learn if we are attentive: *grace is found at the depths and in the death of everything.* After these smaller deaths, we know that the only "deadly sin" is to swim on the surface of things, where we never see, find, or desire God or love. This includes even the surface of religion, which might be the worst danger of all. Thus, we must not be afraid of falling, failing, going "down."

3. *When you go to the full depths and death, sometimes even the depths of your sin, you can always come out the other side—and the word for that is resurrection.* Something or someone builds a bridge for you, recognizable only from the far side, that carries you willingly, or even

partly unwilling, across. All that we hear from reputable
and reliable sources (mystics, shamans, near-death visitors, and nearing-death experiences) indicates no one is
more surprised and delighted than the traveler himself
or herself. Something or someone seems to fill the tragic
gap between death and life, but *only at the point of no
return.* None of us crosses over by our own effort or merits, purity, or perfection. We are all carried across by an
uncreated and unearned grace—from pope, to president,
to princess, to peasant. Worthiness is never the ticket,
only deep desire, and the ticket is given in the desiring.
The tomb is always finally empty. There are no exceptions to death, and there are no exceptions to grace. And
I believe, with good evidence, that there are no exceptions
to resurrection. Love truly is stronger than death.

—ID xx–xxii

Things Learned While Recuperating

*Richard was diagnosed with prostate cancer in 2016 and under-
went a complete prostatectomy. Asking, "What is God trying to
teach me through this?" and trying to see everything as somehow
"another opportunity to learn to love," Richard shares what he
learned in CAC's newsletter.*

The wisdom lessons that God offered me before, during, and
after the surgery were pretty much constant. The experiences
were initially disempowering, sometimes scary in their imme-
diacy, and only in hindsight were they in any way empowering. Prayer was both constant and impossible for much of this
period.

About ten days after the surgery, during my attempt at some
spiritual reading, I opened the Bible to that obscure passage in
the Book of Exodus, where Moses asks YHWH to "Show me
your glory" (33:18), and YHWH shows it in a most unusual
way. "I shall place you in the cleft of the rock and shield you

with my hand until I have passed by. Then I shall take my hand away, and you will see my backside, but my face will not be seen" (33:22–23). In several sermons, I have used that verse to teach that our knowledge of God is indirect at best, and none of our knowledge of God is fully face-to-face. God is always and forever Mystery. All we see is the "backside" of God.

This time, it was not the indirectness that hit me in this passage, but the *afterward-ness*! My best spiritual knowing almost always occurs after the fact, in the remembering—not seen "until God has passed by." I realized that in the moments of diagnosis, doctor's warnings, waiting, delays, and the surgery itself, I was as fragile, scared, and insecure as anybody would be, but if I could stay with *the full narrative,* all the way through, afterward I could invariably see, trust, and enjoy the wonderful works of God (*mirabilia Dei*)—the seeing which Moses seemed to experience as *the very glory of God.*

The foundation of faith is the ability to look at the entire salvation history and *then trust that this pattern would never— could never—change*! It is largely *after the fact* that faith is formed—and gloriously transmuted into hope for the future. Only *after* the fact can you see that you were being held and led *during* the fact. During the fact, you do not enjoy or trust your own strength at all; in fact, quite the opposite. That is when God, for some wonderful reason, is able to fill the gap—like a loving friend secretly depositing much-needed money in your empty bank account.

Because we do not stay with the full narrative of our lives, I am afraid we do not often see the *mirabilia Dei,* the wonderful faithfulness and presence of God. However, the older we get and the longer the narrative unfolds, it becomes easier to believe, to trust, and to have confidence in the process. (I am speaking here not just about protection from disasters, but of the ability to endure and learn from disasters.) The pattern becomes clearer and more compelling: Someone Else is the doer, and it is even that Someone Else who helps you to connect the dots.

After you take your place in the cleft of the rock and allow
God to temporarily shield your sight, you may get a glimpse
of the divine design "after the fact." It is then much easier to
know—*really know*—the patterns of divine love and faithfulness. This is surely why the Jewish people remind us of the
importance of remembering. Until we look back and recollect
for ourselves the disparate moments of our lives, so often taken
for granted, faith remains largely a theory, a memorized Bible
quote, or a line from a sermon, a speculative hope that does
not yet grip our very soul. At that stage, we are not personally engaged, but only mentally obedient. However, these are
probably necessary starting places, so do not dismiss them as
unimportant.

It only gets better! This experienced faithfulness can quickly
morph into love for all others who might be elderly, infirm,
suffering chronic pain, powerless, or even dying at this very
moment. The circle soon widens to include all those who care
for them—for me—along the way: friends, nurses, doctors, family, friars, and the wonderful people who so tenderly and unself-
ishly left messages for me. Right now, my awareness of, and my
empathy for, all human suffering has increased tenfold; I hope
it lasts. I know how much it hurts to hurt, how sad it is to be
sad. At moments, it became even conscious solidarity with the
undeserved pain of all others. In fact, whenever I wanted to feel
sorry for myself, the image of Syrian refugees flooded my mind
and heart. My tiny bit of discomfort became a huge gift and
opportunity—because it offered me a way to experience and to
love my communion with the fate and the state of all humanity.
I wonder if there is any other way to learn such things.

—M 6, no. 1

Contemplation AND Action

I used to think that most of us must begin with contemplation
or a unitive encounter with God and are then led through that
experience to awareness of the suffering of the world and to

solidarity with that suffering in some form of action. I do think that's true for many people, but as I read the biblical prophets and observe Jesus' life, I think it also happens in reverse: first action, and then needed contemplation.

No life is immune from suffering. When we are in solidarity with pain, injustice, war, oppression, colonization—the list goes on and on—we face immense pressure to despair, to become angry or dismissive. When reality is split dualistically between good and bad, right and wrong, we too are torn apart. Yet when we are broken, we are most open to contemplation, or non-dual thinking. We are desperate to resolve our own terror, anger, and disillusionment, and so we allow ourselves to be led into the silence that holds everything together in wholeness.

The contemplative, non-dual mind is not saying, "Everything is beautiful," even when it's not. However, you do come to "Everything is *still* beautiful" by facing the conflicts between how reality is and how you wish it could be. In other words, you have to begin—and most people do in their adult years—with dualistic problems. You've got to name good and evil and differentiate between right and wrong. You can't be naive about evil. But if you stay focused on this duality, you'll go crazy! You'll become an unlovable, judgmental, dismissive person. I've witnessed this pattern in myself. You must eventually find a bigger field, a wider frame, which we call non-dual thinking.

Jesus does not hesitate to name good and evil and to show that evil is a serious matter. Jesus often speaks in dualistic images, for example, "You cannot serve God and mammon" (Matthew 6:24). He draws a stark line between the sheep and the goats, the good and the wicked (Matthew 25:31–46). Yet Jesus goes on to overcome these dualisms by what we would call the contemplative mind. You are honest about what the goats are doing, maybe too honest for most people, but you do not become hateful nor do you need to punish the goats in your life. You keep going deeper until you can also love them.

Beginning with dualistic action and moving toward contemplation seems to be the more common path in the modern era.

We see this pattern in Dorothy Day, Thomas Merton, Martin Luther King, Jr., Mother Teresa, and Jean Vanier. These people entered into the pain of society and had to go to God to find rest for their soul, because their soul was so torn by the broken, split nature of almost everything, including themselves.

The most important word in our Center's name is not Action, nor is it Contemplation, but the word *and*. We need both action *and* contemplation to have a whole spiritual journey. It doesn't matter which comes first; action may lead you to contemplation and contemplation may lead you to action. But finally, they need and feed each other.   —LS

Turning toward the Good

Christianity is not a moral matter; it's a mystical matter. Yet we turned the Gospel into "Monday washing day" and neglected the other days—e.g., "Thursday baking day" and "Sunday feasting day." Humans seem to prefer the six stone cold jars of water for ritual purification to the ecstatic wine of a wedding feast (John 2:1–10). The ego pattern never changes. The mystical mind is the non-dual, spacious, non-counting mind. The ordinary dualistic mind is consumed by counting and measuring how moral I am or you are. It weighs everything up and down—mostly down. The dualistic mind moves toward quick resolution and too easy closure. It is very judgmental. That's why all great spiritual teachers say, "Do not judge." Franciscanism is nothing other than what Francis calls in his Testament "the marrow of the Gospel"—which is love, always choosing the positive over the negative.

As neuroscience suggests, our negative and critical thoughts are like Velcro, they stick and hold; whereas our positive and joyful thoughts are like Teflon, they slide away. We have to deliberately choose to hold onto positive thoughts before they "imprint." Observing my own habits of thought and in counseling others I see this to be profoundly true. The implications are enormous for individuals and for society.

Neuroscience can now demonstrate the brain indeed has *a negative bias*; the brain prefers to constellate around fearful, negative, or problematic situations. In fact, when a loving, positive, or unproblematic thing comes your way, you have to savor it consciously for at least fifteen seconds before it can harbor and store itself in your "implicit memory;" otherwise it doesn't stick. We must indeed savor the good in order to significantly change our regular attitudes and moods. And we need to strictly monitor all the "Velcro" negative thoughts.

Anything which the dualistic mind doesn't understand, it quickly names as wrong, dangerous, sinful, or heretical. The dualistic mind is responsible for most of the disputes, wars, and violence on earth. The dualistic mind sees most opposition as highly justified and necessary, because it judges one side to be superior and one side to be inferior. It always takes sides! The non-dual, contemplative mind abides in God, the Ultimate Positive. It wants the good, the true, and the beautiful so much that it's willing to leave the field of the moment open and to hold onto all parts of it, the seemingly good and the seemingly negative, and it waits for them to fully show themselves.

In some ways, the Gospel of love is so hard to live because it is so very simple. We strangely assume that God has to be complicated. The mind seems to insist on making everything complicated. It wants a job to keep busy. The mind is so biased toward fear and negativity that the common way we try to get control is to descend into some dualistic, right-or-wrong system of morality. We find the perfect excuse for avoiding the wedding banquet that is right in front of us (Luke 14:15), a reason to not sit at the table with "both good and bad" (Matthew 22:10). We would rather slouch in the corner and criticize, all the while feeling moral and superior.

Franciscanism is sometimes called an alternative orthodoxy because it invites us all to sit at God's One Abundant Table, while much of the Christian tradition has set a scarce table for very few. The Church too often assumed that people were very simple and so we had to make the laws complex to protect them from themselves. Jesus and Francis recognized that people are endlessly diverse, complex, and mysterious, and we had best make the law very simple. Just love your neighbor exactly as you love yourself.   —ALG disc 4; EL 155–57; FM disc 3

Heaven and Hell

> *Lord, who then, will be saved?*   —Luke 13:23

> *But remember, some who are now last will be first. And some who think they are first will be last.*
>   —Luke 13:30

A number of saints said that no one is going to hell unless they want to. God condemns no one to hell, unless they choose to live in hatred, evil, and disharmony. Then they are basically living in hell here and now. It's always our choice.

Now, from our side, it looks like God is the one kicking us out of heaven; but the wisdom of the ages seems to be that it is only we who kick ourselves out. If you want to go to heaven—in other words, if you want to live in love (they're the same thing)—you *will* live in love. But it's your decision, and that's the narrow gate.

Pope John Paul II, who certainly was not a liberal, said in 1999, "When will Catholics realize that heaven and hell are not geographical places? They're states of consciousness." Let me repeat it: Heaven and hell are not geographical places; they're states of consciousness. And if that's true, there are probably people reading this now who are in hell. They want to be miserable. They're hateful, negative, and oppositional. They love to exclude people who are different from them. That attitude of hatred is hell, and it's happening right now.

As St. Catherine of Siena said, "It's heaven all the way to heaven; and it's hell all the way to hell." You're choosing *right now*: do you want to live in love and communion with God and your neighbor? Or do you want to live in a constant fight? And as we listen to our politics, that appears to be the only conversation we know—how to fight, how to be angry, how to be hateful, how to tell lies. Who can we exclude now? Which race, religion, or group is unworthy? That's hell. And an awful lot of people, even those who call themselves Christian, are living in hell. That's why Jesus says, "I do not know you" to those who "ate and drank in his company" (see Luke 13:25–27).

Heaven is not about belonging to the right group; it's not about being in the right place. It's having the right attitude. There are just as many Muslims, Hindus, and Jews who are in love—serving their neighbor and the poor—as there are Christians. Jesus says there will be deep regret—"wailing and grinding of teeth"—when we realize how wrong we were, how thoroughly we missed the point. Be prepared to be surprised about who is living a life of love and service and who isn't. "Many who appear to be last will be first" (Luke 13:30). This should keep us all humble and searching and recognizing it's not even any of our business who's going to heaven and who's going to hell. That's the work of God. And as Jesus says, what seems impossible to us is always possible for God (see Matthew 19:26).

—H August 20, 2016

Divinization

If we could glimpse the panoramic view of the biblical revelation and the Big Picture that we're a part of, we'd see how God is forever evolving human consciousness, making us ever more ready for God. The Hebrew prophets and many Catholic and Sufi mystics used words like espousal, marriage, or bride and groom to describe this phenomenon. That's what the prophet Isaiah (61:10, 62:5), many of the Psalms, the school of Paul (Ephesians 5:25–32), and the Book of Revelation (19:7–8, 21:2) mean by "preparing a bride to be ready for her husband." The human soul is being gradually readied so that actual espousal and partnership with the Divine are the final result. It's all moving toward a marriage between God and creation. Note that such salvation is a social and cosmic concept, and not just about isolated individuals "going to heaven." The Church was meant to bring this corporate salvation to conscious and visible possibility.

But how could such divine espousal really be God's plan? Isn't this just poetic exaggeration? If this is the agenda, why were most of us presented with an angry deity who needed to be placated and controlled? And why would God even want to "marry" God's creation? If you think I am stretching it here, look for all the times Jesus uses a wedding banquet as his image for eternity, and how he loves to call himself "the bridegroom" (Mark 2:19–20). Why would he choose such metaphors? The very daring, seemingly impossible idea of union with God is still something we're so afraid of that most of us won't allow ourselves to think it, especially in garden variety religion. Only God *in you* will allow you to imagine such a possibility, which is precisely "the Holy Spirit planted in your heart" (Romans 8:11 and throughout Paul's letters).

The Eastern Fathers of the Church were not afraid of this belief; they called it the process of "divinization" (*theosis*). In fact, they saw it as the whole point of the Incarnation and the precise meaning of salvation. The much more practical and rational church in the West seldom used the word; it was just too daring for us, despite the rather direct teachings from Peter (1 Peter 1:4–5 and 2 Peter 1:4) and John's Gospel being quite clear about it: "I pray not only for them, but also for those who will believe in me through their word, so that they may all be one, as you, Father, are in me and I in you, that they also may be in us, that the world may believe that you sent me" (John 17:20–21). *Jesus came to give us the courage to trust and allow our inherent union with God*, and he modeled it for us in this world. Union is not merely a place we go to later—if we are good; union is the place we come from, the place we're called to live from now.

Paul makes use of the almost physical language of shared embodiment in his single most used phrase "*en Christo.*" Further, Paul offers us the beautiful teaching on the Body of Christ

(1 Corinthians 12), which takes the form of a meal so we can be reminded frequently of our core identity (1 Corinthians 11:17–26). As Augustine said, "We are what we eat! We are what we drink!" Thus I am quite Catholic and conservative in my belief in very "Real Presence" in the bread and wine; otherwise the Eucharist is just a child's pretend tea party. Transformation must be real for persons, for creation, for all that lives and dies. This is summed up in the literal act and metaphor of humans digesting simple elements that grow from the earth. This is perfect and supreme wholism.

At the end, what more fitting conclusion could the "Second Coming of Christ" be if not that humanity becomes "a beautiful bride all dressed for her husband" (Revelation 21:2), with Jesus the perfect stand-in for the Divine Bridegroom (Matthew 9:15; John 3:29)? Rather than denying evolution, Christians should have paved the way and offered a positive image for the end of the world. Instead we largely emphasized the threatening language of Armageddon and Apocalypse.

Divine union will finally be allowed and enjoyed, despite our human history of resistance and denial. When God wins, God wins! God knows how to do victory. The Day of YHWH will indeed be the Day of YHWH, or what Dame Julian called "The Great Deed" that would come at the end of history. *Apokatastasis* or "universal restoration" (Revelation 3:20–21) has been promised to us as the real message of the Cosmic Christ, the Alpha and the Omega of all history (Revelation 1:4, 21:6, 22:13). It will be a win/win for God—and surely for humanity! What else would a divine victory be?

The clear goal and direction of the biblical revelation is toward a full mutual indwelling. The movement toward union began with God walking in the garden with naked Adam and Eve and "all the array of creation" (Genesis 2:1); it continued through inspiration of prophets, teachers, and "secular" history throughout the Hebrew Bible. The theme found its shocking climax in the realization that "the mystery is Christ within you, your hope of glory" (Colossians 1:27). As John excitedly puts it, "You know him because he is with you and he is in you!" (John 14:17). The eternal mystery of incarnation will have finally met its mark, and "the marriage feast of the Lamb will begin" (Revelation 19:7–9). History is no longer meaningless and largely a failure, but has a promised and positive direction. This creates very healthy, happy, hopeful, and generative people; and we surely need some now. All I know for sure is that a good God creates and continues to create an ever-good world.

—NGTS disc 1 and TH 212

The Four Loves

There are many different kinds of love. Ancient Greeks had multiple distinct words for what we try to cover with our single word "love"; these include *philia* (friendship), *eros* (passion), *storge* (familial love), and *agape* (infinite or divine love). I sometimes fear that our paucity of words reveals an actual narrowness of experience.

For Paul, *agape* love is the Great Love that is larger than you. It is the Great Self, the God Self. It's not something you do. It's something that you learn to live inside of even while you already participate in it. This way of being is something you fall into more than you manufacture, just as our wonderful English phrase puts it—falling in love. This love is unconditional, always present, and comes without any stipulations except the falling itself. We will only allow ourselves to fall into love when we give up control, consciously or unconsciously. It will often feel like a falling and a faltering, an ecstatic humiliation.

The ego will resist and say, "Why am I doing this to myself? And yet I long to do it!" Normally, something must lead you to the edge of your present resources so you have to push your reset button to access a power greater than yourself. Most of us just don't go there without a fall or seduction of some kind.

Paul explains how we, precisely in our togetherness and participation, are Christ's Body (1 Corinthians 12). Yet each of us is a different part of this Great Wholeness. He lists the many different gifts of the Spirit. In closing, he writes: "Earnestly desire the greater gifts. And I am going to show you the best way of all" (1 Corinthians 12:31). Then, in his attempt to try to describe this agape or divine love, Paul writes his most poetic chapter in all his letters (1 Corinthians 13). He seems to run out of adjectives and superlatives to express the fullness of love.

Paul is not describing human friendship (*philia*), affection of parents for children (*storge*), or even passionate desire (*eros*); he is describing what it is like to live inside of an Infinite Source—where all the boundaries change, feelings are hardly helpful at all, and all the gaps are filled in from the other side. Any Valentine's Day notion of love is totally inadequate and can even send you down an impossible and disappointing road if you try to conjure up such romantic dedication within yourself. We have to take breathing lessons and develop larger lungs to live inside of such a new and open horizon. It does not come naturally until we draw upon it many times, and then it becomes the only deep and true natural instinct. You have then returned home and can even practice the other kinds of love with much greater ability and joy. —GTP discs 7, 9, 11; H January 31, 2016

Love Never Fails

Paul says some pretty extraordinary things in 1 Corinthians 13. Let's look at some of his points carefully.

If I speak with the tongues of men and of angels, but do not have love, I have become a noisy gong or a clanging cymbal.

This hits close to home for me. Paul makes me realize that I might give a wonderful sermon, but if I don't do it out of God's love for the people right in front of me, it won't be as powerful as when I'm participating in divine love. God will still use even lesser loves, but Paul recognizes that human feelings and preferences are quite unreliable. Our affections are fickle and will finally change and fall short when our conditions or requirements are not met.

If I have the gift of prophecy, and know all mysteries and all knowledge;

Among others, Paul is talking to the intellectuals and the academics, the Greeks of his day—and likely to most of us. This is the common temptation to substitute knowledge for actual love or service.

. . . and if I have all faith, so as to remove mountains, but do not have love, I am nothing.

Here he's challenging religious people who make a task of religion itself, who try to be moral and "believe" through willpower. This often passes for religion, but it is faith without love so it is not true faith. Paul might also be criticizing the common mistake of those we call conservatives or "true believers."

And if I give all my possessions to feed the poor, and if I surrender my body to be burned, but do not have love, it profits me nothing.

Apparently, you can even be a progressive and generous social activist; but if you're just doing it to be holier than thou or out of oppositional energy, you are still outside of the Big Mystery. Self-proclaiming heroics on the Left can be just as unloving as self-proclaiming religion on the Right.

Then Paul tries to describe the mystery of love, and he finally has to resort to listing almost fifteen descriptions. He talks about love not as simply an isolated virtue, but as the basis for all virtue. It is the underlying, generous energy that gives itself away through those living inside of love.

Love is patient, love is kind and is not jealous;

If I'm jealous, then I'm not in love. When you are inside this mystery of love, you operate differently, and it's not in a guarded, protective way.

Love does not brag and is not arrogant, does not act unbecomingly [it is never rude]; it does not seek its own [advantage], is not provoked [it does not take offense or store up grievances],

So every time you and I take offense (how many times a day is that?), we're not "in love."

Love does not take into account a wrong suffered, does not rejoice in unrighteousness [in the mistakes of others], but rejoices with the truth;

The Germans have a word for delighting in someone else's misfortune—*schadenfreude*. Maybe we do not have an English word for it because we take it as normal. I hope not.

Love bears all things, believes all things, hopes all things, endures all things.

And then Paul ends with this: *Love never fails.*[8]

Paul is touching upon something that's infinite; it can therefore include all and has an endless ability to pour itself out. When you're in love, you're operating from this foundational sense of abundance, not from scarcity or fear. There is an inherent generosity of spirit, of smile, of gesture, of readiness, of initial acceptance that you immediately sense from any person who is standing inside this Flow. Honestly, you can tell the difference between someone "in love" and someone "not in love" in the first five seconds of almost any encounter. The all-important point, however, is that if your primary motivation is to love, there is no such thing as failure—except in your failure to draw love from an ever-deeper level.   —TTM and IDM

TO GOD BE THE GLORY

When asked what he would want to be remembered for, Richard thought for a while and then responded:

"Nothing is put on a Franciscan's tombstone except dates of birth and death, but if I were to have an epitaph it would be something like this: 'God allowed me to do everything wrong so God could do everything right.' I look back at my life, founding the New Jerusalem Community and the Center for Action and Contemplation, at how immature I was and how self-serving my motives were and how many mistakes I made. The notion of moral ambiguity has helped me see that most things are not as

---

8. 1 Corinthians 13:1–8, NASB.

black and white as we would like them to be. God always uses very unworthy instruments so we can never think that it is we who are accomplishing the work. The older I get, the more I say, 'God, you were so patient with me! I didn't do it right and you still did it right, you still used me.' I think of that verse in Isaiah: 'All your good deeds are like filthy rags' (Isaiah 64:5). I know that's true and that I didn't know what I was doing most of the time. I stumbled into it and got all this credit. That's why grace is so important. God can always use even bad things. That's what I mean by 'God uses our sin in our favor.'"

Trust God Is Loving in Spite of You

At the end of life, your prayer is largely just praise and admiration and gratitude, thanking whoever this wonderful God is who did this to me, who did this for me, largely in spite of myself. Every one of the Apostle Paul's letters start and end with thanksgiving for the endless ocean of grace that he realizes he is swimming inside of. You do not have to force the flow; you just have to trust it. It will be done unto you.

Paul's prayer in his letter to the Ephesians is perhaps my favorite succinct statement of his wisdom, and it is my prayer for you, as well:

> *I bow my knees before the Father, from whom every family in heaven and on earth derives its name, that [God] would grant you, according to the riches of [God's] glory, to be strengthened in power through [the] Spirit . . . , so that Christ may dwell in your hearts through faith; and that you, being rooted and grounded in love, may be able to comprehend with all the saints what is the breadth and length and height and depth, and to know the love of Christ which surpasses knowledge, that you may be filled up to all the fullness of God.*
>
> *Now to [God] who is able to do far more abundantly beyond all that we ask or think, according to the power*

that works within us, to [God] be the glory in the church and in Christ Jesus to all generations forever and ever. Amen. —Ephesians 3:14–21, NASB

Never doubt that it is all about love in the end. —IFP disc 6

Appendix

The Enneagram

The Enneagram is an ancient personality tool that has roots in several wisdom traditions, including Christianity, Judaism, and Islam. Seven of the nine Enneagram types are associated with the "capital" or "deadly" sins which originated with the Desert Fathers. But it was not until the late 1960s that Oscar Ichazo began teaching the Enneagram as we know it today. From Ichazo's school in South America, a group of Jesuits learned the system and brought it back with them to the United States. Richard Rohr learned about the Enneagram from this group and was one of the first people to publish a book about it in English. Today the Enneagram is widely taught as a way of understanding personality, addiction, relationships, and vocation.

Our deepest sin and our greatest gift are two sides of the same coin. When we are excessively fixated on our supposed gift, it becomes a sin. Maintaining this self-image, this false self, becomes more important than anything else. When used in conjunction with a regular practice of contemplative prayer, the Enneagram can be powerfully transformative. It can open us to deeper and deeper levels of understanding and insight, love and grace.

The Enneagram is divided into nine distinct personality types organized into three Triads: gut (instinctive)—types Eight, Nine, and One; heart (feeling)—types Two, Three, and Four; and head (thinking)—types Five, Six, and Seven.

The ONE

Role: Reformer
Virtue: Serenity
Vice: Anger and resentment

Basic Desire: Goodness, integrity, excellence
Without prayer, love, and nature, Ones can scarcely imagine cheerful serenity and patience, but remain aggressive idealists and ideologues.

The TWO

Role: Helper
Virtue: Humility
Vice: Pride
Basic Desire: To give and receive love
Twos are redeemed from themselves the more they experience God as the real lover and realize that their puny love can only consist in sharing in God's infinite love.

The THREE

Role: Achiever
Virtue: Authenticity
Vice: Deceit (especially self-deceit)
Basic Desire: To feel valuable
Threes need endless successes and feedback to reassure themselves against a very honest and realistic insecurity.

The FOUR

Role: Individualist
Virtue: Equanimity (appreciating life just as it is)
Vice: Envy
Basic Desire: To be uniquely themselves
The essence of the Four is the mystery of our true identity. It feels oceanic, deep, unfathomable, mysterious. Fours live for beauty, intimacy, and depth.

The FIVE

Role: Investigator
Virtue: Non-attachment (not clinging and not avoiding)
Vice: Avarice (for knowledge and for personal privacy)

Basic Desire: Mastery, understanding
The essential core of the Five is the soul's capacity to be illuminated and to illuminate, to make things clear.

The SIX

Role: Loyalist
Virtue: Courage
Vice: Fear
Basic Desire: To have support, guidance
The original blessing of the Six is the quality of awakeness that gives you an unshakable courage to take your place and walk your walk in the world.

The SEVEN

Role: Enthusiast
Virtue: Sobriety (a sober joy despite life's difficulties)
Vice: Gluttony (an insatiable quest for new experiences and options)
Basic Desire: To be satisfied and content
Sevens are people who radiate joy and optimism. Their motto is "More is always better." They are gluttonous for fun and options.

The EIGHT

Role: Challenger
Virtue: Innocence (or mercy)
Vice: Lust (an addiction to intensity)
Basic Desire: Self-protection
Losing the sense of divine Presence makes Eights feel vulnerable, deflated, and dead. The ego tries to force life into feeling real and alive again.

The NINE

Role: Peacemaker
Virtue: Decisive action
Vice: Sloth (lack of focused energy)
Basic Desire: Wholeness, peace, harmony
Nines once knew that reality was all about love, all connected, operative, and effective. Love changes everything; love resolves everything.

(Adapted from https://cac.org/the-enneagram-an-introduction/)

MODERN SPIRITUAL MASTERS
Robert Ellsberg, Series Editor

This series introduces the essential writing and vision of some of the great spiritual teachers of our time. While many of these figures are rooted in long-established traditions of spirituality, others have charted new, untested paths. In each case, however, they have engaged in a spiritual journey shaped by the challenges and concerns of our age. Together with the saints and witnesses of previous centuries, these modern spiritual masters may serve as guides and companions to a new generation of seekers.

Already published:

Abraham Joshua Heschel (edited by Susannah Heschel)
Etty Hillesum (edited by Annemarie S. Kidder)
Caryll Houselander (edited by Wendy M. Wright)
Pope John XXIII (edited by Jean Maalouf)
Rufus Jones (edited by Kerry Walters)
Clarence Jordan (edited by Joyce Hollyday)
Walter Kasper (edited by Patricia C. Bellm and Robert A. Krieg)
John Main (edited by Laurence Freeman)
James Martin (edited by James T. Keane)
Anthony de Mello (edited by William Dych, S.J.)
Thomas Merton (edited by Christine M. Bochen)
John Muir (edited by Tim Flinders)
John Henry Newman (edited by John T. Ford, C.S.C.)
Henri Nouwen (edited by Robert A. Jonas)
Flannery O'Connor (edited by Robert Ellsberg)
Karl Rahner (edited by Philip Endean)
Brother Roger of Taizé (edited by Marcello Fidanzio)
Richard Rohr (edited by Joelle Chase and Judy Traeger)
Oscar Romero (by Marie Dennis, Rennie Golden, and Scott Wright)
Joyce Rupp (edited by Michael Leach)
Albert Schweitzer (edited by James Brabazon)
Frank Sheed and Maisie Ward (edited by David Meconi)
Sadhu Sundar Singh (edited by Charles E. Moore)
Mother Maria Skobtsova (introduction by Jim Forest)
Dorothee Soelle (edited by Dianne L. Oliver)
Edith Stein (edited by John Sullivan, O.C.D.)
David Steindl-Rast (edited by Clare Hallward)
William Stringfellow (edited by Bill Wylie-Kellerman)
Pierre Teilhard de Chardin (edited by Ursula King)
Mother Teresa (edited by Jean Maalouf)
St. Thérèse of Lisieux (edited by Mary Frohlich)
Phyllis Tickle (edited by Jon M. Sweeney)
Henry David Thoreau (edited by Tim Flinders)
Howard Thurman (edited by Mary Krohlich)
Leo Tolstoy (edited by Charles E. Moore)
Evelyn Underhill (edited by Emilie Griffin)
Vincent Van Gogh (by Carol Berry)
Jean Vanier (edited by Carolyn Whitney-Brown)
Swami Vivekananda (edited by Victor M. Parachin)
Simone Weil (edited by Eric O. Springsted)
John Howard Yoder (edited by Paul Martens and Jenny Howells)

Center for
Action and
Contemplation

The Center for Action and Contemplation seeks to awaken a more loving world through prophetic teachings and practices grounded in the Christian tradition. Our conferences, online courses, publications, and the Living School empower people to live out their sacred soul task.

Fr. Richard Rohr founded the Center in 1987. James Finley and Cynthia Bourgeault join Richard as core faculty. Together they are at the forefront of shaping spiritual thought. As role models and teachers, they help us reconnect with our Source of love and engage in acts of justice and compassion.

Join hundreds of thousands around the world in contemplative community. Sign up to receive Richard Rohr's free Daily Meditations at cac.org/sign-up.